Changing Venezuela by
Taking Power

Changing Venezuela by Taking Power

The History and Policies of the Chávez Government

GREGORY WILPERT

VERSO

London • New York

First published by Verso 2007
© Gregory Wilpert 2007
All rights reserved

The moral rights of the author have been asserted

3 5 7 9 10 8 6 4 2

Verso
UK: 6 Meard Street, London W1F 0EG
USA: 20 Jay Street, Brooklyn, NY, 11201
www.versobooks.com

Verso is the imprint of New Left Books

ISBN: 978-1-84467-552-4 (pbk)
ISBN: 978-1-84467-071-0 (hbk)

British Library Cataloguing in Publication Data
A catalogue record for this book is available from the British Library

Library of Congress Cataloging-in-Publication Data
A catalog record for this book is available from the Library of Congress

Typeset in Garamond by Hewer Text UK Ltd, Edinburgh
Printed and bound in the USA by Courier Stoughton Inc.

Contents

For Carol, this is her book.

Acknowledgments

This book was a long time in the making—about five years. My wife and I originally came up with the idea back in 2002, shortly after the coup attempt, thinking that after the coup had called the world's attention to Venezuela, it would be a good idea to write a general overview of what the Chávez government has done since it came into office. However, it proved to be far more difficult to simultaneously work as a freelance writer and to write an unremunerated book than I had imagined. I originally thought I could simply put together an anthology of my articles on Venezuela, but this did not work well. So, I then proceeded to write the book in my spare time, between freelance jobs. As a result and due to a variety of other unforeseen circumstances beyond my control, it took far longer to complete than originally anticipated.

Finally, though, here it is! And the person I have to thank first and foremost for it seeing the light of day is my wife, Carol Delgado. Without her unquestioning support, critical suggestions, dedication, faith, patience, and love, it would never have gotten done. This is her book and if it weren't for the fact that I am the one who ultimately bears responsibility for the book's shortcomings, her name ought to be on the cover too.

Over the years, others have also helped me along the way. Here I should particularly mention the many, many Venezuelans, ordinary and leaders, opposition, pro-government, and "ni-ni" (neither pro- nor anti-Chávez) who allowed me to interview them or casually talk with them for this book, and for my other writing projects that contributed to this book. There are too many to mention and I am bound to leave many out if I try because some of these interviews or conversations took place many years ago. Many of the interviews, though, are transcribed on the website Venezuelanalysis.com.

Others who have helped in a variety of ways to move the project forward, whether via discussions or logistical support, include (in no particular order): Alex Main, Eva Golinger, Marta Harnecker, Michael Lebowitz, Martín Sanchez, Eduardo Daza, Jonah Gindin, Sharmini Peries, Tariq Ali, Michael Fox, Simone Baribeau, Chris Carlson, Steven Mather, Alex Holland, Sarah Wagner, my in-laws: Isabel, Grecia, Luis-Miguel, Margarita, and Luis, and my parents: Bernhard and Czarina.

Also, at various points in the project several individuals reviewed chapters or the entire manuscript and I am very grateful to them for having gone through the trouble and, in many cases, for having provided me with invaluable advice. These include Raul Zelik, Perry Anderson, Michael Albert, three anonymous reviewers assigned by Verso, and my wife Carol. I tried to adhere to their suggestions whenever possible, but was not always able to do so, whether out of stubbornness or lack of understanding.

Gregory Wilpert
Caracas, July 10, 2007

Introduction

La verdad de Venezuela
no se ve en el Country club
la verdad se ve en los cerros
con su gente y su inquietud[1]

—Alí Primera,
Yo Vengo de Donde
Usted no ha Ido

With the general disorientation that today dominates left parties and theorists around the world, following the successive failures of state socialism and of social democracy, one would hardly have expected a small, relatively wealthy, and inconspicuous country in Latin America to boldly announce it will create 21st century socialism. Why and how was this possible in Venezuela? What does it mean? What are its prospects for success? These are the three main questions this book seeks to answer.

The International Context

The election of a leftist president in Venezuela in 1998 foreshadowed what would, in the following seven years, become a wave of successes for left-leaning presidential candidates in Latin America. Leftists who followed Hugo Chávez into the presidency of their respective countries were, first, Luiz Ignacio "Lula" da Silva in Brazil in October 2002, then Lucio Gutierrez in Ecuador in January 2003, Nestor Kirchner in Argentina in May 2003, Tabaré Vázquez in Uruguay in October 2004, Evo Morales in Bolivia in December 2005, Rafael Correa in

Ecuador in November 2006, and then Daniel Ortega in Nicaragua, also in November 2006. While some of these moderated significantly shortly after taking office, such as Gutierrez and da Silva, they represent a wave of left-of-center leaders whose election came as a bit of a surprise given the aforementioned disorientation within the left around the world.

For practically the entire 1990s "the left," ranging from moderate social democrats to leftwing socialists, appeared to be somewhat perplexed as to what their actual political program should be. The fall of the Berlin Wall in 1989 and the subsequent implosion of the Soviet Union and of other state socialist regimes signaled the complete discrediting of state socialism and central planning as an institutional solution for achieving the ideals of socialism. At first, this collapse appeared to vindicate social democrats, who had always argued in favor of mixing state and market, in lieu of a complete abolition of the market.

However, it soon became obvious that social democracy was in a crisis too. In the US, in Britain, and in Germany, left-of-center leaders entered office again in the 1990s, after a long absence, but found that their old Keynesian recipes of state intervention in the market's dysfunctions did not work as well as they used to. The globalization of financial markets and massive indebtedness and deficits made old-style social democratic programs unviable. Capital had become too mobile and the welfare state too expensive for social democratic policies. As a result, Bill Clinton, Tony Blair, and Gerhard Schröder tried to devise a new more moderate program for the left, which essentially accepted the market imperatives that neo-liberals had created in the 1980s and tried to balance budgets and dismantle social programs. At the same time, they tried to keep their left credentials by being slightly to the left of their more conservative opponents. Meanwhile, in Latin America, similarly centrist presidents governed, partly as a result of the left having been purged from politics during the dictatorships of the 1970s and 1980s and partly because of the constraints that massive state indebtedness and financial deregulation placed on governance in Latin America too.

In short, social democracy had become unviable in an age of unrestricted capital flows and lack of financial resources. Instead, neo-liberalism emerged as the dominant political ideology. This economic program had been applied with a vengeance in Latin America throughout the 1980s and 1990s. The results of neo-liberalism, which meant privatization of state assets, free trade, state fiscal austerity, and deregulation of the labor market, were far from as good as neo-liberalism's apostles had claimed they would be. Between 1980 and 1999, during the height of neo-liberalism in Latin America, per capita economic growth of the continent was a paltry 11%, compared to an 80% per capita GDP growth in the previous 20 years (a mostly Keynesian period), between 1960 and 1979.[2] Also, these meager economic results and the material hardship many of the policies implied led to widespread resistance movements and often to their violent repression. As we will see, Venezuela came to be a prime example of neo-liberalism's failures, of resistance, and of repression.

A New New Left?

What remained, then, as an economic program for the countries of Latin America and for the left in general? State socialism, social democracy, and neo-liberalism all seemed to have run their unsuccessful course. By the early twenty-first century no clear answers had emerged, but voters were willing to give the left another opportunity in Latin America, despite the vagueness of their programs. However, of the leftist presidents that were elected in this first decade, only one, President Hugo Chávez Frías of Venezuela, eventually declared that he was following an explicitly anti-capitalist and pro-socialist agenda. At first, despite his somewhat in-flammatory (some would say populist) rhetoric, Chávez's policies were equally moderate as those of his fellow Latin American leftists.

Two things stand out, though, when comparing Chávez with these other presidents. First, Chávez faced far more vehement and even violent opposition to his presidency than the others, even though initially his concrete policies were not much different from those of Brazil's Lula da Silva or Chile's Michelle Bachelet. Second, Chávez's confrontation with the opposition led him to eventually become a far more radical left politician than he started out. It was not until after a coup attempt in 2002, a two-month shutdown of the country's all-important oil industry in 2002–2003, and a presidential recall referendum in August 2004 that Chávez declared his political program to be socialist, in January 2005—a full six years into his presidency.

Of course, just because Chávez announced the pursuit of socialism does not mean that his policies are socialist. Too often have politicians claimed to be in favor of socialism, only to pursue policies that ended either in a centrally planned dictatorship or in capitalism as usual. Thus, to find out whether Chávez's policies match his rhetoric and to see if these policies constitute a real alternative to state socialism, social democracy, and neo-liberalism, it makes sense to examine them carefully. Also, even if they constitute a real alternative, do they actually lead towards a better society?

The Path Towards Twenty-first Century Socialism in Venezuela

Before examining the question of whether Venezuela is actually heading towards something that might be called twenty-first century socialism, the present study first tries to explain how and why twenty-first century socialism came to be on the agenda in Venezuela. That is, Chávez and his Bolivarian movement appeared in Venezuela at a very specific time in the country's history, in a context in which social democracy and neo-liberalism were probably more discredited than in most other countries in the world.

Chapter 1, "The Dialectic of Counter-Revolution and Radicalization," reviews recent Venezuelan history and how this history made a radical project such as that of Chávez's Bolivarian revolution possible.[3] It shows how, ever since the 1920s, Venezuela had grown accustomed to constantly increasing oil revenues, which fueled the development of a strong and economically interventionist state. However, when oil revenues started a long 20-year decline in the early 1980s and they could no longer support its large state sector and a political system that bought political loyalty with oil revenue. Poverty and inequality sky-rocketed to the highest levels in Latin America in this period. The old political system, which had grown increasingly corrupt and repressive and which was held together with an exclusionary two-party pact, began falling apart, eventually giving a complete political outsider such as Hugo Chávez, who promised revolutionary change, the chance to win the presidency in 1998. Another important factor in Chávez's rise to power was that his movement was based on a coalition between progressive sectors of Venezuela's military and Venezuela's traditionally excluded more radical left movements and parties.

As stated earlier, once elected, Chávez gave very radical speeches, promising to eliminate poverty and corruption and to completely overturn the country's ossified political system with a new constitution. It is tempting to believe that Chávez's anti-poverty and anti-corruption program is what incensed the country's old elite to launch an all-out campaign to oust him. However, it was actually his success in completely displacing the old elite from positions of power that provoked their ire. During his first three years in office, Chávez's anti-poverty, anti-corruption, and redistribution measures were actually quite modest. Rather, it was the new constitution, which required the re-legitimation of all branches of government and the resulting complete removal of the old elite from state power that angered them so much.

As a result, Venezuela's old elite refused to accept Chávez as the legitimately elected president and engaged in a no-holds-barred effort to get rid of him. Chávez, though, proved to be a particularly intransigent foe, who refused to concede to the opposition any of its demands. The heightened conflict led to both a polarization of Venezuelan society and to the splitting off of significant chunks of Chávez's coalition and their joining the opposition. The conflict came to its first major confrontation with the April 2002 coup attempt, which demonstrated the extent of the opposition's hubris. Not only did it not recognize Chávez as the legitimate president, but it had also completely ignored his growing constituency among the country's poor and excluded. The opposition's miscalculations about Chávez's popularity among the poor and among the military spelled the coup's failure.

This miscalculation of the opposition, which was rooted in its firm belief that it represented the "reasonable" majority of the country and that Chávez was not a legitimate president, led to several other failed adventures. The next one was the two-month shutdown of the country's all-important oil industry, from early December 2002 to early February 2003, where the opposition lost its power base in the oil industry. Next, it tried to oust Chávez via the legal means of a presidential recall referendum. This too failed spectacularly. Then, in December 2006, Chávez was re-elected in a landslide victory of 63%, to the 36% of his main opponent.

By then, however, the combination of the opposition's implosion as a result of its repeated failures, and the persistence of a new oil boom in 2004, had liberated the Chávez government from the restraints that most leftists face once in office. Economically, the pressure to please international capital in the name of foreign investment and development was practically eliminated thanks to the boom in oil prices. Politically, the opposition had lost crucial bases of power in the polity, the military, the oil industry, and in society in general, thereby freeing Chávez from the need to take opposition reactions to his policies into consideration. Chávez thus discarded his earlier moderation and in early 2005 publicly declared his conversion to a new form of socialism, of "twenty-first century socialism," which he would work on instituting in Venezuela. The parties and sectors that supported Chávez enthusiastically went along with the announcement because they too appeared to have been radicalized by the preceding confrontations with the US-supported opposition.

Identifying Twenty-first Century Socialism in Venezuela

The heart of the book, Chapters 2 to 5, provide detailed descriptions and analyses of the governance policy, economic policy, social policy, and foreign policy of the Chávez government and the extent to which it manages to approximate institutions that fulfill the ideals Chávez talks about. In all four policy areas there are clear indications that indeed the government is pursuing innovative policies that transcend the institutions of capitalism as usual. However, these policies are often contradicted or undermined by contravening policy tendencies. For example, while the Chávez government has embarked on an important project of increasing citizen participation in a wide variety of state institutions, it has also increased the importance and strength of the presidency, which tends to undermine the participatory policies. In the area of economic policy, the government has gone a long way towards establishing economic democracy, but the high oil revenues that cannot be guaranteed, and upon which many of these policies depend, threaten the long-term viability of self-managed enterprises in Venezuela. These types of contradictions exist in all of the main policy areas examined here.

Despite the frequent contradictoriness of the policies, many of them do lay the groundwork for institutions that would fulfill the ideals of twenty-first century socialism. This is a crucial achievement, not only for Venezuelans, because it raises the hope for a Venezuela with more social justice, but it also provides a broader example of what left or socialist politics of the future could look like. An analysis of the Venezuelan institutions that work towards fulfilling society's ideals can help provide orientation and hope to a disorganized, fragmented, and often demoralized left throughout the world.

However, in addition to the frequent problem of contradictory policies, there are even deeper obstacles lurking within the Bolivarian socialist project, which have to do with the Bolivarian movement itself. The last chapter, "Opportunities, Obstacles, Prospects," discusses these obstacles and finds that the three most important impediments for the Chávez government's project are the persistence of a patronage culture, the nearly complete dependence of the Bolivarian movement on Chávez, and Chávez's own top-down governance, which undermine the creation of a participatory society. If Venezuelan society and the Chávez government manage to resolve these three key issues that are internal to the Bolivarian movement, if the policies themselves are made more consistent, and if there is no significant outside interference, then Venezuela might well be the place of greatest hope for establishing freedom, equality, and social justice in over a generation.

Those who are interested in developing a basis for evaluating what twenty-first century socialism might mean in Venezuela and whether the Chávez government's policies could actually lead towards the fulfillment of the ideals of twenty-first century socialism, should read the appendix, "What is Twenty-first Century Socialism?" This first presents some general ideas about this conception of socialism. Unfortunately, Chávez has not clearly defined twenty-first century socialism, other than to say that it is about establishing liberty, equality, social justice, and solidarity. He has also indicated that it is distinctly different from state socialism. However, such ideals, by themselves, make twenty-first century socialism indistinguishable from most other social projects of the twentieth and twenty-first century. Surely, what distinguishes twenty-first century socialism would have to be the institutions it aims to create, not the ideals it is pursuing. At heart, such institutions would be characterized by their democratic and participatory nature. Also, if one establishes that the economic institutions of capitalism—of private ownership of the means of production, the market system, and a pro-capitalist state—are incapable of fulfilling society's ideals, then the new institutions must clearly distinguish themselves from these institutions. This appendix goes on to outline what non-capitalist, perhaps 21st century socialist, political and economic institutions could look like.

1

The Dialectic of Counter-Revolution and Radicalization[1]

Los que mueren por la vida
no pueden llamarse muertos
y a partir de este momento
es prohibido llorarlos[2]

—Alí Primera,
Los Que Mueren por la Vida

The history of the Chávez presidency appears to have been characterized, above all else, by a dialectic of counter-revolution and radicalization, where the country's conservative forces attempted to prevent revolution before one had even begun and Chávez and his followers were then radicalized in reaction. This counter-revolution is much like the one famously described by Herbert Marcuse (1972), in reference to developments in the 1960s in the US and Europe, where counter-revolution is an effort to prevent revolution before one has even taken place and not an effort to undo an already established revolution. That is, Venezuela's old elites, in politics, in the economy, the media, the church, and the labor movement, repeatedly attempted to overthrow Chávez and with every failure merely provoked him, his government, and his supporters among the poor to radicalize. However, why were so many ordinary Venezuelans and why was Chávez open to such radicalization? Why didn't they react in just the opposite manner, as has been so common in other countries throughout history, to moderate their approach?

The perhaps most important reason Venezuela was open to a radical transformation, at first in favor of replacing representative democracy with participatory democracy and later of replacing capitalism with socialism, was Venezuela's rather disappointing experience with both capitalism and representative democracy in the last two decades of the 20th century. That is, while the period from the end of Venezuela's last dictatorship in 1958 to the end of its oil boom days in 1978 caused Venezuelans to believe that their country would soon join the developed world, the period from 1979 to 1999 proved to be two decades of bitter disappointment, not just economically, but also politically. In order to understand where this disappointment came from, we need to understand how Venezuelan's expectations about representative democracy and capitalism were raised during its period of stability and boom, between 1958 and 1978, at a time when most of the rest of Latin America was governed by brutal dictatorships.

Pre-conditions for Venezuela's Transformation

Venezuelan economy, polity, society, and culture are all directly linked to the country's experience with oil. In one way or another one can trace the country's ups and downs to the ups and downs of the oil economy.

Rising Expectations:
The Oil Boom and "Pacted" Democracy (1958–1978)

Between the time oil was first discovered in Venezuela, in the early 20th century, until the 1930s, oil became the country's single most important product, export, and source of private and public wealth. Already by 1920 Venezuela was the world's largest oil exporting country. By 1935 oil exports constituted 91.2%[3] of the country's exports. Prior to that, the economy had been a traditional Latin American agricultural economy, based on cocoa, coffee, sugar, cotton, and tobacco production.

As oil became increasingly important, the country's economy shifted from an agricultural country to a country in which oil production, commerce, and services dominated. While agricultural production made up one third of Venezuela's GDP in the 1920s, by the 1950s this had dropped to 10% and by 1998 to a mere 6% – the lowest percentage in all of Latin America.

As a result of this decline, Venezuela's landed elite, which is traditionally fairly strong in most of the rest of Latin America, lost its power very early in the 20th century. Also, the emphasis on oil and the country's inability to develop a strong domestic industry meant that no strong entrepreneurial class developed to replace the landed elite. Rather, since most economic activity went through the oil industry in one way or another, which was regulated by the state, the real center of Venezuela's power was based in the state itself. No domestic oil barons emerged either, though, because Venezuelan oil production was under the control of foreign oil companies, from the discovery of oil until 1974, when it was nationalized.[4]

The reason agriculture as well as industrial production declined so rapidly with the expansion of the oil industry is that its dominance provoked a so-called "Dutch Disease," as it is known among economists. This economic disease, named after the effect that the discovery of North Sea gas had on Holland's economy, refers to the problems that are associated with the rapid growth in one sector of the economy, where this produces problems in other sectors. Applied to Venezuela's oil industry, this meant that domestic industry and agriculture could not keep up with the rapid expansion of demand for consumer goods and so both industrial and agricultural goods were imported.[5]

Compounding the problem, Venezuela had a fixed exchange rate in the 1970s and early 1980s. As a result, the currency was persistently overvalued and so it was much cheaper to import goods than to produce them domestically. This meant that industrialization in Venezuela never really caught on and agriculture was effectively killed off. Instead, the service sector, whose products cannot be imported as easily, grew dramatically, while agriculture and industry shrank. As a result of the declining agricultural activity, a massive land flight and urbanization process set in, so that Venezuela rapidly became the second most urbanized country of Latin America[6] and the only one to be a net food importer.

Despite these problems of land flight, rapid urbanization, and struggling industry and agriculture, the two decades following the Marcos Perez Jimenez dictatorship (1958–1978) were tremendous boom years for Venezuela, in which per-capita GDP rose to be the highest in all of Latin America.[7] The cause of this boom is directly traceable to the increase in the price of oil and thus of the state's oil revenues. The consequence of the boom was political stability that was unusual for Latin America, although, at the price of a certain level of repression and a dependency on oil production.

The country's economic structure—oil dependency—then shaped its social structure, to produce a weak working class because of the slow industrialization process. Also, it produced a weak landed elite, at least partly because of the rapid urbanization process that did not give much time for such an elite to develop. A weak working class, in turn, meant a relatively demobilized and apathetic civil society, whose support for democracy was based on the benefits of a relatively high standard of living. The weak landed elite meant that even if elections could threaten their interests, there was not too much the elite could do to turn Venezuela towards dictatorship, as had happened in most other countries of Latin America at the time.

Another consequence of the oil-oriented economy was that the state accumulated and directed wealth, rather than an economic elite. This meant that it was the political parties that had control over the country's oil wealth and these kept challengers at bay via a corporatist and clientelist culture, which, in turn, reinforced the strength of the state and of the parties. In addition, this arrangement made the state, due to its power, appear to be "magical" (Coronil, 1997), as if it could solve all of society's problems. This political culture and political structure also contributed further towards the weakening of civil society (of the classes) and the creation of a pragmatic democratic culture.

On the political level, Venezuela's stability was cemented in 1958 with the "Pact of Punto Fijo,"[8] a pact that was signed by the three main political parties of the time, the social-democratic *Acción Democrática* (AD—Democratic Action), the Christian-democratic *Comité de Organización Politica Electoral Independiente* (COPEI—Committee of Independent Political Organization), and the small leftist *Unión Republicana Democratica* (URD—Democratic Republican Union).

The essence of the pact was to share power and resources among the pact's signatories and to exclude any challengers. Part of the reasoning for the pact was, first, to ensure political stability by excluding more radical groups. Second, AD, which was almost certain to win the 1958 presidential elections, realized that it had to share power with at least some of the other parties, if it wanted to avoid a repeat of the 1948 coup that overthrew its democratically elected president Romulo Gallegos. In 1948 AD governed alone and dominated all branches of government, excluding all challengers, which then led them to support a military coup against Gallegos, which eventually led to the Marcos Perez Jimenez dictatorship. The stable Punto Fijo arrangement, though, rapidly led to "rigidity" (Crisp, 2000, 173)[9] and political apathy. Chávez would later rail against the arrangement, blaming the pact for practically everything that was wrong with Venezuela during those years.

Increasing Disappointment: Oil Bust and the Collapse of Pacted Democracy (1979–1998)

A fundamental shift began in Venezuelan society, though, once the oil bonanza began to wane and sputter to a halt. The end of Venezuela's golden years began in 1979, when Venezuela entered its 20-year economic decline. There were occasional oil booms in this period, such as during the Iranian revolution (1980) and the gulf war (1991), but by then the booms could not make up for the lost ground that had already taken place due to heavy indebtedness, increasing oil production costs, declining oil price, and population growth. The decline in per capita oil income and thus also in per capita GDP was steady and unprecedented in the world during this period.

Real per capita income suffered a massive and steady decline over a period of twenty years, from 1979 to 1999, declining by as much as 27% in this period. No other economy in South America experienced such a dramatic fall.[10] Along with this drop, poverty increased, from 17% in 1980 to 65% in 1996.[11] Having such a large proportion of the population slip into poverty was a traumatic experience for Venezuela's middle class, which expected to see their standard of living increase as it had in the previous 20 years, and not decrease.

Eventually not enough resources were available to maintain the clientelistic—corporatistic political culture, which then dealt a deadly blow to the two main political parties and enabled the rise and election of a political outsider. Loyalty to the system had been essentially bought with hard cash rather than earned through political persuasion, so when the money ran out, so did the loyalty. As a result, in the 1993 presidential elections, for the first time in Venezuela's democratic history, a candidate who formally did not belong to the Punto Fijo Pact parties won the election (although, Rafael Caldera, the new president, was one of the original signers of the pact). The votes for Caldera and for another main candidate, Andrés Velasquez, from the leftist *Causa R* party, meant that non-Punto Fijo parties won a majority in that election for the first time.

Another important factor in the decay and rejection of Venezuela's "pacted democracy" was the increased perception of corruption. It is quite common, especially in a situation of diminishing resources, that patronage turns into corruption, since patronage is, in a sense, merely a milder form of corruption. Corruption is, of course, a problem that is endemic to most countries of Latin America and thus does not make the Venezuelan situation distinctive or explain why the political system collapsed there and not elsewhere (though, eventually, it did in some countries). Rather, corruption must be seen as a factor that was both a consequence of the crisis and one that accelerated and deepened it.

A third factor in the fall of Venezuela's Punto Fijo political system was that the parties lacked any kind of innovative capacity.[12] Ossified political structures, a focus on personalism rather than political program, and a general cross-party ideological consensus, made an innovative approach to politics and to the economic crisis practically impossible. Faced with a rapidly changing society and circumstances, the pressure for change grew while an appropriate response to the pressure remained absent. The changes that were introduced were relatively limited, such as introducing elections for governors and mayors in 1989, who were previously appointed. While this allowed for non-Punto-Fijo parties to enter the political arena, such as Andrés Velasquez of *La Causa R* as governor in Bolivar State, it did not introduce change fast enough to allow the Punto-Fijo system to maintain itself.

In addition to the steady decline in oil revenues, one must also add the government's eventual response, which in 1989 consisted of then-president Carlos Andrés Perez turning to the IMF for loans and of introducing neo-liberal "structural-adjustment" reforms. These reforms further hastened the decline of the "pacted democracy" by reinforcing the decline in social spending and of corporatism and clientelism. Also, the fact that the presidents who introduced these reforms, Carlos Andrés Perez (and later, in 1996, Rafael Caldera) instituted them in direct contradiction to their campaign promises, further added to the loss of credibility of, and disgust for, politics and the country's political class.

The Politicization of Hugo Rafael Chávez Frias[13]

It was in the context of economic decline and the deterioration of public institutions that a young soldier by the name of Hugo Rafael Chávez

Frias became politicized. Chávez was born during the Marcos Perez Jimenez dictatorship, in 1954, and grew up in Venezuela's poorest state, in a lower middle class family, during the country's boom years. He joined the military mainly because it was one of the few avenues for upward social mobility, which allowed him to receive a higher education. Venezuela's military was rather unusual in this sense because unlike many other armies of Latin America, it allowed ordinary soldiers from poor backgrounds to rise through the ranks to the highest levels and gave them a university education, often outside of the military academies. As a result, Chávez and many of his peers were exposed to leftist thought at public universities.

In addition to this rather progressive military education, Chávez came face to face with the Colombian civil war and its leftist guerillas and experienced first hand the brutality of this civil war while he was stationed near the Colombian border. Disturbed by this experience, already at 23 years of age, Chávez decided to form his own conspiratorial organization, in 1977, the Liberation Army of the Venezuelan People (*Ejército de Liberación del Pueblo de Venezuela—ELPV*), which had only six members at first. The motivation for creating the group was directly related to his experiences along the border. Chávez tells the story as follows:

> . . . the reflection about the tortures, the strikes against the peasants, the reflection about the corruption of the military, the great Venezuela—so there something happens. . . With three soldiers. . . and two sergeants. . . we formed a group and decided to give it the name: Liberation Army of the Venezuelan People . . . What were we going to do? We did not have the slightest idea at that moment.[14]

Chávez spent several more years in the military, however, before he turned to conspiratorial organizing in all earnestness. During that time, from 1977 to 1982, while Chávez was stationed in Maracay, one of Venezuela's main air bases, the contradiction between the government's effort to create "the great Venezuela" (*La Gran Venezuela*) and the actual reality of economic and institutional decline became ever more glaring. In 1980 he was moved to the military academy in Caracas, where he became a sports instructor. Finally, in 1982, Chávez found several like-minded instructors at the academy, who sympathized with his rejection of the increasingly corrupt Venezuelan social and political system, and founded the EBR–200. EBR, says Chávez, stood for the three ideological roots of the group: Ezequiel Zamora, Simon Bolivar, and Simon Rodriguez. It also stood for Bolivarian revolutionary Army (*Ejército Bolivariano Revolucionario*). The 200 stood for the 200th-year anniversary of Simon Bolivar's birth, in 1783.

Membership of the EBR–200 was based on swearing the same oath that Simon Bolivar swore on Italy's Monte Sacro, when he dedicated himself to fight for Latin American independence: "I swear before you and I swear before the God of my fathers, that I will not allow my arm to relax, nor my soul to rest, until I have broken the chains that oppress us." They were convinced that Venezuelan democracy was not a real democracy, but merely a more sophisticated form of domination. Later, once Chávez started to coordinate with civilians, he renamed his group from EBR–200 to MBR–200 (M for movement).

The key ingredients for Chávez's revolutionary Bolivarianism can be summarized as: an emphasis on the importance of education, the creation of civilian—military unity, Latin American integration, social justice, and national sovereignty.[15] In many ways this is not a particularly different set of principles and ideas to those of any other Enlightenment or national liberation thinker. As a follower of Jean Jacques Rousseau, Bolivar was a classical liberal, except that he tried to apply these ideas to the completely different context of Latin America, where the existence of colonialism, slavery, and an indigenous population made their application more difficult, more radical, and thus more revolutionary than in Europe. Also, compared to the theorists of the US American revolution, Bolivar was far more radical because of his opposition to slavery and his support for indigenous rights.

The Rise to Power of Hugo Chávez

The first real crack in the system, and thus the first push for Chávez to challenge the system, came in February 1989, when the neo-liberal economic shock treatment of Carlos Andrés Perez resulted in rioting throughout the country. Perez reacted to the riots by having the police and the military not only squash them, but also act in retribution against the poor population, for several days, even after the rioting had ended. In the end, the death toll of the so-called "*Caracazo*" was anywhere between 300 and 3,000 dead.[16]

Chávez and his fellow conspirators were unprepared to take advantage of the event by overthrowing the government then. Instead, they used it to redouble their organizing efforts and to find ever more recruits for an eventual attempt to overthrow a government that had just lost almost every last vestige of legitimacy. By February 4, 1992, they were ready and launched their effort to topple President Perez by attempting to take over key military installations and the presidential palace. The effort failed, though, because word of the military rebellion had leaked. Chávez was surrounded in the Caracas historical museum that he had occupied, but couldn't communicate with his comrades. In the end, he surrendered on the condition that he would be allowed to address the nation, to ask his comrades to lay down their arms, so that there wouldn't be any bloodshed. Chávez's one-minute television appearance, which gave a face to a military rebellion that enjoyed widespread popular support, turned him into a folk hero, both for taking responsibility for the failed rebellion—something practically no previous politician had ever done— and for suggesting that he would try again sometime because he said that his group's objectives had not been achieved "for now."

Chávez's coup attempt and the popular support he received among the country's poor and the left were a direct result of the brutal 1989 *Caracazo*, of 12 years of economic decline, and of 25 years of political repression against the country's left. The fact that Venezuela was supposed to be a liberal democracy and one of the continent's richest countries made the contradiction between aspiration and reality all the harsher, thereby legitimating Chávez's actions in the eyes of millions of Venezuelans. A second coup attempt, in November of the same year, while unsuccessful, merely sealed Perez's fate as a failed president and subsequently led to his impeachment over a corruption scandal the following year.

While Venezuela was muddling along economically and politically, unable to get out of its ongoing economic and political decline, Chávez received visitors from the Venezuelan left while spending two years in prison. In 1994, newly elected President Rafael Caldera fulfilled his campaign promise to give an amnesty to Chávez and all other coup participants. Chávez then toured the country and began to realize that much had changed since the time he first began organizing a conspiratorial movement to overthrow the government and that perhaps the electoral route to power and to revolutionary transformation would now be possible. On the urging of various left leaders and with the particular help from Luis Miquilena, a long-time operative of Venezuela's left,[17] Chávez began organizing a political party to help him run for president in the 1998 elections. He thus transformed his movement from MBR–200 into the political party MVR, Movement for the Fifth Republic (using the Latin numeral V, which, in Spanish, sounds similar to "B"). The designation "Fifth Republic" was supposed to signal the complete break from the corrupt and repressive "Punto Fijo Pact," which represented the fourth Venezuelan republic. Allying himself with the union-based party Fatherland for All (PPT—*Patria Para Todos*), Movement towards Socialism (MAS—*Movimiento al Socialismo*), the Communist Party of Venezuela (PCV—*Partido Communista de Venezuela*), and a variety of other smaller parties, Chávez won the presidency on December 6, 1998, with 56.2% of the vote.

With the complete delegitimization of Venezuela's political system and its political class, it should have come as hardly a surprise that a political outsider, who once tried to take the government by force, would be elected on a campaign promise of revolutionizing Venezuela. Hugo Chávez's election to the presidency in December 1998 was thus in many ways the logical consequence of what had come before. Although Chávez did not provide specifics, he promised to completely overhaul Venezuela's political system, beginning with a brand new constitution. He won the vote with support from nearly all classes of society, but especially from the disenchanted middle class, which had been slowly slipping into poverty for the previous 20 years, and from the country's poor.

Counter-Revolution without Revolution[18]

Reasons for Opposing Chávez

Even though Chávez promised a "Bolivarian" revolution, his political program and his speeches attracted the middle class, which desperately wanted someone who would completely overhaul Venezuela's hopelessly corrupt and inefficient political system that they held responsible for their 20-year-long slide into poverty. In the end, Chávez was thus elected largely by the middle class.[19] Not that the poor didn't vote or count—

they did, but the poor in Venezuela, just as anywhere else in the world, turned out to vote in a much smaller proportion than the middle and upper class. In other words, Chávez would never have been elected by the poor by itself in 1998, given its relatively low rate of participation and registration. The source of Chávez's support changed completely by the time of the recall referendum vote in 2004. By then the middle class had practically abandoned Chávez—who had consistently moved towards the left in those five and a half years—and was almost entirely confirmed in office by the vote of the poor.[20]

Exactly how this happened was the result of the aforementioned dialectic of counter-revolution and radicalization that took place during Chávez's presidency. Each effort by the old regime's elite to discredit Chávez caused the middle class to reject Chávez more and to support efforts to overthrow him. Each effort to topple Chávez, though, caused him and his movement to radicalize more, thereby further stiffening his opposition and feeding a growing vicious cycle of counter-revolution and radicalization. Why, though, did the opposition oppose Chávez in the first place? What was it that he did that caused them to engage in counter-revolution when he was enjoying the support of such a broad segment of the middle class when he was first elected?

There are countless reasons why there is such vehement opposition to Chávez. Generally they fall into one of three categories: articulated but mostly fabricated reasons, articulated and real reasons, and, third, unarticulated and perhaps unconscious reasons. The reasons for opposing Chávez that one reads about most often in the media are those that are articulated but mostly fabricated, such as Chávez having supposedly stolen the 2004 recall referendum, that Chávez supports international terrorism, that Chávez is leading the country into a dictatorship, or that Chávez himself engineered the April 2002 coup attempt in a ploy to acquire more power. This is not the place to discuss and rebut fabricated reasons such as these. By and large, one can say that such reasons are the result of an extreme distrust of Chávez (which generally has its roots in the unconscious reasons), combined with a concerted disinformation campaign to discredit him both within Venezuela and internationally.[21]

More important for the sake of the analysis presented here, are the unarticulated and unconscious reasons the opposition wants to oust Chávez, because these are the reasons that give the opposition their force, and fuel the above-mentioned fabrication of reasons for opposing him.

The articulated but perhaps real charges against Chávez, such as accusations of corruption, accusations of the abuse of power by individual government officials, or the charge that there is a personality cult around Chávez are serious, but do not appear to belong to the most important reasons for the opposition. Since these reasons are more relevant to the long-term viability of the Bolivarian project, they will be examined in detail at the end of this book.

The unarticulated and usually unconscious reasons that fueled the opposition's efforts to oust Chávez have their roots in Venezuelan racism/classism and in the old elite's loss of class power. While there is little serious research on racism and classism in Venezuela in general, and on racism/classism that is directed against Chávez and his supporters in particular,[22] the little research there is and the anecdotal evidence for it are overwhelming. Oddly, though, when Chávez first took office, he enjoyed approval ratings of up to 90%, which would suggest that racism and classism for eventual middle class opposition to Chávez could not be an important factor.

The reason, though, that such racism/classism did not play a role early on in Chávez's presidency was that, at first, Chávez was not identified with being a member of a "lower" racial group or economic class. Rather, the racism and classism that worked against Chávez only "kicked in" once Chávez was targeted as deserving of such treatment. How and why, then, was such an attack accomplished? The answer to this is two-fold. First, Chávez himself, via his discourse and behavior, more and more clearly identified with the Venezuelan poor and marginalized, which, in turn, caused him to be seen as belonging to this group. Second, and more importantly, Chávez progressively removed the country's old governing class—in politics, the economy, and culture—from power. It is this loss of institutional class power that, above all else, caused the old elite to oppose Chávez, rather than the actual policies of the Chávez government, as is usually suggested. The old elite then used its control of the country's mass media to turn the middle class against Chávez, creating a campaign that took advantage of the latent racism and classism in Venezuelan culture. In other words, the dramatic loss of political power is what gave the country's old governing class all the reasons it needed to oppose Chávez and to reject him as the legitimately elected president of Venezuela.

Removing the Old Elite from Power: February 1999 to October 2001

The loss of power and the corresponding rejection of Chávez's legitimacy occurred step-wise. The very first such step was Chávez's naming of a cabinet that had little or no ties to the country's elite. According to past practice, key ministers had always come from the sectors that were supposed to be administrated. For example, the economics minister came from big business, the culture minister from a media outlet, the defense minister from the military, etc. Chávez, however, immediately broke with this tradition when he named his first cabinet in February 1999, who almost all belonged to the Venezuelan left.

The next step in reducing the old governing class's power was the writing of a new constitution. Chávez first convoked a referendum asking whether a constitutional assembly should be organized on April 25, 1999, and then convoked the election of constitutional assembly members, on July 25. Chávez and his supporters won both votes with an overwhelming margin, with 92% approving of the convocation of the constitutional assembly, and winning 125 out of the assembly's 131 seats. Chávez's supporters dominated the assembly so easily because the rules, which had also been put to a vote and were approved by 86% of the voters, specified that assembly members would be elected as in-dividuals, instead of via party lists. Following four months of debate, the constitution was put to a vote on December 15, 1999, and was approved by 72% of the vote.

In another act that incensed the opposition, the constitutional assembly appointed a transitional legislature, shortly before its disband-ing, known as "Congresillo." This body immediately went ahead and appointed the new Attorney General, the Human Rights Defender, the Comptroller General, the National Electoral Council, and the Supreme Court. All of these appointments were supposed to be transitional, until there was a new National Assembly which could reverse or ratify them. The move's transitionality, though, did not change the fact that for the opposition it meant the permanent removal of a Supreme Court and an Electoral Council that was part of the country's old governing elite.

The most important consequence of the new constitution that diminished the old elite's power was its requirement for the holding of so-called "mega-elections" to "re-legitimate" all elected officials, including the president, state governors, mayors, National Assembly deputies, and city council members. Also, the new constitution specified social rights that assured greater state involvement in the economy, such as the right to employment, to food, shelter, and to health care. Other important provisions that limited the role of the country's economic elite included the state's commitment to abolish *latifundios* (large and idle landed estates) and the prohibition to privatize the state oil company.

However, it was the "mega-elections" of July 30, 2000 that eliminated the country's old political elite almost entirely from the upper reaches of Venezuela's public institutions and that were the greatest cause of their loss of influence in the country's affairs. Thirty-three thousand candidates ran for over 6,000 offices that day. In the end, Chávez was reconfirmed in office with 59.8% of the vote. Chávez's supporters won 104 out of 165 National Assembly seats and 17 out of 23 state governorships. On the local level Chávez candidates were less successful, winning only about half of the municipal mayors' posts.

Because Chávez's supporters enjoyed a solid two-thirds majority in the National Assembly, it was easy for them to re-appoint the heads of the other three branches of government: the "moral power" (Attorney General, Comptroller General, and Human Rights Ombudsperson), the judiciary, and the electoral power.[23] The transformation of the Venezuelan political arena from one that was once governed by AD-Copei party members to one that was now governed by adherents of the Bolivarian Revolution, was thus complete by the end of the year 2000.

It is this political transformation of Venezuela—the elimination of the country's former governing elite from nearly all centers of political power—that made Chávez wholly unacceptable to this elite, rather than any specific policies that Chávez pursued during his first two years in office. As a matter of fact, his economic and social policies in this time were not particularly different from those of his predecessors. No expropriations, no limitations on making a profit, and no redistribution of wealth had taken place until then. Also, the economy was enjoying a recovery in 2000, largely thanks to Chávez's efforts to consolidate OPEC and raise the price of oil.

Two more incidents, though, threatened to further erode the old elite's power: a forced vote on the leadership of the national union federation CTV and the passage of 49 law-decrees, which the National Assembly had authorized. While Chávez's candidates appeared to have lost the CTV election in October 2001,[24] three of the 49 law-decrees, which were presented in November 2001, proved to infringe on centers of economic power. This is what set the stage for the ensuing "counter-revolution without revolution."

Heightened Resistance, Coup Attempt, and Retreat: November 2001 to December 2002

The outcry against these law-decrees was immediate. The three laws that were the most objectionable, though, were the Land Law, which promised to institute a sweeping land reform of all idle lands of over 5,000 hectares, the Hydrocarbons Law, which raised royalties on oil exploration by foreign companies, and the Fishing Law, which forced large fishers to fish further away from the coast, so that "artisanal" fishers would have a better chance.

Fedecamaras, the country's largest and most important chamber of commerce, complained that these laws were anti-business, undermined private property rights, and were passed without consulting them or anyone outside of government circles. Venezuela's main union federation, the Confederation of Venezuelan Workers (CTV) quickly joined the fray. Ironically, their main argument against the laws was that they were harmful to Venezuela's business community and therefore harmful to Venezuelan workers. A more likely explanation for the CTV's support of the employer federation, aside from their ties to the former governing party AD, was that the CTV had just gone through a pitched battle with the government over control of the organization.

The result of the vehement CTV/Fedecamaras opposition to the government was that the two organizations called for a "general strike" on December 10, 2001. The strike met with moderate success, but the media and the private sector's lockout of their employees for a day gave the "strike" a heightened visible effect.

But it was not only the package of 49 laws that added fire to Venezuela's conflict. Another crucial factor was that the economy suddenly slowed down in the wake of the September 11 terrorist attack on the US. The attack had sparked a worldwide recession and, with it, a decline in the price of oil. This double-blow—low oil prices and a global economic slowdown—forced the government to adjust its budget and cut back spending in all areas by at least 10%. The impact was almost immediately noticeable, as unemployment began inching upwards again, after it had steadily declined in 2000 and 2001.

Meanwhile, an escalation in verbal attacks between Chávez and his opposition began reaching new heights. The economic downturn, the 49 laws, and Chávez's strong discourse against the "squalid opposition" and the "rancid oligarchy," all made it relatively easy for the opposition to chip away at Chávez's popularity, with substantial help from the private mass media. Opinion polls—which can show some trends, but which are not necessarily reliable because their ability to reach into the hearts of the poor neighborhoods is doubtful—indicate that Chávez's popularity rating dropped from around 60–70% to 30–40% between June 2001 and January 2002.

This was the context in which the opposition became convinced that it could oust Chávez—whose legitimacy its leaders never truly accepted—before the end of his presidency. Three concrete attempts thus took place between January 2002 and August 2004. The first was the April 2002 coup attempt, whose apparent detonator was the oil industry management's resistance to Chávez's efforts to gain control over the state-owned oil industry. Crucial to this attempt, however, was a disgruntled sector of the military that, for a variety of ideological and opportunistic reasons, believed that it could and should get rid of Chávez. The failure of the coup, a mere 47 hours after Chávez was removed from office, was emblematic of all subsequent opposition failures to oust Chávez from the presidency. The opposition consistently underestimated the president's popularity, believing instead the mass media's constant claim that Chávez was highly unpopular and incapable as president. However, it was Chávez's support amongst the country's poor and the military that swept him back into the presidency. For the opposition, this was a bitter defeat because it lost an important base of its power in the military.[25]

Chávez's reaction to the coup attempt, after his return, was to moderate his tone and to play it safe. He put a new economic team in charge that appeared to be more centrist and promised to include the opposition more in policy deliberations. Also, Chávez reinstated the old board of directors and former managers of the state oil company PDVSA, whose replacement had been one of the reasons for the coup.

Oil Industry Shutdown and Chávez's Comeback: December 2002 to March 2003

Following a brief period of uncertain calm, the opposition interpreted Chávez's retreat as an opportunity for another offensive against him, this time by organizing an indefinite shutdown of the country's all-important oil industry in early December 2002. While the opposition labeled this action a "general strike," it was actually a combination of management lockout, administrative and professional employee strike, and general sabotage of the oil industry. Also, it was mostly the US fast food franchises and the upscale shopping malls that were closed for about two months. The rest of the country operated more or less normally during this time, except for food and gasoline shortages throughout Venezuela, mostly because many distribution centers were closed down.

Eventually, though, the shutdown was defeated, once again due to the opposition's underestimation of Chávez's support. That is, while about 19,000 or half of the oil company's employees were eventually fired, for abandoning their workplaces, the government managed nonetheless to re-start the oil company with the help of retired workers, foreign contractors, and the military. According to government figures, the industry recovered and as of mid-2003 has been operating at normal levels, producing over 3.1 million barrels of oil per day. The opposition, however, claimed that production never exceeded 2.6 million bpd since the end of the "strike." The opposition thus tried to find solace in another failure. As such, it lost another crucial base of power, this time in the oil industry, whose managers were practically all opposition supporters and were all replaced.

The oil industry's recovery, along with a dramatically increasing price of oil and thus of oil revenues, meant that Chávez now had the resources to introduce new social programs, known as "missions," to address the desperate needs of the country's poor. The first missions Chávez introduced between late 2003 and early 2004 were for literacy training (Mission Robinson), high school completion (Mission Ribas), university scholarships (Mission Sucre), community health care (Mission Barrio Adentro), and subsidized food markets (Mission Mercal).

Radicalization and Defeat of the Counter-Revolution

The Recall Referendum and Presidential Elections:
April 2003 to December 2006

The third and last attempt to oust Chávez during his first full term was the August 2004 recall referendum. After having suffered defeat in two consecutive illegal attempts, the opposition was forced to follow the only democratic and constitutional route for getting rid of Chávez. At the end of the oil-industry shutdown, on February 2, 2003, the opposition had initiated a process for organizing a wide variety of referenda against Chávez, but these were subsequently dismissed by the Supreme Court or dropped by the opposition itself, mostly due to the incorrect manner in which the referendum petitions were formulated or due to the timing of the signature collection process.[26] The agreement to follow a strictly constitutional route for resolving Venezuela's political crisis was formalized in a signed agreement between opposition and government that the Organization of American States and the Carter Center facilitated in May 2003.

Eventually, once a new electoral council (CNE) and the rules governing recall referenda were in place, which took until the end of 2003, the opposition collected 3.1 million signatures in December. Of these, following much political debate, the CNE validated 2.5 million signatures and convoked a referendum for August 15, 2004, only four days before another constitutional deadline (August 19, 2004) that would have lead to the vice-president filling the rest of the president's term, should the president's mandate be revoked.

Shortly after 4 a.m. on August 16, CNE president Francisco Carrasquero announced the first preliminary results of the referendum, giving Chávez a 58% to 42% victory.[27] Immediately after Carrasquero's announcement, opposition leaders held a press conference in which they stated unequivocally that fraud had been perpetrated. They offered no evidence for this claim except to say that they were convinced of it. Despite this claim, the election observer mission of the Organization of American States and of the Carter Center ratified the official result.

For the opposition, this was perhaps the bitterest defeat of all the defeats it had to suffer. Not only did it no longer have a base of power in the executive, the legislature, in the military, or in the oil industry, it now lost its perhaps most important base of power, in the illusion that it was the majority. This loss was later accompanied by a massive loss of support in the middle class. That is, following three years of continuous battle with Chávez, promising its supporters that Chávez was on his way out any day and that he was illegitimate because they represented the majority, opposition supporters saw just how hollow and incompetent its leaders were. Polls after the recall referendum documented a dramatic loss of support for the opposition, so that by July 2005 only 15% of Venezuelans said they identified with them.[28]

Chávez, realizing this near total loss of opposition power, announced in his victory speech that now would begin a new phase of his government. "From today until December 2006 begins a new phase of the Bolivarian revolution, to give continuity to the social missions, to the struggle against injustice, exclusion, and poverty. I invite all, including the opposition, to join in the work to make Venezuela a country of justice, with the rule of law and with social justice."[29] Later, in January 2005, Chávez took this call for a new phase even further, by announcing that from now on his government would seek to build "socialism of the 21st century" in Venezuela. Thus, the continuous efforts of the opposition to oust Chávez, based on its non-recognition of his legitimacy, led to a continuous weakening of this opposition and the concomitant opportunity for Chávez to radicalize his program. An important part of this new program was to push for greater state involvement in the economy, more self-management in the form of cooperatives and co-managed factories, more land reform, and more direct democracy at the local level.

Chávez's call to build twenty-first century socialism received another boost on December 3, 2006, when he decisively won a second six-year term in the presidency. Chávez beat the opposition candidate, Manuel Rosales, with 62.9% to 37.9%. As such, Chávez's 26 percentage point margin of victory was the largest in Venezuela's post-dictatorship history. Also, Chávez managed to double his support from an initial 3.7 million votes in 1998 (56.2% of the total votes cast) to 7.3 million in 2006.

More significant than the increase in support, though, was that the opposition candidate, Manuel Rosales, admitted that he was defeated by Chávez. This is the first time since Chávez's initial election in 1998 that an opposition leader conceded defeat in a confrontation with him. In none of the opposition's previous confrontations with Chávez, whether following the 2002 coup attempt, the 2003 oil industry shutdown, or the 2004 recall referendum, did the opposition take responsibility for its actions. This implies that this was the first time since 2000 that the opposition recognized Chávez as the legitimately elected president and thus opened the path towards the normalization of Venezuelan politics in the Chávez era. As such, the election further smoothed the path for Chávez to lead Venezuela towards 21st century socialism.[30]

If the opposition had merely accepted its defeat in 1998 and had recognized Chávez's legitimacy as the elected president of Venezuela from the start, it is quite likely that Chávez would never have moved towards an all-out effort to create "twenty-first century socialism" in Venezuela. We will never know whether this would have happened for certain, but it cannot be denied that Chávez radicalized his program in reaction to the opposition's actions and not the other way around. At first, following the April 2002 coup attempt, Chávez acted with caution, but then the second attempt to oust him, via the oil industry shutdown in December 2002, taught him that moderation was not the best way to deal with the opposition. From then on he thus kept radicalizing his program, first by pushing forward with the land reform and the social programs, in late 2003, and later, following the August 2004 recall referendum, he pushed ahead with worker takeovers of idle factories and then announced his intention to pursue socialism for Venezuela.

Venezuela's radicalization thus resembles, to a limited extent, the radicalization that occurred in Cuba following its revolution in 1959 and the one that occurred in Nicaragua following its revolution in 1979, both of which occurred in reaction to efforts to defeat these revolutions, rather than as part of an original plan. Unlike these other two efforts, though, it seems that following the 2006 presidential elections, the Bolivarian revolution has soundly defeated its domestic and international adversaries and is now, with the help of its substantial oil wealth—which the other two revolutions lacked—in a good position to implement its vision of socialism with hardly any remaining external obstacles. What, exactly, this vision looks like is the topic of the rest of the book.

2

Governance Policy:
the Constitution, the Judiciary, the
Military, and Participatory Democracy

The Chávez government's policies relating to governance, that is, how political power is exercised in Venezuela, can be divided into four main areas: constitution, judiciary, military, and participatory democracy. In each of these areas the Chávez government has introduced substantial changes, which lay the groundwork for creating a more participatory and just society. Unfortunately, often Chávez and his supporters undermine positive policies with ones that undermine them, such as centralization, as in the case of the president's new powers, the lack of institutionalization, as in the case of the increased civilian duties of the military, or the slow pace at which laws that support participatory democracy have been passed.

The 1999 Constitution of the Bolivarian Republic of Venezuela

One of the first things that Chávez set out to do when he took office was to revamp Venezuela's constitution. As stated earlier, he was able to do this because he won a strong mandate in 1998 to completely reform Venezuela's political system. This mandate was reaffirmed with the April 1999 referendum on whether to convoke a constitutional assembly, with the election of pro-Chávez members of the constitutional assembly, and with the December 1999 approval of the new constitution.

In the process of devising a new constitution Chávez reformed not just the constitution, but Venezuela's entire polity, meaning the institutions that have to do with the exercise of state power, such as the judiciary, the military, and the application of the concept of participatory democracy.

It should be noted that the effort to either completely rewrite or to reform Venezuela's constitution was nothing new in Venezuelan history.

Between 1811 and 1961 Venezuela had 26 constitutions, the largest number of constitutions in Latin America. The 1961 constitution lasted a fairly long time, though, nearly 40 years, until 1999. However, it too has been subject to several reform efforts during the 1980s and 1990s. President Jaime Lusinchi, in 1988, made some changes that allowed for greater citizen participation in Venezuela's political system, by allowing for the election of state governors and mayors, who were previously appointed by the executive. This was the first step that eventually allowed for more parties besides Acción Democrática and Copei to be represented at state and local level. Further changes to the constitution were planned, but never implemented. Then, following Chávez's 1992 coup attempt, the calls for a new constitution were renewed. This too faltered within a few months. During his 1994 presidential campaign, Rafael Caldera brought the issue up again, but again did not get far.

Chávez, however, by making the new constitution one of his primary government program elements and by tapping into the population's tremendous dissatisfaction with the previous political system, managed to introduce a new constitution in record time. By December 1999 Venezuela had a new constitution, which, according to Chávez, marked a radical break from the country's past and inaugurated the start of Venezuela's "Fifth Republic." Concretely, the new constitution brought a number of major changes with it, such as changing the country's name, adding two branches of government, introducing popular referenda, strengthening the presidency in some respects, and introducing local public planning councils.

A Name Change

The new constitution changed the country's name, from the "Republic of Venezuela" to the "Bolivarian Republic of Venezuela." This was a change that Chávez insisted upon, even after his own supporters in the constitutional assembly had rejected it, mainly because it would imply too much of an expense to change all of the government's letterheads, official seals, etc. Finally, however, Chávez convinced the assembly and the name change was included, with the proviso that the old stationery and related official material be used up before fresh supplies with the new name be ordered.

The new name is supposed to signal that Venezuela is just one of the countries that its founder, Simon Bolivar, liberated and that it could, in the future, belong to a federation of "Bolivarian Republics."[1] Given the great importance that Simon Bolivar plays in Chávez's political belief system, it should come as no surprise that he would insist on this change.

Gender Inclusivity

Unlike practically all constitutions ever written, Venezuela's now incorporates the masculine and the feminine versions of all political actors it mentions. That is, the Spanish language, just as most European languages (except English), distinguishes between the masculine and feminine versions of job titles, such as "presidente" and "presidenta." Every time the constitution refers to any individual, such as president, citizen, lawyer, representative, minister, etc., the reference is in both the masculine and the feminine forms. This inclusivity makes the Venezuelan constitution one that can be called "non-androcentric".[2] The implication of constitutions that use only the masculine versions is that either women are not considered to be serious participants in the political sphere or that if they do participate, they ought to be like men. By including both the masculine and feminine versions of the different roles that political actors have, the constitution makes explicit the invitation that women participate equally in politics, without implying their masculinization.

The State of Law and Justice

Article 2 of the new constitution says that "Venezuela constitutes itself in a democratic and social state of law and justice . . ." This stands in contrast to most other countries' constitutions, which simply say that the state is governed by the rule of law.[3] In other words, the Venezuelan constitution highlights the potential differences between law and justice, implying that justice is just as important as the rule of law, which might not always bring about justice.

The constitution's declaration of motives, which precedes the official constitutional text, elaborates on the concept of justice by saying, "the state promotes the well-being of Venezuelans, creating the necessary conditions for their social and spiritual development, and striving for equality of opportunity so that all citizens may freely develop their personality, direct their destiny, enjoy human rights and search for their happiness."[4] Critics have argued that this conception of a state of justice, which contrasts with the state of law, could lead to situations in which a vaguely defined notion of justice prevails over the law, thus opening the possibility for a supposedly benevolent dictatorship. However, given that the concrete consequences of this principle are spelled out in the constitution's sections on affirmative action and in other sections, it seems unlikely that article 2 could be used for interpretations that go that far beyond what the constitution prescribes.

Human Rights and International Treaties

Before Chávez came to power Venezuela was formally bound by human rights standards, but in practice often violated them. Torture, censorship, and violations of the right to assembly were quite common, especially during the second presidency of Carlos Andres Perez (1989–1993). Those who suffered from these human rights violations were to a very large extent the same people who swept into power with the election of Chávez as president. Many of these individuals thus participated in the formulation of the new constitution as members of the constitutional assembly. As a result, they gave human rights a central place in the constitution. However, the human rights that the constitution mentions go far beyond what most constitutions incorporate. Not only civil rights, such as the freedom of expression, assembly, and political participation are included, but so are social human rights, such as the right to employment, housing, and health care. For example, with regard to health care, the constitution states, "Health is a fundamental social right, an obligation of the state, which guarantees it as part of the right to life." In practice, this has opened health care to many Venezuelans who previously did not have access to it.

A further innovation of the new constitution is the inclusion of international treaties as having equal standing with the constitution, meaning that they must be enforced in the same way.

Women's Rights

The constitution incorporates some of the most progressive principles on this issue. For example, the constitution adopts the definition of discrimination that has been set up by the "Convention for the Elimination of all forms of Discrimination against Women" (CEDAW). This definition states that acts are considered discriminatory not only if they are intended as such, but also when they have the effect of producing inequality. Article 21 thus states, "all persons are equal before the law and consequently: No discrimination based on race, sex, creed or social standing shall be permitted, nor, in general, any discrimination with the intent or *effect* of nullifying or impairing upon the recognition, enjoyment or exercise, on equal terms, of the rights and liberties of every individual." What this means in practice is that public policies must be reexamined for their possible discriminatory effects, not just outright discrimination. For example, if women are under-represented at public universities, the state is obliged to examine the causes for this and to eliminate any barriers that exist that cause fewer women than men to attend.

Another important women's right that the new constitution includes is the right of women homemakers to receive social security benefits on account of the work they perform in the home. Specifically, it says, "The State guarantees the equality and equitable treatment of men and women in the exercise of the right to work. The state recognizes work at home as an economic activity that creates added value and produces social welfare and wealth. Homemakers are entitled to Social Security in accordance with law" (Article 88). However, due to delays in passing Venezuela's social security law, this article has not yet been put into full practice. Its spirit is being applied, though, in a new stipend or salary of 80% minimum wage that 200,000 poor mothers have been receiving since early 2006, via the social program known as Mothers of the Barrio (*Misión Madres del Barrio*).

The Right to Information

Article 58, which guarantees the right to information, was one of the more controversial articles while the constitution was being discussed in the constitutional assembly. The reason for this is that it states that citizens not only have the right to information, but that they have the right to information that is "timely, true, and impartial." Members of the opposition read this article as providing the state with the possibility of censoring information that is not considered "true" or "impartial."

However, the next words contradict such an interpretation, by saying that information is to be provided "without censorship, in accordance with the principles of this constitution." Also, at the time of this writing, no effort at censorship has been made by the Chávez government, even though previous Venezuelan governments have done this frequently when the press has criticized them the way it has criticized the Chávez government.[5]

Political Parties

State financing of political parties was eliminated with the new constitution. Previously, the state had provided generous financing to the two main political parties, Acción Democratica and Copei, which enabled these to establish and maintain their dominance in Venezuelan political life for so long. However, with their complete loss of credibility and the corruption associated with state financing, the constitutional assembly decided to eliminate state funding for parties altogether. Given the debate this issue has provoked in northern countries, where progressive forces tend to favor state financing of election campaigns, so that the interests of the wealthy do not predominate in politics, it seems odd that a progressive political movement would enshrine the prohibition of state financing for campaigns in the constitution. But this is not all that strange when one considers how campaign financing was used to exclude all challengers to the old political system.

Referenda

In some ways, articles 71 to 74, which establish the possibility of a variety of different types of popular referenda, represent some of the most important innovations of the new constitution. Four types of referenda are possible: consultative, recall, approving, and rescinding. Each type has slightly different procedural requirements for their implementation. Generally referenda can either be initiated by the National Assembly, the president, or by petition from between 10 and 20% of the registered voters. The consultative referendum is designed to ask the population a non-binding question of a "national transcendent" nature, such as whether the country should join a free trade agreement, or a currency union. The consultative referendum was also the one that the opposition attempted to use in February 2003 to force Chávez to resign, by asking the electorate whether or not he should. The Supreme Court, however, declared the question unconstitutional, since the recall referendum was designed explicitly for this purpose, but carries tougher requirements than the consultative referendum. That is, the recall referendum, which can be applied to any elected office, whether president, state governor, national assembly representative, or city mayor, can only be implemented after half of the term in office has been completed. The approving referendum, just like the recall referendum, is binding and is used to pass important laws or to implement treaties that would infringe on national sovereignty. Also, this referendum is used to approve of amendments to the constitution. Finally, the rescinding referendum is used to rescind existing laws.

Social, Educational, Cultural, and Economic Rights

The new constitution enshrines many more rights besides the usual human rights. Motherhood, for example, is protected from the point of conception on, meaning that prenatal care is guaranteed although thereby making abortion somewhat more difficult). Also, family planning is to be provided by the state. Further, housing, health care, and employment, are discussed at length and are to be guaranteed by the state. Related to employment rights, the constitution states, "Every worker has the right to a sufficient salary that allows a life with dignity and covers his own and his family's basic material, social, and intellectual necessities."[6] In relation to economic rights, the state is obligated to promote and protect economic democracy, such as cooperatives.[7]

As critics have pointed out, many, if not most, of these rights or state duties are impossible for the state to fulfill completely when the state has limited financial resources. Also, the lack of mention of how such rights are to be enforced or what happens if they are not met complicates their implementation further. However, as will be discussed at the end of this section, advocates of the constitution see this section of the constitution (articles 75–129), among several others, as crucial in setting a socialist agenda or political program for the future of Venezuela.

Indigenous Rights

When it came to formulating the rights of Venezuela's indigenous population, the constitutional assembly turned the task over to the representatives of the indigenous population itself. This population of around 500,000, which is relatively small compared to that of some other Latin American countries (about 1% of Venezuela's population), is divided into approximately 26 ethnic groups. During the election of the representatives to the constitutional assembly, Chávez ensured that the assembly's rules would guarantee three representatives to the country's indigenous population.

The new constitution first of all recognizes, for the first time in Venezuela's history, the indigenous population's right to exist, to its languages, cultures, and to its territories. The state thus also commits itself to help the indigenous communities to demarcate their lands. Next, the state guarantees that the exploitation of natural resources in lands of the indigenous population will not negatively affect them.

Also unusual for a Latin American state is that the state is committed to not only protecting, but to promoting indigenous culture and languages, which, among other things, means the funding of bilingual education for the indigenous population. As another part of the protection of indigenous populations, the state must protect their intellectual property, even forbidding outsiders to register patents based on indigenous knowledge.

Finally, just as with the constitutional assembly, the constitution guarantees the indigenous population political representation in the National Assembly and in other elected bodies. Currently they are assured three out of the 167 seats in the National Assembly.

Environmental Rights

Environmental rights are another area where the constitution establishes very progressive standards. For example, it commits the state to protecting the environment, biological diversity, genetic resources, ecological processes, and national parks. Also, it prohibits the patenting of the genes of living beings. Highly unusual for a constitution is the inclusion of the obligation to issue environmental and socio-cultural impact reports for any activities that could cause environmental damage.

Five Branches of Government Instead of Three

Perhaps one of the more unusual innovations of the constitution is the creation of five instead of the usual three branches of government. In addition to the usual three of legislative, executive, and judiciary, the new constitution adds an electoral branch and a citizen branch, which is based on an idea of Simon Bolivar's.

The citizen branch is meant to ensure that the other four branches comply with their constitutionally determined functions. The citizen branch (often also known as the "moral power") consists of the attorney general, the defender of the people (or human rights defender), and the comptroller general. Specifically, the constitution states that this branch should "prevent, investigate, and punish deeds that go against public ethics and administrative morality; watch for good management and legality in the use of the public patrimony, the fulfillment and the application of the principle of legality in all administrative activity of the state . . ."[8]

The division of labor between the three offices is such that the defender of the people is supposed to watch for the state's adherence to human rights. The attorney general's office, in contrast, focuses more on prosecuting citizens' violations of the law. Finally, the comptroller general watches for corruption and the proper administration of public finances.

As for the fifth branch, the electoral branch, it is constituted by the national electoral council (CNE), which regulates and watches over proper electoral procedures. It is principally in charge of state elections, but can also guard over the elections of organizations of civil society, such as unions, either at the request of the organization or of the Supreme Court.

The National Assembly appoints the top members of the judicial, citizen, and electoral branches, following a public recruitment and hearing process and a vote of the National Assembly. In the case of the Supreme Court judges, the National Assembly elects them for a 12-year term, in accordance with a new and controversial Supreme Court law, which establishes that if a judge is not elected with a two-thirds majority in the first three votes, then a simple majority is sufficient. In the case of the three top representatives of the Citizen Power, the National Assembly elects these with a two-thirds majority for a seven-year term. If no two-thirds majority is reached within 30 days, their election is put to the general population. Neither the judges nor the Citizen Power representatives may serve for more than one term.[9]

The Legislature

The biggest change with respect to the legislature was that it was changed from a bicameral system, similar to the US Congress, to a unicameral one, similar to France's National Assembly. The argument behind this change was that Venezuela needed a legislature that would be more responsive to the country's needs by being able to pass laws more quickly. Critics, however, argued that the change favors the centralization of the government because the Senate, which had an equal number of representatives from each state, just like in the US, was eliminated. In practice, the new unicameral National Assembly has not been faster in approving laws than the old legislature. During the period of intense conflict with the opposition, from 2001 to 2004, the legislature fell far behind its legislative schedule. The reason for this, however, can largely be traced to opposition stalling tactics that prevented the conclusion of debates on laws.

The Presidency

Perhaps one of the most controversial topics in the new constitution was the office of the presidency. Chávez insisted on increasing the presidential term from five to six years and on allowing his or her immediate and only re-election. Previously the president was not allowed to run for immediate re-election, but could run again after a minimum ten-year absence. This is what enabled both Rafael Caldera and Carlos Andres Perez to serve twice as president, each during different decades in Venezuela's history.[10] Chávez's argument for extending the president's term and for allowing immediate re-election was that the task of rebuilding Venezuela is so great that a single five-year term is not enough. Often Chávez even says that the task will last until the year 2021 or until 2030, which has led many of his opponents to accuse him of wanting to remain in office until then. While Chávez at first denied such accusations, since early 2006 he has backtracked on this and proposed a constitutional amendment that would allow for an indefinite number of re-elections of the president. Following his re-election on December 3, 2006 Chávez announced that he intends to run for President again in December 2012. As will be discussed in the final chapter, such plans directly undermine efforts to create a progressive social movement that is self-sustaining and is capable of pursuing twenty-first century socialism because of the force of its ideas and not because of the force of Chávez's personality.

State Role in the Economy

Some analysts argue that the new constitution assigns a much larger economic role to the state than the previous constitution did.[11] Indeed, section VI of the constitution, on "the socio-economic system," outlines that the state is responsible for promoting national industry, agriculture, and various other smaller branches, such as fishing, cooperatives, tourism, small businesses, crafts, etc. The promotion of a diversity of economic activity appears to show an awareness of Venezuela's problem, that its economy needs to diversify if it is to be sustainable in the long run. Beyond the state's obligation to promote various aspects of the economy, though, the type of socio-economic system or even its general characteristics are not spelled out, despite the section's title.

Civil Disobedience

Not much attention was paid to the section about civil disobedience when the constitution was first written. However, following the April 2002 coup attempt, the opposition relied heavily on articles 333 and 350 to justify its questionable or illegal actions, with the argument that these articles give citizens the right to civil disobedience. Also, during the December 2002 oil industry strike, oil industry managers made reference to these articles to justify their shutting down of the oil industry.

These two articles basically state that citizens have an obligation to reestablish the applicability of the constitution, should the current government fail to follow the constitution. However, while the opposition has tended to use the term civil disobedience, which has a long established meaning in the context of civil rights struggles in the US and elsewhere, the constitution merely uses the terms "obligation to reestablish the validity of the constitution" (article 333) and "people of

Venezuela . . . disavow any regime, legislation, or authority that contradicts the values, principles, and democratic guarantees or impairment of human rights" (article 350). Pro-Chávez constitutional lawyer Carlos Escarrá has thus argued that neither of these articles permits the breaking of laws and that the disavowal of the "regime" or the reestablishment of the democratic order must remain within the framework set by the constitution.

Common Criticisms of the Constitution

One of the more common and serious charges leveled against the 1999 constitution is that it strengthens the military's role in Venezuelan society. Perhaps most importantly in this respect is that rather than having the legislature approve of military promotions, the task has now been placed solely and directly with the armed forces itself. Critics argue that this places the military more directly at the service of the president and of his political program because he wields tremendous influence within the military.[12] Specifically, they say that Chávez is interested in a military that actively supports his political program and that only those who do so are promoted. Also, the new constitution has given the members of the military the right to vote, something that was previously denied to them, so as to keep them completely out of politics. The Chávez government augmented these constitutional changes with some administrative changes, such as placing around 200 active duty officers at different levels in various government institutions. Also, he ordered the military to devise and implement plans for combating poverty, such as the Plan Bolivar 2000.

Chávez has often argued that a key element of his political program is to revise the relationship between the population and the military, so that the military acquires a more useful function in society, which goes beyond merely military defense and takes advantage of its huge resources to help solve social problems, with the argument that the country should be defended not only against military attack, but also against poverty and injustice. Critics say that as a result of Chávez's policies, civilian society has become more "militarized." Some have even gone so far as to argue that the real rulers in Venezuela are the military, not Chávez. In contrast, Chávez and his supporters, though, argue that the military has become more "civilian" in its functions.

Chávez has said that this process is based on the principle of "civil—military unity" (*unidad civico-militar*).

However, how can one tell if civilian society is becoming more militarized or if the military is becoming more civilian? In either case, it is certain that the strict separation between military and civilian sectors has been blurred. One indication that the military is not in control of the government and hence that the military is becoming more civilian instead of the other way around is that Chávez, for the first time in Venezuela's history, appointed a civilian as minister of defense, José Vicente Rangel. Also, while Chávez has many retired military officers actively involved in programmatic and ideological functions of his government (such as Diosdado Cabello, a former vice-president of Chávez's and now Governor of Miranda State), these are still by and large controlled by civilians. Active duty officers are mostly in charge of administrative functions in the Chávez government.[13]

Another area of criticism of the 1999 constitution is that it has centralized presidential power even more than the already somewhat presidentialist constitution of 1961. The increased presidential powers include the ability to dissolve the National Assembly, following three no-confidence votes by two thirds of the National Assembly, to declare a state of emergency, to freely name ministers and their area of responsibility,[14] the extension of the president's term from five to six years, and allow for an immediate consecutive re-election.[15]

While clearly some presidential powers have been increased, one must keep in mind that the constitution balances these through increases in the population's power via its ability to independently call for referenda to change the constitution, to abrogate laws, and to recall the president's mandate. In addition, numerous other means for increased citizen participation exist, such as via the local public planning councils, the naming of judges, and via what is being called "social comptrol" (*contraloria social*). In contrast to the US president, the Venezuelan president cannot veto laws or name Supreme Court judges.

Summary

There is a large consensus both within Venezuela and among foreign observers that Venezuela now has one of the world's most "advanced" constitutions. However, what does this mean? For the most part those who praise the constitution mean that it provides for broad citizen participation, making Venezuela a "participatory democracy," rather than merely a representative one. Also, the constitution provides for some of the most comprehensive human rights protections of any constitution in the world. Next, its inclusion of special protection for those traditionally marginalized, such as women and the indigenous population, and protection of the environment makes Venezuela's constitution one of the most inclusive and responsive to the needs of the less powerful. Also, the placing of justice on an equal footing with the rule of law lays the groundwork for more social justice. Finally, the creation of two new independent branches of government, the citizen branch and the electoral branch, places the protection of human rights and of free and fair elections on a firmer footing.

Skeptics of how important Venezuela's new constitution is for the social and political transformation of the country are quick to raise the point that most state socialist countries had "advanced" constitutions, with extensive human rights and social welfare guarantees, but that in practice this meant little for the well-being and/or political opportunities of these countries' citizens. Ultimately, what makes the difference between a constitution that is actually implemented and one that is merely a formality on paper is the country's political culture. If the institutions, citizens, political leaders, and state officials generally abide by the letter and spirit of the constitution, as part of the population's world view and political culture, the constitution will be very significant because infraction of the law will be caught and prosecuted. This is especially relevant for the functioning of the judiciary, of course. However, if there is a political culture in which the law is regularly subverted and interpreted in ways that violate its spirit, as was the case in state socialism, then the constitution will be mostly meaningless.

Given the foregoing, what kind of political culture and judiciary does Venezuela have? As a measure of political culture and the adherence to the rule of law, one could take Venezuela's Corruption Perception Index, as measured by Transparency International,[16] where Venezuela ranks in 114th place, making it a country that is perceived as one of the world's most corrupt, in the same rank as Congo, Honduras, Uzbekistan, and Zimbabwe. Of course, these are merely perceptions among business leaders, who are heavily influenced by the oppositional private mass media.

Another measure of corruption and the rule of law in Venezuela is the survey conducted by Latinobarometro, which, in 2005 found that Venezuelans give their country higher marks than their fellow Latin Americans do for their respective countries. On a scale of 1 to 10, with 1 being complete disregard for the law and 10 being complete adherence to the rule of law, Venezuelans self-rank their country as having a score of 5.8, which is well above the Latin American average of 5.1. Uruguay comes highest with a score of 6.3, followed only by Costa Rica, Colombia, Chile, and Venezuela. Brazil (4.4), Peru, Paraguay, and Ecuador (3.9) bring up the rear.[17]

Nonetheless, it is probably fair to say that in Venezuela corruption and disrespect for the rule of law is quite widespread, which does not bode well for the new constitution. The April 2002 coup attempt, the consequent suspension of the constitution, and the acceptance of these acts by a large part of the population further reinforces the impression that Venezuela's political culture often plays fast and loose with the rule of law.

Despite the problems with Venezuela's political culture and the implications these have for the effectiveness of the constitution, the 1999 constitution was not in vain. Another important aspect of Venezuela's political culture is the intensity and the high regard with which the country's poor see it. As anyone who comes to Venezuela can see, the constitution is sold in small format (approx. 5cm × 10cm) at almost every street corner. At pro-government demonstrations participants wave it as though it were their party's banner. In pro-government political study groups (such as the Bolivarian Circles), people read and study the constitution. None of this can be said for the 1961 constitution, which few in the general population had ever read. In other words, the 1999 constitution has become more than "just" a constitution. It is a political project towards which pro-Chávez Venezuelans want to move the society. Roland Denis, a long-time political organizer in the barrios of Caracas and former vice-minister for local planning, puts it this way:

There was no real central revolutionary organization here. What we had was a mass rebellion movement—first a rebellion of the masses [in 1989] and then rebellions of the military [two in 1992]. These were very heterogeneous, dispersed, fragmented. What united them was the project to develop a new basis, a new constitution. No one would have been able to centralize this movement's program, not even Chávez. His leadership was and is undisputed, but his ideas would not have been enough to bring together the movement. The constitution fills this gap. It is a political program and simultaneously serves the purpose of providing a framework for the process. This constitution is not simply a dead text. It reflects values and principles. Perhaps not enough, perhaps one will have to reform it, maybe later one will not need it anymore for the revolutionary process. But at the moment it has the function of *Mao's Little Red Book*: It represents the demands and goals of the grassroots movement.[18]

Ideally, of course, a constitution should not be a political program. Rather, its requirements and provisions should be a social reality, not something to be strived for. However, given that constitutions and the rule of law are rule systems with which Venezuelans, and many Latin American peoples in general, have a relatively loose relationship, it is better to have a constitution that the people aim to make a reality than to have one that everyone ignores, both in its present and future implementation. While a constitution that is not an actual practical reality seems, just as it was in the Soviet Union, worthless, it is not worthless if the general population actively strives to make it a reality. In Venezuela, the politically active portion of the population, for the most part both in the opposition and among government supporters, are indeed using the constitution as Roland Denis suggests, as something to be made a reality.

Judicial Reform

Of all of Venezuela's public institutions, its judicial system has historically perhaps had one of the worst reputations. According to a study by the Lawyers Committee for Human Rights:

> In many ways, the judiciary symbolized all that had gone wrong with Venezuela's political system. The roots of the crisis in the judiciary intertwine several areas: political interference, corruption, institutional neglect, and the failure to provide access to justice for the vast part of the Venezuelan population.[19]

During the early 1990s, the World Bank offered to help Venezuela's justice system, thus providing the Bank's first loan for this type of task. However, due to the political turmoil of the 1990s, with the 1992 coup attempts, the impeachment of President Carlos Andres Perez, and President Rafael Caldera's unwillingness to work with the World Bank, nothing ever came of the Bank's reform plans.

When Chávez was elected, the new government launched on a major reform program, completely overhauling the country's judicial system, along with the new constitution. From the legal perspective, the judicial system was changed such that the new constitution made the judiciary more independent from the other branches of government. That is, the entire judicial system would be under the control of the Supreme Tribunal of Justice. Also, there were tighter requirements for candidates to become nominees in the first place, such as public hearings and minimum years of service in a legal profession. Finally, so that the legislature's budgetary power cannot be used to put pressure on the judiciary, the new law that regulates the functioning of the judiciary ("*Ley Organica del Poder Judicial*") requires that a fixed percentage of the overall government budget automatically goes towards the judiciary.

In terms of overcoming the existing, mostly corrupt, structures and judges, Chávez, under the principal guidance of one of his main advisors, Luis Miquilena, created a "Judicial Restructuring Commission," which was to review all of the country's judgeships and replace judges wherever necessary. Given the widespread unhappiness with the old judicial system, Chávez's moves to reform the judiciary were welcomed by the vast majority of the population. The unmanageably large workload of this committee and its understaffing, however, made it practically impossible to carefully review all judges. Instead, an expedient was put in place, such that all judges that had eight or more charges of corruption pending against them would automatically be removed. As a result, around 80% of the country's judges were removed from office within a very short amount of time, mostly during the year 2000.

To replace those who were removed, the restructuring commission to a large extent placed provisional judges, since it did not have time to fully review the new appointments. Towards the end of the year 2000, about 70% of the judges in the capital region (Caracas, Miranda and Vargas states),[20] were provisional. This, of course, led to the very credible charge that the new judges will be even more beholden to their political benefactors, Chávez and Miquilena, than judges ever were before, since the provisional judges can be removed almost at will. The Andean Commission of Jurists, in its annual report on the Venezuelan judicial system said, for example, that "It is premature to conclude that in Venezuela the institutions that form part of the judicial system are autonomous."[21] In other words, the suspicion is that rather than actually reforming the judicial system to make it better, the reform consisted merely in a replacement of old governing party judges with judges loyal to the new governing party.

It appears that the main reason the reform effort did not advance at first was because the Supreme Court was politically evenly divided (10 to 10, opposition versus Chávez supporters), so that no clear decisions were made on restructuring the judiciary. Ever since the court dismissed the charges against the coup officers in August 2002, Chavistas felt that the Supreme Court was essentially a pro-coup court, even though it was split right down the middle. The events in the country for those two years, from August 2002 until August 2004, were full of activity and much stalemate in the National Assembly, so nothing could be done about the court. In early 2004, though, the National Assembly managed to change some of its rules of order, so that it could more easily end debates in the Assembly and thus pass more laws. One of the laws that was on the top of the list of the pro-Chávez majority in the Assembly was the long overdue Law of the Supreme Court,[22] which it finally passed, a year and a half after its first reading, in May 2004.

Finally, more than four years after the first reform efforts, in early 2005, under the tutelage of a newly expanded and thus no longer paralyzed Supreme Court, its new president, Omar Mora, announced that a new reform effort would be launched. The primary goal of this new effort would be to turn the provisional judges into lifetime appointments. Despite on-going charges of politicization,[23] Mora's reform effort made some progress in 2005, so that by the end of the year, the number of provisional judges had been reduced to 40%, with the rest receiving permanent appointments. By the end of 2006 the percentage of provisional judges had been reduced to 20%.

However, the 2004 Supreme Court law became perhaps one of the most controversial laws since the 2001 passage of the 49 law-decrees. The opposition, Human Rights Watch, and the US government all severely criticized it, saying that it was a "court-packing law." The main reason for dubbing this law that way was that it increased the number of Supreme Court judges from 20 to 32. By adding twelve new judges to the court, the pro-Chávez majority in the Assembly was able to establish a solid pro-Chávez majority in the court. The argument for expanding the court in this way was that many of the court's chambers were hopelessly overloaded and thus needed additional judges to take over some of the workload.[24]

Part of the reason the slim pro-Chávez majority was able to appoint new judges without making concessions to the opposition had to do with another controversial provision in the new court law, which said that a two-thirds majority for the approval of new judges would only be required for the first three rounds of voting. If no two-thirds majority was reached by the third vote, a fourth vote could approve new judges with a simple majority (50% +1). Predictably, the twelve new judges were approved with a simple majority and were all nominated by the pro-Chávez coalition in the National Assembly.

A third important controversial measure of the new law stipulated that the National Assembly could dismiss judges with a simple majority under certain circumstances. Normally, the impeachment of a judge required a two-thirds majority, such as when the judge is accused of having committed a crime. However, the new law says that under some circumstances, such as having lied about one's qualifications for the judgeship or an attack against the "prestige" of the Supreme Court, a simple majority vote of the National Assembly could nullify the judge's appointment. Only a Supreme Court ruling could, in turn, nullify such a decision.[25]

Critics argued that not only did the new Supreme Court law constitute a "packing" of the court, but the last provision mentioned above would seriously affect the court's independence. Given that the constitution does specify that a judge can only be removed after having been charged by the Citizen Branch (Attorney General, Human Rights Defender, and Comptroller General) and then following a two-thirds vote of the National Assembly, it would seem that the law's provision for nullifying judgeships ought to be unconstitutional. According to the procedures for passing "organic" laws (laws based on the constitution), the constitutional chamber of the Supreme Court ought to declare this provision for nullifying judgeships unconstitutional, but at the time of writing this has not happened. In any case, this is a serious problem for the judicial independence of Venezuela's Supreme Court, if judges can be removed with a simple majority vote by the National Assembly.

As for adding twelve new judges, also via a simple majority vote, this sets a dangerous precedent, but it is, technically, well within Venezuela's legal framework. That is, the precedent it sets is that whenever there is a court that the legislature opposes, it could, in theory, add judges to regain a majority it favors. One should note that US President Franklin Roosevelt once attempted to do the same with the US Supreme Court, but was rebuffed by the public's reaction. Ever since then, it has been practically unthinkable in the US to increase the court's number so as to change the balance of power in the court. On the other hand, if US military officers were ever to attempt a coup against the US President and the Supreme Court let them free, then it is quite probable that an anti-coup majority in the US Congress would try to change the balance of power in that court.

One could thus argue, as Chavistas generally do, that the old Venezuelan Supreme Court set a dangerous precedent when it dismissed the case against clearly identifiable coup organizers, essentially stating that the coup was not a coup. Its ruling legitimated the impunity of overthrowing a constitutionally elected government. The question thus became one of which precedent is more dangerous, that of allowing a coup to go unpunished or that of fixing a dysfunctional court by "packing" it.[26]

The more immediate consequence of the new Supreme Court law was thus that the newly enlarged constitutional chamber of the Supreme Court decided to revisit the dismissal of the case against the coup generals. On March 11, 2005, the constitutional chamber decided to nullify the August 14, 2002 decision, declaring that the full court had violated the constitution when it dismissed the case because two of the court's judges had been recused who should not have been recused from the case. The Attorney General, Isaias Rodriguez, immediately declared that a new case would be opened against the officers, but this time no pre-trial in front of the Supreme Court's plenary would be required as the accused were no longer active duty officers. Also, according to Rodriguez, holding a new trial would not violate prohibitions against double jeopardy because the first trial was a pre-trial and not a regular trial.

The Military

The Military's Role in the Chávez Government

Ever since Chávez first took office in early 1999, military officers have played an important role in staffing key positions within his government. Active duty and retired officers serve throughout the Chávez government, including as ministers, vice-ministers, and heads of state-owned companies. Of the 61 ministers that have served in the Chávez government between 1999 and 2004, 16 (or 26%) were military officers.[27] Also, Chávez supported the election of retired officers to numerous governor's and mayor's posts. Following the 2004 regional elections, of the country's 24 governors, 22 belonged to the Chávez camp. Of these, nine (41%) have a military background.

When asked why it is that his government has such a high presence of military officers, Chávez responds that the main reason is that he lacks qualified civilians who support his project. That is, there are plenty of qualified civilians and plenty of civilians who support Chávez, but all too often most of the civilians who support Chávez have no experience in running large complicated state bureaucracies. As a result, Chávez makes use of the military, since, in theory at least, they have some degree of training and experience in running large institutions efficiently and he has a fairly good idea as to who he can trust in the military.

The presence of so many military officers at all levels of government has provoked much critique from the opposition, some of whom even suggest that the Chávez government is really a military government in disguise. Chávez, however, has said that Venezuela's higher education system has to prepare more civilians who are capable of working in public administration and as soon as this is the case, more would be employed there. It is generally assumed that the Bolivarian University of Venezuela is supposed to play an important role in this preparation, especially since it is seen as a pro-Chávez university.

Civilian—Military Relations and Military Policy

Aside from appointing military officers in his government, thereby apparently militarizing civilian institutions, there has been a much stronger trend towards "civilianizing" the military. That is, under

Chávez, the military has taken on many more civilian functions than it ever had before. For example, one of Chávez's first projects to alleviate poverty was to institute the Plan Bolivar 2000, which was essentially an assignment for the military to propose projects that would help combat poverty.

The plans were met with quite wide popular approval and contributed to Chávez's early popularity ratings, especially among the poor. However, not too long into the plan, rumors began to spread about poor oversight over budgets and that the plan was feeding a lot of corruption in the military. Eventually the comptroller general, who was allied with the opposition at that time, published a report that accused many officers of suspicion of corruption. Following an internal investigation, numerous officers were removed from their posts. A shadow of suspicion remained over the whole plan, however.

By 2002, the plan was phased out and, following the coup attempt and the oil industry shutdown of that year, other plans, the "missions," took its place in mid-2003. While these missions received some help from the military, they were mostly civilian-directed programs and thus different from the Plan Bolivar 2000.

Chávez's rationale for programs such as Plan Bolivar 2000 is to promote "civilian—military unity." In numerous speeches Chávez has pointed out that one of his main ideological anchors is the unity of civilians and armed forces. When referring to this he often quotes Mao, who said, "The people are to the military as the water is to the fish."[28] In other words, the military cannot be separate from the general population, but must be an integral part of it. According to Chávez, the separation of the military from civilians is an artificial one that enables the military to repress the civilian population and also stands in the way of the country's development. Venezuela must "break with this type of artificial division that sometimes turns into a terrible obstacle for the development of the country, for the process of national unification."[29] Put another way, Chávez says that he wants: "The participation of the Armed Forces in the development of the country and the participation of civil society in the development of the Armed Forces."[30]

In practice this policy agenda has meant two things. First, it has meant the aforementioned involvement of the military in what are normally civilian duties, such as in the Plan Bolivar 2000 and in the missions. The military was also heavily involved in the rescue operations during the

Vargas mudslides of 1999. The second aspect of civilian—military unity has been the involvement of civilians in military tasks. This expresses itself most directly in the government's mobilization of military reservists. About 93,500 reservists are mobilized via the *Misión Miranda*, named after General Francisco de Miranda, who fought for Venezuela's independence in the early 19th Century. In 2005 the government reported that it had 85,000 Army reservists, 5,000 from the National Guard, and 1,500 from the Navy.[31]

In addition to *Misión Miranda*, Chávez announced on February 4, 2005, on the 13th anniversary of his 1992 coup attempt, that his government would mobilize "popular defense units" of various sizes that would be organized according to neighborhood and workplace. This new plan is meant to be an application of the ten-point "new strategic plan" that Chávez had announced shortly after the October 31, 2004, regional elections.[32] These units would be placed directly under Chávez's command. The recruitment goal for these reservists was first supposed to be one million Venezuelans and was later expanded to two million.

Chávez's comments regarding the units suggest that their purpose is to prepare for a possible US invasion, for an "asymmetric war."[33] This speaks directly to the fear of a US invasion of Venezuela that has become quite real among Chávez supporters. Many have thus begun to actively prepare for such an eventuality and greatly welcomed Chávez's initiative for the creation of popular defense units in this regard. Opposition analysts, however, have argued that the popular defense units would just be another step in the "Cubanization" of Venezuela because they remind them of the Cuban committees for the defense of the revolution.

Another purpose of the military that amplifies the Chávez government's concept of civilian—military unity is their role in assuring not only the security of the country in terms of defending it from foreign threats, but also in the sense of assuring the security of Venezuelans in having food and shelter. That is, the idea is to expand the concept of security to include the general well-being of the population and not just their physical safety from outside attack. This expanded notion of security is also reflected in the new Law of the National Armed Force,[34] which stipulates that Venezuela's military is to have an active role in assuring the economic and social development of the country.

Clearly, Venezuela's opposition has repeatedly attacked Chávez's concept of civilian—military unity, accusing Chávez of essentially militarizing Venezuelan society. Compared to 1989 and 1992, though, when President Carlos Andrés Perez temporarily instituted martial law, suspended constitutional guarantees, and placed the military on just about every street corner, the military now, at least subjectively, hardly seem to be present at all in Venezuelan society. Rather, a strong argument can be made that rather than militarizing civilian society, Chávez has been civilianizing the military. Whether this dissolution of the boundary between military and civilians is a good idea is a larger philosophical question. However, given Latin America's history of military repression, which was to a large extent made possible precisely because of the military's dissociation from civilian life, it might be a good idea to blur the boundary in favor of civilian society.

But there are other issues that Venezuela's opposition has criticized with regard to the Chávez government's military policies, which mostly involve greater centralization of military command, a reduction of civilian control and oversight, and, with that, a greater independence of the military. For example, the 1999 constitution changed Venezuela's National Armed Forces (plural) into a single National Armed Force. The idea behind this was to bind the different branches of air force, navy, national guard, and army into a single force that was under more centralized command. The danger, according to critics, is that a more united military would be in a better position to coordinate and to exert pressure on the civilian government. Another change that the 1999 constitution introduced was that promotions would be solely decided within the military and not by the legislature, as was previously the case. This again increases the military's independence with regard to civilians.

Finally, critics say that Chávez has politicized the military, largely due to the influence he exerts over the promotion lists and indirectly through the general polarization that has occurred in the country, which tends to force people to choose sides. Chávez supporters, though, respond that Chávez needs to control the promotion lists (and thereby politicize them) because of the tendency of some officers to conspire against him. In other words, the same question as already exists in the larger society is also an issue with regard to the military: Is the polarization that exists within the military a consequence of Chávez's uncompromising governance or is it a consequence of the opposition's unwillingness to accept Chávez as the democratically elected president and commander in chief?

However, in addition to the government's and the opposition's politicization and polarization of the military, one has to take into consideration that Venezuela's military has a history of being divided, as was described earlier. Also, opposition analysts say that many in Venezuela's military resent that they are being asked to take on civilian duties. On the other hand, Chávez supporters argue that Chávez has increased the prestige of Venezuela's military because for the first time the population sees the soldiers being put to practical use. That is, Chávez has vindicated the role of Venezuela's military, following the tremendous loss of prestige they went through in the wake of the 1989 *Caracazo.* Also, since Chávez himself clearly identifies with the military,[35] the soldiers, by and large, also identify with him.

In sum, there are clearly contradictory tendencies at work with regard to the Chávez government's military policy. On the one hand, there is a clear trend towards increasing military participation in civilian tasks and an increasing participation of ordinary citizens, via the military reserve, in military tasks. As such, the military is indeed being civilianized, in terms of the inter-penetration of civilians and military in each other's affairs. On the other hand, there is a trend towards centralization and independence of military control, so that the president has more control over the military, via promotion lists and the subordination of the reserve under the president. This means that as long as the president supports the "civilizing" of the military, which Chávez clearly does, this will be the prevailing trend. However, as soon as there is a president who opposes this practice, the military is in danger of becoming once again a force that is isolated from the rest of the population. That is, the positive changes Chávez has instituted within the military are hardly institutionalized to outlast the personal preference of whoever happens to be president. In contrast, a policy that seeks to assure citizen participation in all levels and institutions of the polity, including the military, should examine how it can institutionalize the democratization of military command structures, so as to assure citizen participation in all aspects of their polity, including the military.

Participatory Democracy

The participation of the people in the formation, execution, and control of public administration is the necessary means for achieving the involvement that ensures their full development,

both individual and collective. It is the obligation of the State and
the duty of society to facilitate the generation of the most favorable
conditions for putting this into practice.

—Article 62, Constitution of the
Bolivarian Republic of Venezuela

Despite the poor institutionalization of participatory principles in the
military, advocates of Venezuela's Bolivarian project refer to Venezuela's
new political system, the Fifth Republic, as a "participatory and
protagonistic democracy." The term "protagonistic" (*protagónica*) does
not translate well, but it means to say that citizens are not only supposed
to participate in the democratic process, but that they also take an
actively involved (a protagonist's) role. But why this emphasis on
participation and exactly how and where does it manifest itself in the
political system of the Fifth Republic?

Participatory Democratic Theory

To understand why supporters of the Bolivarian project place so much
emphasis on the participatory aspect of their democracy, one needs to
understand how they perceive representative democracy. For the Bolivarian movement, representative democracy is the kind of democracy
that predominated during the Fourth Republic, before the 1999 constitution, which meant the exclusion of ordinary citizens and their non-
participation in the country's political affairs. Citizens could vote once
every five years and other than that they were expected not to get
involved in politics. According to this analysis, the consequence was that
politicians were free to do as they pleased, since there was no-one looking
over their shoulders. This then made corruption and the abuse of power
almost a necessary consequence of representative democracy.

The constitution's "Elucidation of Reasons" for establishing a participatory democracy expresses this conception of representative democracy and its improvement with participatory democracy as follows:

This regulation [in favor of participatory democracy] responds to a
felt aspiration of organized civil society that strives to change the
political culture, which so many decades of state paternalism and
the dominance of party heads generated and that hindered the

development of democratic values. In this sense, participation is not limited to electoral processes, since the need for the intervention of the people is recognized in the processes of formation, formulation, and execution of public policy, which would result in the overcoming of the governability deficits that have affected our political system due to the lack of harmony between state and society.

To conceive public administration as a process in which a fluid communication between governed and the people is established, implies a modification of the orientation of state-society relations, so as to return to the latter its legitimate protagonism.[36]

In other words, for opponents of Venezuela's Fourth Republic, its representative democracy was synonymous with "partyarchy" (*partidocracia*), in which the two dominant parties divided up the spoils of Venezuela's political and economic system amongst themselves and used their power to exclude all challengers. According to this interpretation, the only way to overcome this system is to bring the people back into politics, via participation and their protagonism. More than that, the constitution also places limits on political parties to prevent their "vertical organization" that in the past has "obstructed the deepening" of democratic values.[37]

The participatory aspect of Venezuela's democracy comes up in a wide variety of places, in its laws and its constitution. Perhaps the five most important areas are: referenda, local public planning councils, social oversight (*contraloria social*), citizen assemblies, and civil society involvement in a wide variety of state institutions.

Participatory Democratic Practice 1: Referenda

The referenda are in some ways both the center of Venezuela's participatory democracy and its most superficial aspect. That is, they are at the center in the sense that they represent the most visible and dramatic difference from the previous constitution and are potentially the most powerful means by which "partyarchy" and ossified representative democracy are subverted. Citizens can directly petition for referenda and, if they meet the necessary requirements, can impose their will between regular elections and against the will of the political parties and those who are in public office. However, it is a process that is bound to be used fairly rarely because it is difficult to implement and so its practical effect will be rather limited. Much more important, thus, for the day-to-day operations of the government and for transforming Venezuela's political culture will be the other four mechanisms of participatory democracy.

Participatory Democratic Practice 2: Local and Communal Councils

The Local Public Planning Councils (CLPP—*Consejos Locales de Planificación Pública*) and the Communal Councils (*Consejos Comunales*) potentially represent the most far-reaching transformation of Venezuelan political life on the day-to-day level. The Local Councils are modeled to a large extent after the participatory local budgeting process first pioneered in Porto Alegre, Brazil over 15 years ago. While the Local Councils took most of their inspiration from Porto Alegre, they also bear some similarity to planning councils that exist in many communities in the US. The key difference, however, is that while in Venezuela the constitution and a national law guarantee their existence, in the US they are entirely dependent upon community charters and local laws for their existence.[38]

In Venezuela, CLPPs were first called into existence via article 182 of the new constitution. Then, in June 2002, the National Assembly passed the CLPP law, which regulates the functioning of the CLPPs. According to the law, the CLPPs are formed by each municipality and are constituted by the mayor, the municipal council, the presidents of the district councils (a smaller geographic unit that make up the municipality), representatives of neighborhood groups, and representatives of other civil society organizations, coming from sectors such as healthcare, education, sports, culture, ecology, security, formal and informal businesses, women, transportation, land committees, the elderly, people with disabilities, etc. The elected officials (mayor, district council presidents, and city council representatives) and civil society representatives are supposed to outnumber the representatives of neighborhood groups and other organizations by one vote. Participation in the councils is on a volunteer basis.

The central purpose of the councils is to gather and evaluate proposals for community projects, to work on the municipal development plan, to develop a map of the community's needs, to elaborate the municipality's investment budget, and to coordinate with other municipalities and with state authorities, among others.[39] The key difference between the CLPP's areas of responsibility and those of the mayor is that it is the mayor's task to execute the plans, while the CLPP plans and oversees the mayor's execution of these.

The implementation of the CLPPs ran into numerous serious problems, however, due to larger political events, the poor formulation of the law, and resistance from elected officials. The interfering events included, first, the April 2002 coup attempt, which occurred just before the law was passed, then the December 2002 oil industry shutdown, and, finally, the mayoral elections of October 2004. Nonetheless, many communities managed to get the CLPPs off the ground, despite these interferences, but most have, at the time of writing, yet to do so. The practical implementation of the councils, though, has left much to be desired for several other reasons. Long-time community organizer and former vice-minister of local planning, Roland Denis, outlines three serious obstacles to the functioning of CLPPs.[40]

First, basing the CLPPs at the municipality level makes them far too large in some cases. At its worst extreme, the main municipality of the heart of Caracas, Libertador, has at least two million inhabitants, which is larger than many states in Venezuela. To apply local planning in a participatory manner on such a large scale is impossible and defeats the entire purpose of the CLPPs. Members of the Libertador CLPP are every bit as removed from the communities they represent as the governors of some states, if one goes by the number of people they represent.

Second, the financial resources allocated to each district are not based on population size. Large districts receive more or less the same financial resources as very small ones. Considering that the size difference between districts can be enormous, activists consider this to be extremely unfair. For example, the Caracas municipality of Sucre, with its 1.2 million inhabitants has three districts, while the Caracas municipality of Libertador, with its 2 million inhabitants has 22 districts. If each district receives more or less the same amount of funding, then the three Sucre districts receive about one quarter of what the Libertador districts receive. Similarly, a rich neighborhood, such as Chacao, also in Caracas, with only 75,000 inhabitants, receives, per capita, five times the amount Sucre inhabitants receive. As such, the CLPPs will be much more effective in small upper-class districts such as Chacao, than in the densely populated and poor districts of Sucre. This was surely not the original intention behind the law.

Partly to address this problem, Chávez announced on January 10, 2007, during his swearing-in ceremony for his second full term in office, that he plans to reorganize Venezuela's municipalities. The idea would be to address the above-named disparities, to reconfigure the territorial "geometry of power" in Venezuela.

The third problem with the CLPPs is that the law that governs them does not give them sufficient power. That is, decisions of the CLPPs can still be overruled by the mayors or district councils. Overruling CLPP decisions, though, can act as a deathblow to these, as the volunteers who participate in them are hardly going to feel motivated to put much hard work into any project that then ends up being overruled. "The Councils create a lot of hope," says Roland Denis, "but when they try to apply this law they are going to realize that it is flawed, I would even say that it is criminally flawed because now that the Councils are appearing it is becoming apparent that they don't have power or legitimacy."[41]

A fourth problem with the CLPPs is that they presuppose citizen education, interest, skills, and dedication that are often not available. Unless citizens are well informed about the functioning of CLPPs and have the skills to participate in them and the motivation to put in countless hours of volunteer work, they will fall apart. Unfortunately, for many districts and municipalities in Venezuela, there is often a lack of qualified citizens for this work. The CLPP law ought to take this into consideration, so that training and some sort of compensation is available for those who work in CLPPs.

Finally, there is a fifth problem which has nothing to do with the CLPP law, but with the fact that mayors and city councils often feel threatened by the planning councils. Rather than seeing the councils as a welcome help in guiding their decisions, they see them as challengers and usurpers. As a result, mayors often create obstacles for the organization of CLPPs or they try to manipulate them, so that their buddies control them. When this happens, of course, community activists rapidly lose interest in working on the planning councils at all.

As a result of these numerous problems with the implementation of the local public planning councils, two camps have developed with regard to what to do with the CLPP law and the CLPPs. On the one hand, there is a maximalist position,[42] which says that the law ought to be completely scrapped and that one should pass a new CLPP law that is introduced via popular referendum, since there are too many entrenched interests in making the CLPPs impossible. On the other hand, there is a more moderate position,[43] which says that citizens should begin work in and with the CLPPs, but should, at the same time, strive to reform the CLPP law through the National Assembly, so that it would work much better in the future. According to this more moderate view, the CLPPs, even if flawed, are a better tool for mobilizing communities and for developing a true grassroots movement in favor of participatory democracy than if one did not take advantage of the existing albeit flawed legal framework.

A third approach to the local planning councils has been in the works since early 2005, by which these would be supplemented by communal councils. That is, the constitution mentions the possibility that citizens also create citizen assemblies on a much smaller scale than the local councils that exist on the municipal level. This project has been spearheaded by the Ministry for Popular Participation and Social Development,[44] which has implemented the idea in seven communities, as an experiment, forming 3,700 communal councils. Over the course of 2006, though, over 16,000 communal councils were created throughout the country's 335 municipalities. These councils have several advantages over the municipal councils, such as that their decisions are binding, so that if a majority of communal councils make a decision, then the mayor must abide by it. Also, they exist on a much smaller scale, of about 200 to 400 families in urban areas and starting with 20 families in rural areas, thus enabling manageability and direct democracy.

Anyone over the age of 15 may participate in the communal council meetings, which are constituted by general assemblies of all participating families. The general assembly then elects communal council spokespersons, decides on work groups, and elects a finance committee and an audit or oversight committee. For the general assembly's decisions to be valid, at least 20% of all voting age members of the community must participate.

Perhaps the most interesting innovation of the communal councils is that they are designed to integrate the wide variety of committees that have formed in communities over the course of the Chávez presidency. For example, various social programs have, in the name of citizen participation, required communities to form committees that would help implement social programs, such as the missions. As such, most barrio communities now have urban housing committees, for the urban land reform, health committees for the community health program, water committees for the planning of water connections, etc. Each of these committees would now become a work committee of the community council. Each work committee then sends one representative to the executive council, which oversees the decisions of the general assembly.

In April 2006, the new communal council law was passed, which spelled out the procedures for communities to set up these councils. Communities began rather quickly to set them up and by the first half of 2006 Chávez had handed out grants for 653 community improvement projects to the initial group of communal councils. Over the course of the year, a total of approximately $1.5 billion was turned over to these councils for their projects. Additional funds would come from local and state governments, donations, and other fundraising activities of the councils. Chávez announced in early 2007 that the funds for community councils would be increased to $5 billion that year.[45] This represents a significant redirection of state funds, away from governors and mayors and towards the communal councils. Currently about 30% of the funds for local and regional governments go to communal councils, but Chávez supporters in the National Assembly are proposing to increase this to 50%.[46]

If successful, these communal councils could transform the nature of the Venezuelan state in the long run because of the way their decisions are binding for the next higher level. That is, according to one of the designers of the program,[47] future reforms would involve the creation of associations of community councils, where each community council sends a spokesperson to a higher-level body, which would coordinate large-scale projects for all of the member councils. As such, this council system would create a governing structure that runs parallel to the existing representative democratic structures, but which is based on direct democratic councils. In January 2007 Chávez referred to the implementation of this idea as one of the "five motors" for the next phase of the Bolivarian revolution, the creation of 21st century socialism.[48]

Participatory Democratic Practice 3:
Social Audit/Comptrol (Contraloria Social)

One of the key tasks of the Local Public Planning Councils is to exercise social audit of the work of the public administration. The principles and legal base for social audit, though, apply not just to CLPPs, but the social audit is a right that any Venezuelan citizen may exercise. What is meant by social audit is that citizens have the right to request an accounting (financial and non-financial) of all activities of any public administration. That is, if someone has reason to believe that a public office is not being administrated properly, a citizen may place a request with the attorney general's office to have the office audited. The individual or group making the request may then fully participate in the audit.

The principle of social auditing is a key element in Venezuela's concept of participatory democracy because it forms the basis of direct citizen involvement in and oversight of the public administration. That is, it is not good enough for citizens to be able to propose and perhaps implement projects and programs, but, via social audits, they also can make sure that those projects and programs are being run properly.

Venezuela's public administration law describes social audits as follows:

> The national public administration . . . must establish systems that will supply to the population the broadest, most timely, and accurate information about its activities, so that social auditing may be exercised over the public administration. Anyone may solicit from the organisms and bodies of the public administration the information that they desire about their activity, in conformity with the law.[49]

The entire legal framework for social auditing is covered by a wide variety of laws,[50] which is perhaps why it rarely gets mentioned as an important aspect of Venezuela's participatory democracy. However, more and more organizations and individuals have recently been taking advantage of this right. For example, the Vargas Hospital in Caracas underwent a social audit because neighborhood groups suspected that many of the hospital's resources were being diverted due to corruption. In another example, in 2003, Venezuela's National Council on the Rights of Children and

Adolescents was socially audited for similar reasons. A new law which gathers and deepens all of the existing regulations around social audits was supposed to have been passed by the National Assembly in 2006.

Participatory Democratic Practice 4: Citizen Assemblies

"Citizen Assemblies" represent yet another attempt to introduce participatory democracy in Venezuela. The inspiration for citizen assemblies comes from a movement that emerged following the 1989 *Caracazo*, when citizens in the barrios got together for "barrio assemblies." Following the riots, these assemblies attempted to articulate the grievances of the people living in the barrios, such as inadequate utilities in their neighborhoods, insecurity, and the general lack of attention from governmental authorities. The citizen assemblies of the Fifth Republic address the frustration of the barrio assemblies by giving citizens a forum in which such assemblies would be more effective than the barrio assemblies ever were.

Citizen assemblies are briefly mentioned in the constitution, in article 70, which states that citizens have the right to convoke citizen assemblies that have a binding character. The details of how these assemblies are to be convoked, though, and exactly what this "binding character" means is left to a separate law. This law, which was introduced in the National Assembly in 2001, has, at the time of this writing, not yet been passed. Nonetheless, citizens have already begun gathering in citizen assemblies, following the law project's legal stipulations.

According to the proposed law, citizen assemblies may be convoked by at least 1% of a district's or municipality's registered voters. All decisions at such an assembly are binding for the district's or municipality's authorities and must be implemented within 90 days of being made. If the authorities fail to do so, the next higher level of government is supposed to take the matter and implement it. Finally, if higher authorities fail to implement the decision/s, matters may be taken to court, which can then issue an injunction.[51]

The previously mentioned communal councils are based on the same article of the constitution and are thus somewhat similar, except that the communal councils constitute permanent governing structures of a community, while the citizen assemblies represent more ad-hoc decision-making bodies.

Participatory Democratic Practice 5:
Civil Society Involvement in Government

Organizations of civil society in Venezuela have the right to become involved in a wide variety of governmental operations, ranging from public institutions such as the Councils on the Rights of Children or the Directorate for Social Responsibility in Television and Radio, to nominations processes for Supreme Court judges and members to the National Electoral Council. For example, half of the members of the Councils on the Rights of Children and Adolescents, which are regional bodies that are supposed to work for protecting children's rights in Venezuela, are appointed by representatives from civil society organizations that have to do with children's issues. Similarly, for the nominations of Supreme Court judges, a nominations commission is set up with five members from the National Assembly and six from civil society organizations that have to do with legal matters. Other entities of the public administration that are set up similarly include the National Electoral Council and the Citizen branch of government (Attorney General, Human Rights Ombudsperson, and Comptroller General).

In addition to these examples of citizen and civil society involvement in the highest levels of government, citizen participation is also sought out at much lower levels on a regular basis. For example, for the redistribution of rural and urban land, as part of the land reform programs, citizens are encouraged to form land committees that help governmental institutions in many of their tasks of measuring the land that is to be redistributed and in deciding who gets which plots of land.[52] Also, in another example, the capital's water company, Hidrocapital, has encouraged communities to set up "technical water committees" that can help the water company determine where there is a need to improve service and how to best organize this service for the community. As a result of this community consultation process, it has been possible for the water company to significantly expand its service from 60% of the population to over 90% in six years.[53] Other examples of community involvement in public services have been the health committees, which have helped shape the *Misión Barrio Adentro* program of community doctors and clinics in the country's poorest neighborhoods.

Similarly, many other missions, such as the *Misión Robinson*, which provides literacy training to the country's illiterate and *Misión Ribas*, which provides adult education to those who did not finish their primary schooling, also involve a large degree of citizen participation in their execution. This participation ranges from actual decision-making, to volunteering with the teaching programs, to providing one's homes for the necessary courses.

Participatory Democratic Practice 6: Cooperatives

Finally, the last major area in which the Chávez government has promoted participatory democracy is in the area of supporting the creation of cooperatives. With the help of technical advice, small business loans, and the creation of a legal framework for cooperatives, over 100,000 cooperatives have been founded[54] since Chávez has become president, in all areas of business, with over one million members. Cooperatives, due to their governance system in which the members are able to elect the managers and have a constant say over the decision-making within the organization, represent an important instance of participatory democracy. While cooperatives are not governmental institutions and thus do not contribute to the participatory democratic governance of the state, they do promote a political culture of partici-patory democracy and lay the foundation for a participatory democratic economy. Also, insofar as the government's greater goal is to empower people in general and to eliminate poverty and exploitation, cooperatives represent a significant step in this direction.

A proposal that would further strengthen workplace democracy in Venezuela is a new law that would be passed sometime in 2007 to create workers' councils in all public and private workplaces. These councils would allow workers "processes of control over production, planning, and the efficient use of resources," according to Oscar Figueroa of the Communist Party of Venezuela, who is drafting the law.[55] It remains to be seen, though, if Chávez and more moderate factions of Chavismo will support such a project.

An Assessment of Participatory Democracy and Constitutional Presidentialism

There has been in Venezuela, without a doubt, a tremendous move towards empowering ordinary citizens, from recall referenda, to land, water, and health committees, to civil society participation in nomination processes, to legally binding citizen assemblies, to the creation of communal councils and public planning. The opportunities for Venezuelans to become involved in politics have expanded as never before. During the Fourth Republic, in the *Punto Fijo* political system, Venezuelans were expected to be spectators of the political game, not participants. Now, as a result of the political transformation that has occurred since Chávez's election, Venezuelans have become more involved in the political life of their country than ever before. In Caracas, this involvement extends from the poor barrios of the mountainsides of Caracas, such as Petare, Catia, and La Vega, to the relatively wealthy upper middle-class neighborhoods of Altamira, Prados del Este, and Cafetal. In all social-economic classes, but especially among the poor, Venezuelans are organizing themselves.

However, there are three dampers on this development. The first is a relatively simple issue that will be overcome with time, which is the relative inexperience of many of these activists. That is, although there were many active civil society organizations prior to Chávez, with a substantial experience base, many of the leaders of these organizations have been absorbed into the government. Also, with the rapid growth of new community organizations and committees for land, water, health, and education, the number of groups has increased dramatically in a very short amount of time. The experience base for building and maintaining effective organizations thus needs to be built up.

More importantly, though, than the lack of experience, is that the government's ideals of participatory democracy, as expressed in the constitution and in new laws, have yet to be fully implemented. That is, while the constitution and official pronouncements celebrate the arrival of participatory democracy in Venezuela, many of the necessary laws are either still in discussion, such as the law of Citizen Participation, or have been poorly written and are in serious need of fundamental revision, such as the law of the Local Public Planning Councils. Added to this, there are still plenty of local government officials who are not particularly interested in participatory democracy and have sabotaged the CLPPs or, perhaps, are intentionally not advancing the passage of the Citizen Participation Law in the National Assembly.[56] The lack of official support, in the form of lacking or inadequate laws, poorly enforceable laws due to a dysfunctional judiciary, official obstructionism, or just general official disinterest is proving to be a serious damper on the government's participatory democracy project.

Certainly, participatory democracy is not something that can be decreed from above and perhaps it is too much to expect a government to implement it. Just as with most advances in political rights, participatory democracy has to be the result of political struggle. A key to making participatory democracy a reality will thus be for civil society to use the government's platform in favor of participatory democracy as a tool in its organizing activities, despite the obstacles that come from within the government and within civil society itself. This has, to some extent, already been happening.

Unfortunately, there is a third and perhaps even more serious impediment for the realization of this participatory goal, which is the constitution's, the government's, the Bolivarian movement's, and Venezuelan culture's tendency towards presidentialism and clientelism. As was described at the outset of this chapter, the constitution represents a combination of participatory and centralizing tendencies. The extension of the presidential term from five to six years, the president's ability to dissolve the National Assembly, to freely name ministers and create ministries, and to declare a state of emergency, all contribute towards strengthening Venezuela's presidency, which historically already was one of the strongest in Latin America. This constitutional presidential orientation combines with Chávez's strong and charismatic personality and a strong culture of clientelism to further strengthen the president's role in Venezuela's political system. The result is that it is difficult for Venezuela's civil society and social movements to find a voice that is independent of that of the president, without automatically becoming branded as being part of the opposition.

Civil society's relative lack of influence on the upper reaches of government is also a result of two other factors. First, the Bolivarian movement and civil society in general are relatively poorly organized and thus unfocused. Second, avenues of influence into the upper reaches of governmental power, where key policy decisions are mainly made by Chávez and his cabinet, are relatively underdeveloped, meaning that there is an absence of the normal tug and pull of interest groups, as is common in less presidentialist democracies. On the other hand, while informal channels of civil society influence on the government are lacking, the concept and practice of participatory democracy is gradually opening formal avenues of influence, which need time to take root in the population and that need to learn to overcome presidentialism and clientelism.

Despite the above mentioned limitations, Venezuela's political system is definitely in the midst of a process of moving away from merely liberal, representative democratic governance towards a more participatory democracy. After nearly eight years in office, this movement has been very slow, but it has been accelerating ever since the opposition's defeat in the August 2004 presidential recall referendum. And, according to an initial draft of Chávez's governing program for 2007–2013, Chávez plans, if re-elected, to further "strengthen and create institutional mechanisms that privilege popular participation."[57]

3

Economic Policy: Macro-economic Policies, Social Economy, and the Oil Industry

Although Chávez has said that he wants to institute twenty-first century socialism not just in the economic sphere, but also in the political sphere, it is in the economy where one is most likely to see the extent to which Chávez is moving towards something that can be called twenty-first century socialism. As we saw in the previous chapter, Venezuela's movement towards a socialist or participatory democracy contains many internal contradictions, but generally appears to be developing in the right direction for the fulfillment of this goal. The same can be said, in broad terms, about the direction of economic policy, even though here the internal contradictions are, at first glance, more serious than in the political sphere.

In the course of Chávez's presidency, from 1999 to 2006, the government has made significant strides in redistributing wealth, via the land reform programs and social policies, and in democratizing economic activity, mostly via workplace self-management. The other key achievement of the Chávez government's economic policy has been to re-assert economic sovereignty, mostly by gaining control over the state-owned oil industry and by resisting the US push for free trade and by instead promoting Latin American economic integration. However, these achievements stand to be significantly undermined by the power of transnational corporations and domestic big business in Venezuela, the lack of a clear conception of how to gain control over the market and its dynamics, and the inability of the government to deal with the "Dutch Disease" effects of the booming oil economy, which tends to strangle off all non-oil industrial and agricultural economic activity.

According to the government's official development plan for 2001–2007,[1] economic policy is designed with the intent to achieve six interrelated objectives. First, just as in almost any country, the main objective is to achieve a sustainable and continuous level of economic growth. Second, given Venezuela's past history of high economic volatility, especially in reaction to fluctuations in the price of oil, the objective is to eliminate economic volatility. Third, the government intends to "internalize" oil production. What this means is that it wants to use the expertise which exists in the oil sector to further develop the industrialization of oil production, so that Venezuela produces more oil-related products, rather than merely exporting crude oil. The hope is that such a national industrialization of oil production would lead to spin-off industries which would then cause industrialization in other sectors. The fourth objective is to develop a strong "social" economy, meaning the democratization of capital, the promotion of production cooperatives and community enterprises, strengthening small and medium-sized businesses, and instituting a comprehensive micro-credit program to support all of these. Fifth, the government aims to achieve fiscal sustainability, which means balancing the government budget. Finally, sixth, in order to achieve greater economic productivity, the country must increase its savings and investment rates.

Sustainable Economic Growth

Sustainable economic growth is to be achieved through a combination of diversifying the economy, integrating production chains, guaranteeing food security, strengthening small and medium-sized businesses, incorporating and adopting new technologies, and consolidating and rationalizing the public finance sector. It is impossible at this point to go into detail about the meaning of each of these programs, evaluating the extent to which they have all been implemented or are effective. Just a few key programs designed for improving the country's economic growth will thus be highlighted.

Perhaps most important for overcoming Venezuela's "Dutch Disease" is the effort to diversify the economy. One way the government has tried to do this is by encouraging the integration of the Latin American economies and by protecting itself from other economies. The idea is that Venezuela would compete against economies that are more similar to its own, while keeping at bay economies that could dominate Venezuela, such as the US. In other words, Venezuela would initiate a "rational and not generalized opening to international competition."[2]

One of the main areas where the Venezuelan state can directly intervene in the diversification of production is the state-owned oil industry. Here, for example, the goal is to strengthen the vertical integration of oil production and commerce by focusing on producing more of the oil sector's downstream products, such as petrochemical products. To do this, in mid-2005 the government spun off the state oil company's petrochemical subsidiary, Pequiven, into an independent state-owned enterprise. Its specific mission is to more than double petrochemical production in the seven years following its founding, from 11.5 million tons per year to 25 million tons. Also, it would focus on producing petrochemical products for national consumption, instead of for export, as had previously been the case. When Chávez signed the decree for creating the new company, he bemoaned the insanity that Venezuela exports the fertilizer it produces and imports fertilizer from other countries.[3]

Another example of greater diversification via the vertical integration of the oil industry is the effort the Chávez government is making to produce its own refinery pipes, which it has traditionally always imported from first-world countries, but which it could just as well produce itself, given Venezuela's large iron and steel production. Similarly, in 2004 Chávez announced that PDVSA would repair and even build tankers in Argentina instead of the US or other countries of the North. This represents a tremendous boost to Argentina's shipbuilding industry and makes regional economic integration more of a reality. Later, in mid-2006 the government announced that it would create its own shipbuilding industry, mostly to service the many tankers it is purchasing from Brazil, Argentina, and China (62 new tankers in total).

Other important areas where the government is focusing its economic diversification efforts are the agricultural sector, the support of small and medium-sized businesses, and the expansion and improvement of basic infrastructure. The focus on infrastructure is nothing new in Venezuelan economic policy, but will be examined more closely below. With regard to the support of small and medium-sized businesses, the Chávez government has issued several decrees, ordering all state institutions to prioritize their purchasing with small and medium-sized businesses and especially with cooperatives and with Latin American businesses.

The government spends billions of dollars every year in state purchases, which represents an important boost to the private economy. The small and medium-sized industrial business chamber of commerce, Fedeindustria, has repaid the favor by actively supporting Chávez quite loyally, even through the worst of the opposition offensives, such as during the April 2002 coup and the December 2002 to January 2003 oil industry shutdown. Finally, the government has tackled the diversification of agriculture largely via its land reform program, which has benefited hundreds of thousands of peasants. This program is being complemented with training, credits, equipment, and commercialization programs. The government's goal is thus to raise agriculture's percentage of GNP from 6% to 12% by 2007.[4] This target has been completely missed, though, in that agriculture still only made up 6% of GNP in 2006.[5] This gives rise to the suspicion that the Dutch Disease has not been overcome in the least, despite the government's efforts to diversify the economy.

Part of the problem is that while agricultural production has indeed increased, by 21.5% between 2003 and 2006, sectors that are not affected by the Dutch disease, such as commerce, have developed three times as rapidly, by 68.2%,[6] thereby drowning out agriculture relative to the rest of the economy. The other problem is that as the government's main strategy for overcoming the Dutch Disease is to keep sectors such as agriculture and industrial production afloat, it relies mostly on subsidizing them, which accounts for their growth, but was not enough to make them grow more than other sectors.

Another important element in creating sustainable economic growth has been the prevention of capital flight and maintaining the stability of the country's currency. Until the banking crisis of 1984, Venezuela kept a fixed exchange rate with the dollar. However, once the banking crisis hit and the banks were bailed out with newly minted money, this fixed exchange rate could no longer be maintained and the reins were gradually let go, at first with different types of exchange rates, depending on the type of economic activity for which the dollars were to be used. By the late 1990s the currency was fluctuating quite wildly and devaluing almost constantly, especially every time a crisis hit and then the government would impose currency controls. When Chávez came into office the currency was floating against the dollar, but the central bank tried to keep fluctuations under control by purchasing the national currency, the bolivar. In the lead-up to the 2002 coup, though, this was no longer possible because the Central Bank was losing too much of its foreign currency reserves, due to massive capital flight. The government thus had to let the currency float completely and the currency devalued by nearly 40% from January to February 2002. It then held steady for a while, until the oil industry shutdown, when it dropped precipitously again, in January 2003, and the government decided to impose a strict currency control, for the first time during the Chávez presidency.

This currency control made it relatively difficult for Venezuelans to exchange the local currency, the bolivar, into dollars and thus kept a tight lid on capital flight. Only those who could prove that their business taxes had been paid in full and who needed to import goods for their business were allowed access to dollars. This had several beneficial consequences for the economy, such as steadily increasing foreign currency reserves, which by 2006 had reached $35 billion, which is as high as Canada's (which has only a slightly larger population) and on a per capita basis is far larger than Germany's ($55 billion). Also, the control prevented capital flight and thus forced Venezuelans to seek domestic investment opportunities, instead of foreign investment opportunities, as was common. As a result, Venezuela's stock market, whose index tripled between 2002 and 2005, experienced a major boom. High stock prices mean that more capital is available for Venezuelan businesses to invest, which, in turn, can mean a greater incentive for diversifying the economy.

Ultimately, the diversification of the economy is supposed to counter Venezuela's Dutch Disease problem by creating a greater degree of balance in the sources of the nation's wealth. Also, should Venezuela's oil revenues decline, it would be in a better position to manage the decline with an economy that is not based purely on oil production. The success of this strategy has been thwarted, though, in the more recent years of Chávez's Presidency (2004–2006), due to the extraordinarily high oil revenues, which intensify the problems of the Dutch Disease and reduce incentives for economic diversification.

Reducing Economic Volatility

Reducing economic volatility, the second main objective of the government's economic program, is also an important area for countering Venezuela's persistent "Dutch Disease," in that economic volatility, especially in exchange rates, tends to make investment in Venezuela unattractive, thus leading to more imports and a greater reliance on Venezuela's principal industry. There are two key means for combating economic volatility. The first is by maintaining a stable price of oil, via a strong OPEC and its price bands for oil. The second is supposed to be via a "Macro-Economic Stabilization Fund" (FEM in the Spanish initials). The idea of the fund was that whenever the price of oil rose above the average price of the past five years, the extra income would have to be deposited in the FEM, which is administered by the country's Central Bank. If the price of oil drops below the five-year average, then the central government would have the right to withdraw funds from the FEM.

The idea was initially proposed by the Caldera administration and the law for the FEM was passed in 1998, just before Chávez's election. Chávez was a strong supporter of this concept and it represented an important plank in his economic policy platform. However, Chávez and his supporters disagreed with the specifics of the law and so Chávez had it re-written five times during his presidency. Each re-write weakened the obligatory nature of the savings and increased the government's ability to use the fund at its discretion.[7] Originally contributions to the FEM were based on a five-year average of income, so that any income in excess of this average would be automatically transferred to the FEM. The fund did accumulate significant savings in the years of 2000 and 2001, reaching a savings high point of $7 billion at the end of 2001. The combination of recession in late 2001, the coup of April 2002, and the oil industry shutdown of early 2003 meant that revenues were very low for that period, so that the government could draw down on the FEM savings, which dropped down to $700 million by August 2003.

A modification to the FEM law, made in 2003, stipulated that no deposits to the FEM would have to be made until 2006. This meant that despite the high oil revenues in 2004 and 2005, no new savings were placed in it at all by early 2005, despite the steadily rising oil revenues. However, already before the moratorium on new deposits had ended, Venezuela's finance minister suggested in February 2005 that perhaps the law should be changed again, so that the state oil company would first make its deposits into its social fund, before calculating its excess revenues.[8] This change was subsequently made in July of that year. When the FEM requirements kicked in again, in

2006, oil revenues were dropping again and so once more no further deposits were made for a year.

It would thus seem that while the FEM was of some use in smoothing out the rough economic ride of 2002 and 2003, it has been left quite toothless since then. Ever since the price of oil went up in 2003, Chávez and his oil and energy minister, Rafael Ramirez, have suggested that oil prices will remain high for the foreseeable future. If true, the implication is that Venezuela will no longer experience economic volatility and that therefore a strictly managed FEM is no longer necessary. At least, the numerous changes to the FEM law to address contingencies and changes of opinion of the moment undermine the basic idea of the FEM, which is to force Venezuelan governments to save during economic good times.

More or less in place of the FEM, the pro-Chávez National Assembly created a different kind of special spending account, in July 2005, known as Fonden (Fund for National Development), which would be funded from so-called "excess" Central Bank reserves. That is, since Venezuela's Central Bank reserves were sky-rocketing to over $30 billion ever since early 2004, the National Assembly, at the behest of Chávez, modified the country's Central Bank law, so that all hard currency reserves above a certain level would be deposited into Fonden, to be used at the discretion of the executive.

Opposition critics immediately criticized the idea as being a violation of the Central Bank's and the economy's basic operating principles, since the reserve money has, technically, already been spent by the central government and any further re-use of this money would only mean the printing of more Venezuelan currency, flooding the money supply, and leading to hyper-inflation.[9] However, when the legislature revised the Central Bank law, it stipulated that the Fonden money could not be used for expenditures denominated in the national currency, but could only be used for expenditures abroad, such as for the purchase of equipment or for paying off the external debt.[10] In effect, Fonden represented a means of exchanging the backing of the country's national currency from dollars,[11] to other forms of capital, which could, in theory, be exchanged back again, should it be necessary.

The revised Central Bank law identified $30 billion as being the necessary limit to Venezuela's foreign reserves in 2005 and thus allowed the transfer of the "excess" $6 billion, which had accumulated by then, to Fonden. Chávez immediately decided that about $2.5 billion would be used for improving the country's hospital equipment and $1.5 billion for paying off a portion of the country's external debt. Other funds are going towards the construction of two new thermo-electric plants, among other projects. For 2006 another $7 billion was authorized for transfer from the currency reserves to Fonden.

Creating a Social Economy

This aspect of Chávez's program has undergone an important evolution in the six years that Chávez has been in office. Originally the emphasis was on creating a social economy in the sense of strengthening micro-enterprises and cooperatives and by democratizing ownership of rural and urban land. Along with the emphasis on creating a social economy, Chávez had originally placed much emphasis on developing and supporting national private enterprise, along the lines of the theory of "neo-structuralism" of Osvaldo Sunkel, the director of CEPAL.[12] However, this strategy was quite well within the capitalist framework, since it was no more than a "free market model helped by the state."[13] As Chávez radicalized, largely as a result of his own ongoing self-education in socialist literature and as a result of the opposition's providing an opening for radicalization, due to its failures to oust him, Chávez moved towards a much more anti-capitalist position. The role of the social economy and of endogenous development thus came to occupy center stage in the construction of an alternative to capitalism.

According to the government's Economic and Social Development Plan for 2001–2007, the social economy

> is an alternative and complementary way to that which is known as the private economy and the public economy. Put another way, the concept serves to designate the production sector of goods and services that arrange economic and common social interests, supported by the dynamism of local communities and in an important participation of citizens and workers of the so-called alternative enterprises, such as the associative enterprises and self-managed micro-enterprises.

Other terms that the government has used for social economy are the "solidaristic economy" and the "popular economy." In other words, within this economic sector, economic activity is organized on the basis of solidarity and the common good, rather than on the basis of self-interest.

Altogether, the social economy encompasses at least five closely inter-related programs: redistribution of wealth (via land reform programs and social policies), promotion of cooperatives, creation of nuclei of endogenous development, industrial co-management, and social production enterprises.[14]

The Redistribution of Wealth and Micro-Credit

One of the main ways the government is attempting to correct for problems of unequal market allocation is via redistribution, mostly in the form of the urban and rural land reform programs and the numerous social programs. Another important form of redistribution is occurring via the extensive micro-credit program for the country's poor, enabling them to create their own micro-enterprises (usually of one person or one family). In order to do this, the government has created numerous micro-credit banks, such as the Banco del Pueblo (People's Bank), Banco de la Mujer (Women's Bank), and Fondo de Desarrollo Microfinanciero (Fondemi—Fund for Micro-Finance Development). In addition to these, the 2001 banking law stipulates that all banks have to set aside at least 3% of their credit portfolio for micro-finance projects.[15] The increase in micro-credits has been dramatic, so that between 2004 and 2005 private banks alone gave out 140% more micro-credits, for a total value of $500 million in 2005.[16] This figure is in addition to the micro-credits that come from state banks, such as the ones named above.

Promoting Cooperatives

A second measure for facilitating the growth of a social economy is the government's support for cooperatives, which is often combined with the micro-credit program. State promotion of the cooperative movement occurs largely via Sunacoop, the National Superintendancy of Cooperatives, which is supposed to promote, supervise, and legalize cooperatives in Venezuela. In the first seven years of the Chávez government, cooperatives have mushroomed throughout Venezuela, with the help of training programs, logistical support, and credits. Their numbers increased from 762 in 1998 to over 100,000 by 2005.[17] According to

Sunacoop, it hopes that over 200,000 cooperatives will have been created by the end of 2006. The number of people involved in cooperatives increased similarly, from about 200,000 in 1998 to well over one million in 2005. This means that about 16% of formally employed Venezuelans are employed in a cooperative.

It should be noted, though, all too often cooperatives are phantom cooperatives, created just so that their directors can gain access to preferential loans and other government services. The actual number of functioning cooperatives could thus be significantly lower than the official figure states. A 2006 census of cooperatives suggests that as much as 50% are either not functioning properly or never were real cooperatives in the first place. While this figure is high, the total number of cooperatives is impressive nonetheless.[18]

Part of the reason that cooperatives are flourishing in Venezuela is that the government is giving preferential treatment to cooperatives in all of its state purchasing of goods and services, including purchasing from state-owned enterprises, such as PDVSA. Also, one of the government's main social programs, *Misión Vuelvan Caras* (Mission About Face), provides work training and prepares participants for creating cooperatives once they complete the program. In September 2004 the government even created an entire ministry devoted to the promotion of the social (or popular) economy (*Ministerio de la Economia Popular*—MinEP).

Industrial Co-Management

The third dimension of the social economy developed only once Chávez had already been in office for three years: worker-managed factories.[19] That is, in 2002, shortly after the April 2002 coup attempt, the Chávez government embarked on an experiment in worker-state co-management of Venezuela's main electricity company, CADAFE. The experiment is still relatively small, though, as only two worker representatives are on the five-member company coordinating committee, which is an advisory body to the management. Another electricity company, CADELA, was also turned over to worker co-management, where worker participation is much more substantial and meaningful.

In late 2004 the government embarked on another experiment when it nationalized a paper production plant, Venepal, and allowed workers to co-manage the plant with the state (renamed as Invepal—*Industria*

Venezolana Endógena del Papel). A little later, a similar move was made with a valve manufacturer, CNV (renamed to Inveval). Both of these companies had entered into bankruptcy largely due to their participation in the ruinous oil industry shutdown. The fifth and perhaps most important experiment in worker co-management is the state-owned aluminum company, ALCASA, which was turned over to workers also in early 2005. These are relatively small efforts compared to the overall dimensions of Venezuela's state-owned industrial sector, but they are a sign of probable future developments, especially considering that the government announced that it is investigating over 800 other recently bankrupt businesses for possible worker takeovers.

The reason these enterprises are co-managed, between workers and the government, instead of completely self-managed, the way cooperatives are, is that large enterprises touch on interests that go far beyond the workers within these industries. As such, according to the government, the interests of society at large ought to be represented in the running of these enterprises, via the participation of society's representatives, in the form of the state. Left to their own devices, especially in the context of a competitive market economy, large self-managed enterprises would have little to no incentive to internalize costs, such as pollution, or to pursue larger social interests of the common good. In some cases this model seems to be working, such as at ALCASA, where the state is giving the workers a large amount of say. Unfortunately, in other cases, such as INVEPAL, the state ends up with a majority vote on the governing boards of these enterprises and, as a result, workers end up being marginalized.[20]

Nuclei for Endogenous Development (NUDE)

Before we can examine the Endogenous Development Nuclei, we have to first clarify what endogenous development is supposed to mean. This is a relatively new concept within the development literature, which emerged largely as a complement to the concept of sustainable development. While sustainable development is meant to focus on making sure that development does not destroy the resource base of the area that is being "developed," it was still an open question as to how this development would come about. Often, especially in the context of neo-liberal theory, development comes about when countries or communities open themselves up to outside investors, thus implying an exogenous development. The concept of endogenous development, though, implies that the resources, in terms of skills and materials, come from within the country or community that is being developed.

The Chávez government defines endogenous development as follows:[21]

1. based in existing capacities and necessities
2. motivates community participation in the planning of the economy, via new forms of organization, such as cooperatives and social networks
3. is organized from below towards above
4. is based on the values of cooperation and solidarity
5. uses appropriate technologies of the region without compromising the ecological equilibrium.

Endogenous development, as the Chávez government intends to practice it, is supposed to be applicable to both the nation as a whole and to individual communities. On the community level it is mostly being applied in the Nuclei of Endogenous Sustainable Development (Nudes), which are specific communities that have been chosen for special government attention. These communities are thus supposed to become places where the endogenous development of the country as a whole is moved forward. However, unlike the general theory of endogenous development, which proposes that development should only come from within the community, governmental support for the Nuclei takes the form not only of educational programs, but also of financial start-up support for projects. The individual projects within the different nuclei are supposed to fit within one of five priorities for national development: agriculture, tourism, industrial production, infrastructure (transport, communication, education, health, etc.), and services. The emphasis, though, is on agriculture (50%) and industrial production (30%), paying particular attention to achieving self-sufficiency with regard to the production of food, clothes, and shoes. By March 2005 there were 149 nuclei of endogenous development throughout the country.[22]

Mission About Face (Vuelvan Caras)

The Nuclei for Endogenous Sustainable Development were created relatively early in the Chávez administration. Two or three years later, in early 2004, the government added the *Misión Vuelvan Caras* (MVC— Mission About Face), which has been designed to provide support to the nuclei. Actually, this mission has become one of the most important missions, according to government officials, because it represents the most tangible and practical effort to transform Venezuela's capitalist economy into a socialist economy. According to the government's literature, MVC is "the government's strategy to transform the existing economic model into one of endogenous and sustainable development."[23] As such, one of its main tasks is to integrate all of the other missions in the service of MVC. The primary function of the MVC is to provide skills training and logistical help for unemployed Venezuelans to start cooperatives, if possible, in the context of a Nucleus of Endogenous Sustainable Development.

Elias Jaua, who was the first Minister of Popular Economy, which is in charge of MVC, says that 300,000 Venezuelans will have found work through the mission by May 2005. One million more Venezuelans will have passed through the MVC program and found work, according to Jaua, by mid 2006. Jaua insists, though, that the mission is much more than an employment program. One of its key tasks he says is "the cultural transformation of the way in which society produces."[24]

Social Production Enterprises (EPS)

Increasingly, while Chávez was publicly advocating twenty-first century socialism, he was also placing greater emphasis on the need for communities to be involved in the creation of this socialism. Chávez argued that workers needed to develop a new socialist ethic, which would be in solidarity not just with their fellow workers, but also with the larger community.[25] Chávez's recognition of the importance of community appears to have come from his reading of a book by the Marxist theorist Istvan Mészáros, which talks about the need to base exchange in a "communal system of production and consumption."[26] That is, Chávez began to recognize and talk about how, in capitalism, consumption and production occur on the basis of the individual self-interest of buyer and seller and thus exclude concerns of those outside of the immediate exchange process. Production and consumption, thus, should be communally based, so that the concerns of the entire community are taken into account.

The primary means for making sure that social and communal concerns are included in the production and consumption process would thus be the newly formulated concept of Social Production Enterprises (EPS). Officially the concept of an EPS was first introduced with a decree in September 2005, which stated that enterprises organized as an EPS had to fulfill a list of requirements, such as to, "privilege the values of solidarity, cooperation, complementarity, reciprocity, equity, and sustainability, ahead of the value of profitability."[27] Furthermore, they had to invest at least 10% of their profits in the communities in which they operate and produce "goods or services in which work has its own meaning, without social discrimination nor privileges associated with one's position in a hierarchy, in which there is substantive equality between its members, planning is participatory, and they should operate under either state, collective, or mixed ownership."[28] In other words, pure private companies cannot qualify as EPS. Companies that do fulfill these requirements are then eligible for special financing, state purchasing, and other preferential benefits from the state. As of mid-2006, 500 EPS had registered, with another 7,000 in the process of doing so.[29]

The Social Economy—A Preliminary Evaluation

Taken all together, the policies of promoting micro-credits, cooperatives, worker co-management, nuclei of endogenous and sustainable development, *Misión Vuelvan Caras*, and the EPS are all supposed to create and expand the social economy in Venezuela. To what extent this program will succeed is still too early to say. The plans are ambitious, though. Many plans for these projects have only been elaborated relatively recently and already for 2006 the Ministry of the Popular Economy hopes to incorporate well over one million Venezuelan workers in the social economy. If successful, this would mean that at least 16% of the workforce would be occupied in the social economy. As an employment program this would mean much for a country that has been suffering an unemployment rate of 10–15% between 2004 and 2006 and an informal employment rate of 45–50%.

However, the compatibility and therefore durability of this social economy with the larger capitalist economy still needs to be proven. If the social economy only survives by virtue of government subsidies then any downturn in Venezuela's volatile oil revenues could cause these jobs to evaporate in an instant. It is thus still an open and crucial question as to whether this social economy can compete with the regular economy, with other Latin American economies, and with the world economy (if exposed to these).

Another issue the social economy faces is in the cultural dimension. Government representatives such as President Chávez and Popular Economy Minister Elias Jaua repeatedly emphasize that these new forms of organization of production are meant to not only increase democracy and equality, but they must also create a new culture that values solidarity and cooperation above individualism and competition. Experiments in other places, most notably in the Basque region of Spain known as Mondragon,[30] have shown that it is possible to successfully foster a new culture of solidarity and cooperation that also enjoys economic success. However, they have also shown that the economic success of such experiments can suffer setbacks when that very success increases exposure to global market forces, which then causes the experiment's adaptation to the global market, which in turn means the adoption of competitive market values in the place of cooperative and solidarity values.

So as to ensure the long-term success of cooperatives and the social economy in general it becomes important to think about whether other forms of exchange and allocation are possible besides those governed by the market system. There is a recognition in the Chávez government of the problem that markets undermine the social economy and some effort has been made to deal with this. One of the ways of overcoming this problem is the aforementioned involvement of the state in purchasing products that come from the social economy, which are then re-sold in government stores, such as the Mercal grocery stores. Another idea that has been implemented only since September 2006 is the introduction of a special currency used for trading goods only between cooperatives. This idea is based on the LETS (Local Exchange and Trading System) and local currency concept, which allows participants to trade goods without using regular money, but also without resorting to barter.[31] Since this idea is merely in its initial phase, it is too early to say whether it can truly avoid the problems of the competitive market, but it could be the start for moving towards more cooperative forms of exchange, such as a participatory economy.[32]

The government's plans for the future do, however, indicate that no matter the obstacles for a social economy, it intends to expand this social economy significantly during Chávez's 2007–2013 term. A draft of the government's program for this term states that while the coexistence of social economy, state enterprises, and capitalist enterprises is expected to continue, the enterprises of the social economy are to grow in number and size to such an extent, so that sometime in an unspecified future this sector is equal in size to that of the other two more or less equally sized sectors. Exactly how this is to happen, whether via nationalizations of private enterprises, by increasing government support for the social economy, or some other means, is not entirely clear. The program does suggest, though, that this transformation is to happen gradually and at least partly by converting some private enterprises into social economy enterprises. The draft program also states that state enterprises will be transformed into social production enterprises (EPS). If successful and if market allocation is overcome with de-centralized and participatory allocation mechanisms, then indeed, a path towards the ideals of 21st century socialism will become more visible.

Fiscal Sustainability

If, however, the social economy is being supported mostly by subsidies, then fiscal sustainability is important not just for the state, but also for the new economic projects the Chávez government has created. Fiscal sustainability is thus also a key goal of the government's 2001–2007 development plan. Ironically, ever since the oil boom of the late 1970s, Venezuela has been struggling with large state deficits and a large public debt. Part of the reason for this is that policymakers generally felt that they could count on oil income that was as high, at least, as it had been in the previous year. However, with the constantly declining oil prices, this was rarely the case and so governments got in the habit of borrowing and running a budget deficit, thinking they could pay the debt off the next year. Eventually it became clear that this was not going to happen and governments were forced to cut back, which they did, and which led to the gradual dismantling of Venezuela's welfare state between 1980 and 1998.

For the Chávez government, one of the most important elements in achieving fiscal sustainability was, first, to increase the government's revenues. This, according to the government's plan, was to be done by increasing both the oil revenues and the non-oil revenues. Oil revenues were to be increased via higher oil prices and higher oil industry taxes. Non-oil revenues were to be increased by enforcing the existing tax laws more strictly. The second element in achieving fiscal sustainability was supposed to be to increase the efficiency of the state, so that expenditures on the public administration would go farther. This was to be done mainly through tighter control over accounting of state expenditures. Finally, the third element was improving the management of the public debt, mostly by spreading out the repayment schedule (which had repayments lumped together in short periods of time, making them almost unpayable) and by taking greater advantage of the domestic credit market instead of the international one—that is, transforming foreign-held debt into domestically held debt.

With regard to the first element, the Chávez government has been able to increase both its oil revenues and its non-oil revenues, except for during the two crisis years. From the time that Chávez first came into office, in 1999, until 2001, oil revenues increased from $6 billion to $11 billion. But these revenues dropped back to $8 billion in 2002 and $9.7 billion in 2003. Then, with the price of oil climbing steadily, oil revenues were significantly up again, at $13.5 billion for 2004 and $18.9 billion for 2005. Similarly, non-oil revenues increased from 1999 to 2001, from $14 billion to $19.5 billion, dropped in the crisis years to $10 billion and $14 billion, only to rise to $17 billion for 2004 and $20 billion in 2005.[33] Venezuela used to see such wild fluctuations in its revenues in the past, due to fluctuations in the price of oil. During the Chávez presidency, though, oil price fluctuations were overshadowed by the economic effects of the political conflict.

With regard to controlling Venezuela's debt, the Chávez government has been less successful than it was with augmenting its revenues. In some senses Venezuelan history is thus repeating itself, as its earlier period of greatest indebtedness, the late 1970s and early 1980s, corresponded with its period of greatest state revenues. Recently, though, Venezuela managed to pay down some of its debt during the 1990s, so that by 2006 its foreign debt was lower relative to other Latin American countries, at $26.7 billion and 22.3% of

GDP.[34] Still, it is about $3.5 billion higher than when Chávez first came into office.

During the first three years of his term Chávez pursued a relatively fiscally conservative strategy and also transferred a significant amount of the public debt from foreign to domestic.[35] His fourth and fifth years in office (2003–2004), however, were characterized by deficits, mainly because revenues dropped dramatically due to the opposition's coup and the oil industry shutdown. Total public indebtedness (foreign and domestic) thus rose from 27% of GDP in 2000 (the lowest level in 18 years)[36] to 39% in 2004. In absolute terms, the foreign debt was lowered from $23.4 billion in 1998 to $22 billion in 2001. But it rose again in the subsequent years, to $31 billion in 2005 and dropping in 2006 to $26.8 billion. Total debt, as a percentage of GDP, thus increased slightly from 29.6% to 32.0% in the first seven years Chávez was in office. Once again, though, the leaps in indebtedness are all traceable to the two crisis years of 2002 and 2003.

Finally, as for the government's plan to increase the state's efficiency in its economic and fiscal activity, not much improvement could be seen here. On the one hand the government slashed secret discretionary budgets by 80%. These were often used in the past by ministers and other government officials as one of the main sources of corruption in the Venezuelan state. Also, oversight was improved in many areas, mostly via *contraloria social* (social oversight, described in chapter 2) and the comptroller general is now formally independent of the executive and thus freer to pursue accusations of corruption. On the other hand, the state seems staffed with countless numbers of inexperienced or poorly skilled public servants, as many who used to be in the public admin-istration were either forced to leave or left voluntarily because they identified with the opposition. Also, many of those who sympathize with the opposition and did not leave, are often known to actively or passively sabotage the implementation of government policies. The consequence of this, of course, is a greatly diminished efficiency of the state. The sum of the positive changes and the negative ones with regard to public administration thus tend to cancel each other out.

What Venezuela would need to do in order to truly improve the efficiency of the state apparatus is have a total reform of the public administration. So far, though, no clear strategy has emerged as to how such a reform could be undertaken. Chávez has repeatedly expressed the need for a reform, but little has happened, except in a few notable areas, such as the tax collection office (SENIAT) and the identification office (ONIDEX). The draft 2007–2013 government plan mentions the need for state reform, but other than stating objectives such as "guaranteeing the protagonic participation of the population in the national public administration," "elevating the levels of equity, efficacy, efficiency, and quality of state action," "constructing a new ethic of the public servant," and "combating corruption systematically in all of its manifestations," no details are provided as to how these things should be achieved.[37]

The Politics of Oil

In contrast to the rather problematic efforts to reform the public administration, the Chávez government has had some significant success in reforming its oil industry. This reform turned out to be absolutely crucial for enabling Chávez to turn Venezuela into an experiment for twenty-first century socialism. Without the massive oil revenues that oil provides it is quite unlikely that Chávez would have been able to steer the country in an increasingly more radical direction.

There are two things one must know about oil in Venezuela. First, Venezuela is the world's fifth largest oil exporting country, with the largest reserves of conventional oil (light and heavy crude) in the western hemisphere and the largest reserves of non-conventional oil (extra-heavy crude) in the world. Second, oil production is a relatively unusual industry because it is one of the single most lucrative industries there is. Since oil is the life-blood, almost literally, of modern society, practically no other economic activity is capable of generating as much profits as the oil industry. The ratio between the cost of producing a unit of oil and its market price usually tends to be far higher than for most other industries (with the late '90s being a notable exception). As such, oil is an area of tremendous conflict. Not only does oil's potential for generating massive profits frequently cause conflict, but, since it still is the most efficient source of energy for modern society, its significant geo-strategic value also generates conflict.

In order to understand the Chávez government's oil policy, it makes sense to first take a brief look at the history of Venezuela's oil industry. One can divide this into five periods: the discovery and initial production of oil (1912–1943), Venezuela's assertion of control over the oil industry

(1943–1974), the oil boom and nationalization of the oil industry (1974–1983), the internationalization and gradual de-nationalization of the oil industry (1983–1998), and the Chávez government's attempt to regain control over a largely independent state-owned oil industry (1999–2004).

The Birth of the Petro-State (1912–1943)

That Venezuela had abundant supplies of oil was already known since the earliest pre-Colombian times, when the indigenous peoples of Venezuela made use of oil and asphalt, which seeped to the surface, for medicinal and other practical purposes. However, it was not until 1912 that the first oil well was drilled. Shortly thereafter, Royal Dutch Shell and then Rockefeller's Standard Oil became the main producers of oil in Venezuela. Within a few years, by 1929, Venezuela was the world's second largest oil producer, after the US, and the world's largest oil exporter. Between 1920 and 1935 oil's share of Venezuelan exports went from 1.9% to 91.2%.[38] This, of course, had an immediate and dramatic impact on the country's economy in the form of the earlier mentioned Dutch Disease. Agricultural production declined to almost nothing in a relatively short amount of time and the country fell behind in industrializing, relative to other Latin American countries.

The Strengthening of the Petro-State (1943–1973)

In 1943 Venezuela passed a vast reform of its oil policy with the Hydrocarbons Act, which tied the Venezuelan state's income more tightly to the extraction of oil. While previously oil income was mostly based on concessions and customs, the new hydrocarbons act related oil revenues to taxes based on income from mining. The law established that the foreign companies could not make greater profits from oil than they paid to the Venezuelan state. The continually increasing oil income led to an ever-increasing reliance of the state on this source of income in lieu of individual income taxes.[39] By the 1950s, however, the world oil industry began to feel the effects of the over-supply of oil, especially following the increased production of oil in the Middle East and the imposition of import quotas in the US. The consequence was a chronically low price for oil. So as to combat this problem, in 1960, the world's main oil exporting countries, largely due to the prodding of the Venezuelan government, decided to form the Organization of Petroleum Exporting Countries (OPEC). Also in 1960, Venezuela created the Venezuelan Oil Corporation, which later formed the basis for the nationalization of Venezuela's oil industry.

The Oil Boom and the (Phony) Nationalization of the Oil Industry (1973–1983)

With the Middle East oil embargo of 1973, world oil prices and, along with it, Venezuelan government revenues, quadrupled from 1972 to 1974. This sudden and sizable increase in government income was unprecedented for Venezuela. It allowed the newly elected president, Carlos Andrés Perez, to promise Venezuelans that Venezuela would become a developed country within a few years. His project was known as "*La Gran Venezuela*" and was supposed to "sow the oil" through a combination of fighting poverty, via price controls and income increases, and the diversification of the country's economy, via import substitution. Part of this plan was also the nationalization of Venezuela's oil industry, which became nationalized over a two-year period, ending in 1976 with the creation of Petroleos de Venezuela (PDVSA).

Many analysts who are critical of this nationalization process argue that the nationalization of Venezuela's oil industry was a phony nationalization because it merely transferred ownership over the industry, without transferring management or management culture and policies.[40] That is, the industry continued to be run by the same management, under the same principles and goals as it did before it was nationalized, even while it was under new ownership. PDVSA maintained an anti-statist and transnational corporatist management culture throughout its existence. The ties of the nationalized Venezuelan companies to the former owners were maintained primarily through technical assistance contracts and through commercialization contracts, which heavily discounted the price of oil to the previous owners. This explains why the industry never actually pursued Venezuelan interests. The management simply felt no loyalty to Venezuela, but only towards the oil company and thus sought to maximize production and sales, but not profits, which would have to be turned over to a, from their perspective, wasteful state. Another dimension of the lack of governmental control over PDVSA during this time was the relative unimportance of the Ministry of Energy and Mines (MEM). Formally, PDVSA is subordinate to the ministry. However, in practice PDVSA completely overpowered the ministry. PDVSA regularly ignored MEM directives, such as the installation of modern measuring equipment to determine oil production levels or to adhere to OPEC quotas. Also, employees of the MEM earned less than half as much as their counterparts in PDVSA and in some cases PDVSA even paid a supplemental income to MEM employees, thus making them beholden to PDVSA's interests.

The government's lack of control over the oil industry was further institutionalized in PDVSA's board of directors. While normally a board of directors is supposed to represent the interests of the owners vis-à-vis the management, in the case of PDVSA the board of directors, almost in their entirety, was appointed from PDVSA's upper management, who, due to their backgrounds, tended to represent management. This is why, when Chávez appointed a board of directors who were oil experts and who did not come from PDVSA, the PDVSA management protested and joined the April 2002 work stoppage against the government. Chávez was breaking a decades-old tradition that regarded board membership as the highest promotion a PDVSA manager could receive.

The Internationalization and De-Nationalization of the Oil Industry (1983–1998)

With the currency crisis and the implementation of a currency exchange control in 1983, the central government looked towards PDVSA to help bail out the government by using the company's investment fund. This move, combined with the lack of investment opportunities within Venezuela, caused PDVSA executives to re-think their strategy with regard to the Venezuelan state and to find ways to protect the company's revenues from what it perceived as an increasingly incompetent and failing state. The solution was to internationalize the company by investing outside of Venezuela. During this period PDVSA bought numerous refineries in the US and in Europe (such as the US refinery and gas station chain Citgo). Also, with the use of "transfer pricing"— the sale of Venezuelan oil to its own subsidiaries—PDVSA wrote up long-term contracts where oil was sold at a discount, indirectly transferring PDVSA's profits abroad. By the late 1990s, PDVSA was transferring as much as $500 million per year from Venezuela to its foreign subsidiaries.[41] Also, during this time, the subsidiaries never paid any dividends to PDVSA.

In 1989 PDVSA adopted a worldwide combined accounting method, so that costs and losses outside of Venezuela would be balanced against the revenues and profits within Venezuela. Previously the accounting for transactions within Venezuela and for those abroad was done separately. The result of the account consolidation was a large-scale import of costs that were incurred abroad. Since PDVSA's tax rate within Venezuela is about twice that in the US, for example, the company had to transfer a much smaller proportion of its revenues to the government.

The internationalization program from the early 1980s to late 1990s was carried out under the banner of vertically integrating the company on a global level. While other state-owned oil companies also initiated vertical integration projects, Venezuela's was the most ambitious. One of the official reasons for this was that Venezuelan oil is mostly of a very heavy crude variety, with many components that are undesirable for finished oil products, such as sulfur, nitrogen, and several metal elements. In other words, Venezuelan crude requires a fairly sophisticated refining process, which not all refineries can handle. The logic of acquiring foreign refineries was that such refineries could be retrofitted to process Venezuelan crude and to then provide finished oil products to the market closest to the refinery. The idea thus was to guarantee a market for Venezuelan heavy crude oil.

However, many, if not most, of the refineries that were acquired were purchased at a bargain price, mainly because the vendor could not find a way to make it profitable. As a result, PDVSA tried to avoid losses in these refineries either by providing Venezuelan crude at below market rates or by avoiding the costly retrofitting process altogether and providing the refinery with lighter crude from other countries, such as Russia.[42] The net result of the internationalization process and of the new accounting procedure was that tremendous PDVSA costs that were incurred outside of Venezuela were "imported" to the national branch of PDVSA, thus lowering overall profits and transfers to the government.

Another strategy that PDVSA managers developed to escape government taxes during this period was to undermine OPEC quotas, thereby contributing to the decline of the price of oil and the lessening of oil revenues. First, starting in 1983, quotas were measured at the country's ports instead of at the wells, as used to be the case. This meant that oil used domestically was no longer measured or part of the OPEC quotas. Also, the government no longer knew exactly how much was produced and so PDVSA avoided paying royalty payments on some of the oil. Finally, oil production was opened to international investment for the first time in the 1990s. These operating agreements with transnational oil companies were also not counted towards the country's OPEC quota and were taxed at a lower rate than PDVSA's oil production. Thus, when OPEC quotas required a lowering of production, it was PDVSA's higher taxed oil production that was cut and not the lower taxed operating agreements. Also, PDVSA classified the extra-heavy oil reserves in the Orinoco Oil Belt as bitumen and thus its production also did not fall under the OPEC quota system. Increasing production of extra-heavy crude further allowed PDVSA to lower its tax commitment because this was taxed at a far lower rate than conventional oil production.

Another source of increased costs developed as a result of outsourcing (or operating service agreements), whereby PDVSA opened up marginal oil fields to private investors. The program was known as the *Apertura*, or "Opening." Beginning in the early 1990s, so as to attract private investors, PDVSA negotiated lower taxes and royalties for foreign oil companies on oil production in less profitable fields. While on the surface this makes sense because marginal fields are much more costly to operate, the result was the production of extremely costly and in some cases unprofitable oil. Of the 3.2 million barrels per day that Venezuela produced, about 500,000 barrels per day came from costly outsourced oil fields.[43] In mid-2005, PDVSA announced that many of the operating agreements were producing losses for the oil company because transnational oil companies were charging more for the oil extraction process than the oil could be sold for on the market. The average charge for extracting a barrel of oil was at 52% of what it could be sold for—a far higher percentage than PDVSA-operated oil fields.[44] By the end of Rafael Caldera's presidency in 1998, PDVSA thus paid only 39% of its gross revenues in taxes, compared to the 71% it paid in 1981.[45]

PDVSA's low efficiency is also visible when one compares PDVSA with other state-owned oil companies. According to rankings of the business magazine, *América Economía*,[46] PDVSA was the largest Latin American company in 2000, but in terms of efficiency it ranked among the lowest of the fifty most efficient companies, far below any of its state-owned competitors, such as Petrobras of Brazil, Pemex of Mexico, or Petroecuador of Ecuador.[47] Other measures of profitability show similar results. For example, in terms of the dollar revenues provided to the government per barrel of oil produced, PDVSA paid only about a quarter ($8.34) of what Mexico's PEMEX paid out to the government ($24.66) in 2001.[48]

Ironically, PDVSA has a fraction of the number of employees that Pemex does, something that might be traced to PDVSA's more extensive use of automation, outsourcing, and sub-contracting. Still, it is well known within PDVSA that it had nearly twice the number of administrative workers that it needs. In 1997 PDVSA merged three of its holdings, Corpoven, Lagoven, and Maraven, into PDVSA proper. According to Carlos Rossi, a former PDVSA economist, the Caracas headquarters of PDVSA acquired the nickname "Hollywood" because, "everyone there [in PDVSA Caracas] seemed to have a double."[49]

The foregoing sets the stage for showing just how extremely important the country's conflict over oil is. At the most overt level, the conflict between the Chávez government and the oil industry is one about who controls PDVSA. But beyond that, the specific issues that control is being fought over have to do with the company's efficiency, its internationalization program, its outsourcing and subcontracting practices, OPEC membership, and special oil contracts.

The PDVSA and the Chávez Government (1999–2006)

When Chávez was first elected in December 1998, it did not look like he had any particular plans for PDVSA. He did, however, have very clear plans for OPEC, which, under the leadership of Alí Rodríguez, was to be turned into a strong cartel once again. Until Chávez came to power, OPEC had turned into a shadow of its former self, with member states regularly ignoring or evading their quotas. Venezuela, especially, had turned into one of the member states' most unreliable partners. Production over allotted quotas, combined with the expansion of oil production in non-OPEC countries, such as Russia and Mexico, led to a steep decline in the price of oil. Chávez promised to put an end to this by organizing OPEC's second-ever meeting of heads of state in Caracas, in 2000. Also, Chávez spent the first years of his presidency visiting the leaders of OPEC and non-OPEC countries to convince them to adhere to production quotas, so as to maintain an oil price of between $22 and $28 per barrel.[50] Chávez's efforts bore nearly immediate results, when the price of oil rose for the first time, since 1991, to over $27 per barrel (in nominal prices).

Very soon, however, Chávez ran into conflict with the management of PDVSA, which, for the past fifteen years, had been focusing on producing as much oil as possible, regardless of OPEC quotas. The result was, first, a steady rotation of PDVSA presidents and, later, an all-out confrontation between the Chávez government and the oil industry. Chávez used this conflict to argue that what the oil industry needed was a complete "re-nationalization" because it had become too independent of the state and had turned into a "state within a state." The Chávez government's effort to transform Venezuela's oil industry thus encompassed four main areas: solidification of state ownership of the oil industry, tax reform, strengthening of OPEC, and the general subordination of the oil industry to national interests.[51]

"Re-nationalization"

The 1999 Constitution, which was written by Chávez's supporters, anchors state ownership of PDVSA in the constitution. It is well known that the government of Rafael Caldera, Chávez's immediate predecessor in the presidency, wanted to privatize PDVSA. With the new constitution, however, Chávez tried to make sure that PDVSA would remain a state-owned oil company. The new constitution thus clearly states that "for reasons of economic and political sovereignty and of national strategy, the state will maintain the totality of the shares of PDVSA or of the entity created to manage the oil industry . . ."[52] This article of the constitution was supposed to mark a definitive break from neo-liberal economic policies that PDVSA and the government had been pursuing prior to Chávez's election.

Related to state ownership is a provision in the hydrocarbons law which specifies that all state activity related to oil exploration and production is to be dedicated to the "pubic interest."[53] More specifically, it states that all oil related activity must be oriented to support "the organic, integrated, and sustainable development of the country, paying attention to the rational use of resources and the preservation of the environment." Income derived from oil "for the most part" must be used to finance health care, education, and the FEM (the fund for macro-economic stabilization).

While bringing PDVSA under state control was formalized with the new constitution, it was still far from being achieved in practice. In 2000 and 2001 Chávez made constant efforts to find out about the company's finances and to break its resistance to change.

The company's unwillingness to go along with the government's plans to increase taxes on the oil industry, to reduce costs, to increase transparency in its international operations, and to appoint a pro-Chávez board of directors, came to a head during the April 2002 coup attempt, when PDVSA managers actively supported the coup by shutting down one of Venezuela's main refineries during that crisis, among other things. Later, when Chávez was back in office, he tried to reconcile with the PDVSA management and reappointed the old board of directors, all the while continuing to pursue his key policy aims for the industry. However, Chávez was unable to make any changes until after the December 2002 to February 2003 shutdown of the oil industry, when he fired about 18,000 striking managers, engineers, administrative employees, and other professionals. It was only then, with a largely compliant staff and board of directors that Chávez was able to push through major changes in the way the oil industry was run.

Tax Reform

The main target for reform, following the subordination of PDVSA to the state, was the way that the Venezuelan government extracts revenue from the oil industry. Here the Chávez government introduced a change in taxation. Since 1943 the government had required a royalty payment of 16.6% for every barrel of oil that either PDVSA or a foreign company extracted. In many cases this royalty had even been negotiated to drop to 1% for some foreign investors, such as in the case of extra-heavy crude production in the Orinoco Oil Belt. A new oil reform that PDVSA was working on in 1998 even suggested eliminating royalty payments entirely. With the new oil reform law of 2001, however, royalty payments were nearly doubled to 30%. At the same time, the government lowered the income tax levied on oil extraction from 59% to 50%.

When the government introduced this change, the opposition cried out that the doubling of royalty payments would ruin Venezuela's cooperation with foreign investors and would practically eliminate foreign direct investment in Venezuela. The government's main argument for increasing the royalty payments is based on the fact that it is much easier for it to collect royalty payments than it is to collect taxes on oil income. That is, the government can more easily track how much oil is being extracted, and what the royalty payments should be based on the current price of oil, than it can track taxes on oil production profits, which involves far more variables. That is, taxes on profits are much more difficult to control because expenses are not that easy for an outside auditor to track, where the tax payer can attempt to inflate expenses, in order to lower tax payments.

Another way to increase oil revenues is to force oil companies to be more efficient. That is, by making fewer expenses tax deductible, which is what the shift from income tax to royalties does, the company is given a strong incentive to make its operations more efficient. In other words, the "royalty makes the interests of the natural resource owner [the state] and of the investor [the company] coincide."[54]

Another policy shift involving revenue increases has to do with the shift from operating agreements to joint ventures. In early 2005 PDVSA announced that all 32 private companies that have operating agreements with PDVSA must transition these into joint ventures with PDVSA, where PDVSA would control 60% of the joint venture. The companies had one year, until the end of 2005, to negotiate a transition agreement with PDVSA. All companies with operating agreements, with the exception of ExxonMobil, signed such transition contracts by the designated deadline. ExxonMobil was the only company to challenge the forced transition in court, while their fields were taken over entirely by PDVSA. The new joint ventures no longer have an opportunity or incentive to inflate their operating expenses, as they did before, because now they have to pay royalties as well as taxes on their oil production.

OPEC Reform

When Chávez first came to power, in February 1999, among his highest priorities was to strengthen OPEC and to raise the price of oil. Venezuelan oil had dropped to less than $10 per barrel, to a large extent because PDVSA was evading its OPEC oil production quotas during the previous government of Rafael Caldera. Also, non-OPEC members such as Mexico and Russia were increasing their production considerably, further driving down the price of oil. Chávez immediately put Alí Rodríguez—a former leftist guerilla fighter and oil industry expert for Chávez's coalition partner PPT—in charge of the Ministry of Energy and Mines. Within the new government's first 100 days, Rodriguez visited most OPEC and non-OPEC oil producing countries and returned with a commitment from most of them to abide by their OPEC quotas. The price of oil immediately went up, from an average price of $12.28/barrel for 1998 to $17.47/barrel for 1999, one of the largest non-war related increases of the past decade. Later, Chávez and Rodriguez managed to convince OPEC to introduce a price band system, of $22 to $28 per barrel, which OPEC would try to maintain.

The following year, 2000, Chávez spent much time also traveling to both OPEC and non-OPEC countries, to consolidate their commitment to restrained oil production and to convince them to attend the second-ever gathering of OPEC heads of state, to be held in Caracas.[55] On September 27 of 2000, Chávez opened and hosted this second-ever OPEC summit. For the Chávez government, the summit had the following six objectives:

1. Reestablish a dialogue between Venezuela and its partners in OPEC
2. Recuperate the credibility of Venezuela in OPEC
3. Strengthen OPEC
4. Defend oil prices
5. Reassume a leadership position within OPEC
6. Consolidate relations between Venezuela and the Arab/Islamic world

Given the strengthened position of OPEC in the world today, it is safe to say that the summit's objectives were largely achieved.[56]

INTESA

Another dimension of the lack of state control over the oil industry emerged during the 2002–2003 shutdown of the oil industry. Not only had PDVSA outsourced some of its oil production, but also some of the general operations of PDVSA. Perhaps the most important instance of outsourcing, in terms of the management of PDVSA, is the joint venture it engaged in with the US-based company SAIC (Science Applications International Corporation) to create INTESA (Informática, Negocios, y Tecnología, S.A.) in 1996. INTESA was to manage all of PDVSA's data processing needs. After four years of outsourcing this important task to INTESA, it became increasingly clear that INTESA was costing PDVSA much more than it expected, when it should have brought savings.[57]

Following the April 2002 coup attempt, Alí Rodríguez, the new PDVSA president, assigned Juan Fernandez, who was later to be the leader of the December 2002 PDVSA shutdown, to cancel the contract with INTESA. Fernandez negotiated that the contract would end, perhaps not so coincidentally, by the end of December 2002. INTESA joined the strike, however, and shut down all of its services to PDVSA, well before the contract expired. The result was that PDVSA could not transfer its data processing to new systems, nor could it process its orders and invoices for oil shipments. PDVSA ended up having to process such things manually because passwords and the general computing infrastructure were unavailable, causing the strike to be much more damaging to the company than it would have been if the data processing had been in PDVSA's hands.

An investigation into INTESA and into its majority owner SAIC (60%), revealed some information that ought to have been quite disturbing to the government of Hugo Chávez.[58] That is, INTESA, which controlled all of PDVSA's information, is in turn controlled by SAIC, a Fortune 500 company (revenues in 2002: 6.1 billion) that is deeply involved in the US defense industry, particularly as it relates to nuclear technology, defense intelligence, and computing technology. Its managers included two former US Secretaries of Defense (William Perry and Melvin Laird) and two former CIA directors (John Deutch and Robert Gates). Its current Board of Directors includes the former commander of the US Special Forces (Wayne Downing), a former coordinator of the National Security Council (Jasper Welch), and the former director of the National Security Agency (Bobby Ray Inman). Whether or not SAIC was actively involved in the PDVSA strike and whether it passe crucial company information on to other oil companies is unknown. However, the very fact that these connections existed should have been a cause of great concern to PDVSA and the Venezuelan government.

Latin American Integration via Energy Integration

The Chávez government's most recent initiative with regard to oil policy has been to promote Latin American integration via energy integration. At various points in his presidency, Chávez had proposed the creation of a Latin America-wide oil company, which would merge all of Latin America's main state-owned oil companies. However, it was not until late 2004 that Chávez took the first concrete steps in this direction, with the signing of the Petrosur agreement with Argentina's state oil company Enarsa in December 2004. Later it was expanded to include the state oil companies of Brazil (Petrobras) and Uruguay (ANCAP).

The main purpose of the agreement is to, "minimize the negative effects the price of energy has on the countries of the region—prices that have their origins in speculative and geo-political factors—via the lowering of transaction costs (elimination of intermediaries), access to preferential financing, and the taking advantage of commercial synergies to solve the economic and social asymmetries."[59]

A common misunderstanding of the agreement and of the other agreements that followed was that Venezuela had agreed to provide discounted oil to the countries of Latin America. This, however, has no basis in truth. Rather, the agreement merely tries to lower costs by eliminating intermediaries and providing preferential financing of oil invoices. Another important element is that countries may pay their oil bills in goods and services instead of cash. The most prominent example of such a move was with regard to Argentina, which was allowed to pay for Venezuelan oil with cattle. Later, tractors and other products were added to the deal.

The next major move towards energy integration was the Petrocaribe agreement, which Chávez and PDVSA signed in June 2005 with fourteen Caribbean countries. Similarly to Petrosur, the agreement's main element was that it provided preferential financing for the payment of most Caribbean countries' oil invoices. Buyers have up to two years to begin paying their oil bill, with financing of 1% over seventeen to twenty-five years for that portion of the bill that exceeds 40 per barrel. This is somewhat similar to an earlier agreement that Venezuela and Mexico signed with Caribbean countries in 1980, the San José pact, but with a lower interest rate.[60] Just as with the Petrosur agreement, countries are allowed to pay their oil bill in goods and services. Also part of the new agreement was that Venezuela's PDVSA would help Caribbean countries expand their storage facilities, so that they would be less dependent on transnational oil companies for their reserves.

Shortly after the signing of the Petrocaribe agreement, in July 2005, Chávez signed a third oil agreement, this time with the Andean countries of Bolivia, Colombia, Ecuador, and Peru, to form Petroandina. This agreement was much more general, in that it merely stated that it would "promote electrical and gas interconnection, the mutual provision of energy resources, and joint investment in projects." The details of the agreement were to be ironed out later, and at the time of writing have still not been worked out.

The three agreements, Petrosur, Petrocaribe, and Petroandina, are together supposed to be the backbone of Petroamerica, which would be the continent-wide energy integration of Latin America. Included in the long-range vision of this project is the creation of an "energy cone" for Latin America, which would lay a network of electricity lines and gas and oil pipelines.

One of the first major projects in this longer term vision is the proposal to create the world's longest gas pipeline, running from Venezuela's Caribbean coast, through Brazil, to Argentina's Rio de la Plata estuary. The total length would be between 7,000 and 9,300 kilometers and would cost $20 to $25 billion to construct over a period of seven years. Despite objections from environmental groups because the pipeline threatens to destroy much wildlife in the Amazon jungle and despite objections from analysts who said the pipeline would be too expensive to be worthwhile, the governments of Venezuela, Brazil, and Argentina pledged in March 2006 that they would conduct a detailed feasibility study for the project. A few months later Paraguay and Bolivia also joined the project. The governments hope that the pipeline would enable Latin America to fully exploit its tremendous reserves of natural gas over the next several decades.

The long-term strategy of promoting Latin American integration via energy integration is interesting in that it at least partially mimics European integration, which also began as an integration of energy supply and trade in Europe and only later expanded into all areas of trade and then into gradual political integration. In other words, Petroamerica aims to feed into ALBA, the Bolivarian Alternative for the Americas, Venezuela's proposal for a Latin American Community of Nations. In the shorter term, though, such integration aims to boost Latin American economic development by ensuring that the provision of energy, whether electric, gas, or oil, is distributed evenly throughout the continent, whereby energy resource rich countries such as Venezuela would prioritize resource poor areas of Latin America over energy supply to the developed north. Chávez explained the reasoning as follows, "It does not seem fair to us that with us having so much gas, so much oil, that there are frequent blackouts in the Dominican Republic, that northern Brazil does not have sufficient energy for development, that Colombia does not have enough energy for its towns at its borders . . ."[61]

An Economic Policy for Twenty-first Century Socialism?

The Chávez government's economic policies can be divided into two categories: reformist and potentially transformative. In the first category fall all those policies that are essentially social democratic or Keynesian in character, in that they involve state intervention in the capitalist economy but do not fundamentally alter the capitalist dynamic of private capital accumulation and of market competition. That is, policies such as the currency control, the redistribution of wealth via land reform, progressive taxation, and social programs; the efforts at import substitution via subsidies and trade restrictions; and the providing of microcredits, all fall into this category of economic reform. The bulk of the government's policies, that is, those that so far have had the largest impact, thus fall into this category.

To the second category, of potentially transformative economic policies, which could change the capitalist dynamic of competitive private capital accumulation into a dynamic that is instead based on human needs and cooperation, fall far fewer policies. The creation of worker cooperatives and of worker co-managed enterprises, if greatly expanded and if linked to each other within a cooperative framework of solidarity and mutuality between enterprises, could end up transforming the capitalist market dynamic.

Another transformative dynamic that the government has begun to introduce, but which has not been discussed yet, is its decision to switch to free software. In September 2004 the government announced that the entire public administration had to switch its software from proprietary software to free software, unless no free software alternative was available.

Chávez explained that the move was being made in the name of "national scientific independence, so that we do not depend on privately owned software. If knowledge does not have owners, then intellectual property is a trap set by neo-liberalism."[62]

This might seem like a minor practical issue that is designed to save the government some money because it would no longer have to purchase expensive Microsoft software. However, the implications of such a policy are more far-reaching than that because free software transforms the conception of intellectual property rights, which in capitalism is based on private intellectual ownership and capital accumulation, to one based on free exchange and equality.

In other words, in two key dimensions of the economy, of property relations, via cooperatives and co-management, and of knowledge and technology, via free software,[63] the Chávez government has made important but small steps towards a non-capitalist economy. A third essential economic dimension, though, the functioning of the market has only been touched via state intervention in the market, whether through the power of state-owned enterprises or more direct forms of intervention, such as subsidies and targeted state purchasing. As we will discuss later, a more far-reaching transcendence of the market, with the newly conceived "communities of production and consumption," still needs to be developed.

These moves towards transforming the economy will fail, however, if three tightly interrelated persistent economic problems are not overcome. First, despite the government's constant efforts, the economy is further removed from becoming less dependent on oil production than it has been in a long time. The main reason for this, of course, is that the price of oil has tripled in recent years, thus increasing the revenues significantly during the Chávez presidency. The higher oil price combines powerfully with the government's efforts to increase control over the oil industry, giving the government more revenues than Venezuela has seen since the oil boom years of the 1970s.[64] These new revenues should, in theory, allow the government to "sow the oil," to invest in its people and in material infrastructure, so that new non-oil economic activity might develop.

However—and this is the second obstacle, the Dutch Disease—just as happened in the 1970s, the huge oil revenues undermine non-oil sectors because the revenues represent an increase in Venezuelans' incomes that is not matched by increased productivity. That is, it ends up being cheaper (again) to import agricultural and industrial products than to produce these in Venezuela. In other words, high oil revenues, the very phenomenon that allows Chávez to "sow the oil," also undermine the non-oil economy. This fundamental contradiction cannot be resolved as long as the government allows market mechanisms to play a predominant role in determining allocation.

Third, the continued strength and large size of the oil industry in the economy raises serious questions about whether Venezuela's experiments with economic transformation for twenty-first century socialism can survive outside of the context of a well-heeled oil economy.

4

Social Policy: Land Reform, Education, Health, Housing, and Social Security

Beginning again with the Social and Economic Development Plan 2001–2007, the Chávez government's social policy objective is to achieve social justice in Venezuela. To achieve this, the plan proposes three sub-objectives, which are: the universalization of social rights, the reduction of the inequality of wealth, income, and quality of life, and the appropriation of the public realm as a collective good. In what follows we will see how the government has approached the pursuit of these objectives and to what extent the social policies might contribute to the aim of creating twenty-first century socialism.

Key to this discussion is that the Chávez government sees social rights as being equally important as political rights. That is, the 1999 constitution guarantees Venezuelan citizens the right to education, health care, housing, employment, and social security. Often liberal political theorists question these kinds of social rights because they argue that it is unclear exactly how the state and the society would guarantee their fulfillment. In the case of Venezuela's constitution, though, this is more or less spelled out, in that the constitution specifies how the state is expected to work towards the fulfillment of these rights. In the case of health and education, for example, it says that the state must provide these free of charge to all citizens. In the case of employment, though, it simply says that the state must develop economic and social policies that aim towards full employment. It does not say that the state must provide everyone who needs work with a job, as was the case in state socialist societies. Another important specification in the constitution in this regard is that it says that the fulfillment of social rights is on the basis of co-responsibility. What this means is that both the state and citizens in general have the responsibility of fulfilling these rights. Exactly how co-responsibility is carried out in practice will become clearer in the ways in which some of the policies are formulated.

The social policy areas examined here are grouped into land reform, education, health care, housing, social security, and social assistance. To have a basis of comparison, we will first examine social policy and the general poverty trend before Chávez came into office. This chapter concludes with an assessment of how poverty in Venezuela during the Chávez presidency evolved and whether these policies represent something fundamentally new, something that is better suited to fulfill the goals of twenty-first century socialism than the policies typical of pro-capitalist governments.

Social Policies before Chávez

The evolution of social policies in Venezuela before Chávez came into office followed the overall development of the economy, going through a build-up phase during the boom years, from the mid '70s to the mid '80s and a decline (as marked by the decline in social spending) during the bust, from the late '80s to late '90s. Prior to the oil boom, the main government program against poverty was the rural land reform program, which redistributed land to 150,000 families during the early 1960s. However, with the oil boom, Venezuela was intent on becoming a modern industrialized country and neglected the land reform program in favor of programs that would move the country away from agriculture. Primarily, during the boom years, anti-poverty policies meant providing free universal education, free health care, a decent minimum wage, and massive public works projects. All of these were dependent on high oil revenues and ended up having a clear impact on reducing poverty in Venezuela. Other social assistance programs existed as well, but all of them suffered from clientelism and paternalism, so that beneficiaries were often expected to become members of one of the two dominant parties, AD or Copei, before receiving benefits.

With Venezuela's 20-year economic downturn, though, which began in the mid 1980s, the most important measures, which were originally meant to benefit the country's poor, ended up benefiting the middle class. As the country became poorer and poorer and median wages declined dramatically, the middle class could no longer afford private health care and private education. As a result, the middle class gradually took over the country's public education and public health system. Also, other programs originally targeted for the working class, such as the home buying assistance program, international study abroad grants, or the tax-free automobile, increasingly became policies that supported primarily the middle class.

An important factor in the gradual class shift in beneficiaries of government programs was that the services were no longer free. Public education, for example, gradually instituted registration fees and ever increasing costs for school supplies. Similarly, public health care, while nominally free or low cost, required patients to pay for all treatment supplies. The government's sporadic shifts towards neo-liberal economic measures during the Carlos Andrés Perez administration (1989–1993) and towards the end of Rafael Caldera's presidency (1996–1998) aggravated the problems of poverty in Venezuela due to privatization measures, social spending cutbacks, and the increasing costs of public services.

Not only did the beneficiaries of government policies gradually shift towards the middle class, but poverty itself gradually changed. In addition to encompassing an ever-larger proportion of the population, poverty began affecting people who would, based on their education, normally be considered part of the middle class. Poverty thus became much more diversified and generalized. Also, with large streams of migration coming from Colombia and other Latin American countries, the poor became ethnically more diverse. By the time of the second Caldera government (1994–1999), the state's resources for alleviating poverty had become so scarce that hardly any programs were left that directly benefited the poor.

Poverty in Venezuela

The decline in social programs for alleviating poverty and the accompanying economic decline had an immediate impact on increasing inequality in Venezuela and on decreasing per capita income. These two trends combined have produced in Venezuela the greatest poverty rate increase of any country in Latin America.

The standard measure for inequality, the so-called "Gini Coefficient," which measures income inequality in any country, did not show a significant change over the course of almost thirty years in Venezuela.

From 1971 to 1997 it fluctuated irregularly, but generally remained between .45 and .50, ending at almost the exact same level in 1997 as it was in 1971.[1] However, the Gini index only measures wage and salary income, not capital income. Other data shows, for example, that the share of capital income (income from capital investments) increased substantially more than wage and salary income increased over the past thirty years in Venezuela. One study, for example, shows that labor lost 11% of GDP to capital between the seventies and the nineties.[2]

Thus, if one takes capital income into account, Venezuela's inequality increased quite dramatically, so that Venezuela is now one of the world's most unequal societies, surpassing the inequality of even South Africa and Brazil.[3] The reason for this can be traced to several factors, the most important of which are an increasing concentration of capital and a collapse in wage rates during this period.

The collapse in wage rates is related to the declining per capita oil income in Venezuela. Even though per capital oil exports doubled from 1973 to 1983, per capita oil income declined. The main reason for this can be traced to declining oil prices, which dropped from a high of $15.92 per barrel in 1982 to $3.19 per barrel in 1998 (both figures in 1973 prices).[4] The value of oil exports, per capita, thus dropped from $955 in 1974 to $384 twenty years later, in 1993.[5]

Since oil is Venezuela's principal source of income, its decline, combined with growing inequality in Venezuela, had a significant impact on the poverty rate. Depending on which statistics and measurement methods one uses, poverty increased dramatically from about 33% of the population in 1975 to 70% in 1995.[6] While poverty more than doubled, the number of households in extreme poverty increased three-fold, from about 15% to 45%. Other poverty measures, particularly ones that are not just based on income, are lower, but all of them paint the picture of a large increase in poverty in Venezuela over the past 25 years.[7] Compared to other countries in Latin America, Venezuela has the largest increase in poverty in this time period and among the larger countries of Latin America, it has the largest proportion of the population living in poverty by the time Chávez was elected.

Trends which accompanied this increase in poverty are a dramatic decline in real industrial and minimum wages, which dropped to 40% of their 1980 levels in twenty years, leaving them at a level below that of the 1950s.[8] Overall government social spending dropped from 8% of GDP in 1987 to 4.3% in 1997. Also, the percentage of people working in the informal economy grew from 34.5% in 1980 to 53% in 1999. Finally, the level of unionization dropped from 26.4% in 1988 to 13.5% in 1995.

When Chávez came into office in 1999, his first order of business was to introduce some "quick-fix" programs, collectively known as Plan Bolivar 2000, to deal with the country's terrible levels of poverty. His more long-range programs, though, were the rural land reform program and the reform of the country's education system. While these early programs generated much disapproval from the country's old elites, and contributed towards the April 2002 coup attempt, the Chávez government's more far-reaching programs did not start until after the opposition had been defeated in the coup attempt and the oil industry shutdown. To some extent, these new programs, known as "missions," were in preparation for the August 2004 presidential recall referendum and partly they were the result of increased government revenues, due to the oil boom, and partly they were the consequence of Chávez's and his supporters' ideological radicalization in the post referendum period.

Land Reform[9]

A social and economic program that was common throughout Latin America in the 1960s and 1970s was land reform. However, their poor design, which usually provided for insufficient support for new farmers, such as in skills training, credits, technology, and access to markets, caused most of these programs to fail miserably, so that by the 1980s they had little to show for themselves. The unequal distribution of land and thus of wealth in Latin America largely remained the same despite these programs. Practically no government in the region, following the dominance of neo-liberal economic theory, took up the issue of land reform again. The notable exception, though, is Chávez, who made land reform one of the central issues of his government program. More than that, land reform was not to be just a rural issue, which in Venezuela affects only a small proportion of the population, but also an urban issue, with the institution of an urban land reform.

Rural Land Reform

Venezuela's rural land reform program probably represents one of the key policies and turning points of the Chávez presidency. When it was introduced in November 2001, it was one of the laws that the opposition objected to the most of the package of 49 laws which were passed as part of the "enabling law." The land reform basically states that all adult Venezuelans have a right to apply for a piece of land for their family, as long as they meet some basic prerequisites.

Venezuela already had some experience with land reform, when in 1960 a land reform law was passed which eventually benefited up to 150,000 small farmers. This reform program, however, quickly fell apart in the 1970s, when the government lost interest in it during the oil boom years and stopped implementing it. This earlier land reform also failed because it did not provide for adequate mechanisms for farmers to acquire credit, technical assistance, or help with marketing their products. The new land reform law is supposed to change all that.

Since the first land reform in 1960, however, Venezuela has become a much more urbanized country, just like the rest of Latin America. Only about 12% of the population is rural now, compared to 35% in 1960. Also, agriculture's share of economic activity, as a percentage of Venezuela's GDP, declined from 50% in 1960 to only 6.1% in 1999, the lowest in Latin America. This statistic is also reflected in the fact that Venezuela is Latin America's only net importer of agricultural products.

Oil, of course, is the main reason why Venezuela's agricultural production declined so dramatically, ever since oil became the country's main export. Awareness of this problem has been the main reason that all Venezuelan governments since the oil boom of the early 1970s have unsuccessfully tried to diversify the Venezuelan economy. The Chávez government has even gone so far as to enshrine economic diversification in the constitution, in the sense that the government is constitutionally required to work towards the alimentary self-sufficiency of the nation.[10]

Another important goal of the land reform is to achieve greater social equity. 75% of the country's private agricultural land is owned by only 5% of the landowners, while 75% of the smaller landowners hold only 6% of the land.[11] The government wants to achieve greater equity, first, by making land available to almost anyone willing to work it. Second, it wants to "completely eliminate the *latifundio* regime, as a system that is contrary to justice, the general interest, and social peace in the country-side."[12] *Latifundio* (sometimes translated as plantation) is defined by the land law as any property that exceeds 5,000 hectares of idle agricultural land.

Finally, a third major motive for the land reform has its basis in the realization of most agricultural experts that smaller family farms are generally more efficient than large farms.[13] The hope is that by redis-tributing land to smaller family farms, the country can increase its agricultural production.

Land reform, however, is an extremely tricky business. The Food and Agriculture Organization (FAO) reports that most land reform programs that have been carried out since 1945, throughout the world, have failed. According to the FAO, most of the time there is a tremendous gap between theory and practice, where the laws and intentions of land reform do not keep up with their effective implementation. So what guarantees that the Venezuelan reform program will succeed where others have failed?

With regard to this problem of turning law and theory into practice, the president's brother, Adán Chávez, who was president of the Land Institute for a brief period in 2002–2003, says that the main reason land reform had only limited success in Venezuela in the past was that the program did not create a series of institutions that had clearly defined responsibilities in the land reform process. Also, there was a lack of political will. However, the new land reform law creates three new institutions, the National Land Institute, which is responsible for land tenancy and redistribution; the National Rural Development Institute, which is responsible for technical assistance and infrastructure; and the Venezuelan Agricultural Corporation, which will provide assistance with distributing and commercializing the agricultural products of farmers who have benefited from the land reform. According to Adán Chávez, "The new law assures, first, in theory, that the productive chain does not break. But then, in practice, we still have to make it reality—through our promise to the people, we are going to follow through."[14]

The most controversial aspect of this whole process is, of course, the process of land redistribution and the possibility of expropriations. According to the law only high-quality idle agricultural land of over 100 hectares or lower quality idle agricultural land of over 5,000 hectares can be expropriated. Supporters of the law, such as Adán Chávez, argue

that the opposition completely exaggerates the possibility of expropriation because expropriation is only a measure of last resort. There is plenty
of government-owned property that will be transferred before any private
property would have to be expropriated. Also, the law commits the
government to convincing landowners to put land into agricultural
production before it is expropriated. Finally, unlike many other land
reform programs around the world, the government would compensate
expropriated land at market value.

Any Venezuelan citizen who is either the head of a family household
or is between 18 and 25 years old may apply for a parcel of land. Once
the land has been productively cultivated for three years, the applicant
may acquire full ownership title to it. However, full title does not mean
that the owner can sell their land, only that it can be passed on to
descendants. The prohibition against selling titles acquired through the
land reform is another issue that land reform critics find fault with
because it easily leads to a black market in land titles. And, just as in all
black markets, because the titles are not completely legal, they end up
being traded far below their true value and thus lead to making poor
farmers even poorer than they otherwise would be. Olivier Delahaye,
professor of agronomy at the Central University of Venezuela, says, "the
campesino who transfers 'his' land obtains for them a price significantly
below (40–60%) the price he would obtain in the formal market. Such a
prohibition [against selling land] cannot be implemented in practice and
disadvantages the poorest."[15] On the other hand, the government's fear
that people will acquire land through the land reform and then sell it at a
profit, leading to renewed land distribution inequality, is not unreason-
able.

At first, the land reform program got off to a slow start, mainly because
the necessary infrastructure needed to be put into place. While the
government distributed very little land in 2002, the next year it went into
high gear and turned over 1.5 million hectares to about 130,000 families.
This makes about an average of 11.5 hectares per family and a total
beneficiary population of 650,000 (based on an average of five persons
per household). By the end of 2005 a total of 3 million hectares of state-
owned land had been distributed to over 200,000 families.

It was not until early 2005, though, that the Chávez government
turned its attention to privately held land. Until that point only state-
owned land had been distributed. For this task, Chávez put Eliecer

Otaiza, who is known as a radical of the Chávez government in charge of the land institute in early 2005. This thus represented the government's first major challenge to Venezuela's landed elite, since the passage of the land reform law in 2001.

The first effort to engage in this renewed land reform effort began in March 2005, when the land institute declared that five estates were to be "recovered." That is, rather than declaring the land as a "latifundio" and expropriating it on the basis that too much of it was idle, the land institute argued that all or part of these lands actually belong to the government because the current occupants cannot properly prove their ownership of it. This, of course, generated much controversy, especially since some of the owners claimed to be able to prove their ownership with documents dating back to the mid 19th century. The government, though, said that some of these documents were false.

Part of the reason for this controversy is that land ownership in Venezuela, just as in most of Latin America, is an extremely murky affair. Large land owners often expanded their territory far beyond its original boundaries, claiming land that either belonged to the state or to absentee landlords. Part of the reason they could do this is that the descriptions in old land titles are very vague about demarcating territory. Also, sometimes a land owner might have legitimately bought land, but the person who it was bought from did not have a legitimate title. The main task now for the Chávez government is to sort all of this out and to develop a coherent and accurate registry of land titles. This, though, is an extremely difficult, time-consuming, and conflictive process.

Already, in many cases landless peasants have on their own challenged the ownership of large land owners, saying that they are not the rightful owners and have occupied their land. For example, in one controversial case a large group of peasants decided to occupy the estate of El Charcote, which belongs to the British cattle ranching company of Lord Vestey. The cattle ranch owners, who say that the occupation has cost them beef production losses of one third of their pre-occupation output, have said that they have ownership documentation that goes back to 1850. In the end, the land institute took up the case and ruled that the owners indeed did not have proper title to the land, but since about two thirds of it was not idle they could continue to use that land. The other third, which the institute declared to be idle, however, would be turned over to peasants; although, not necessarily the ones who were occupying it.

In another case, one of the country's largest and best-known latifundios, known as *La Marqueseña*, the owner negotiated with the
government and eventually agreed to turn over 85% (8,490 hectares)
of the estate to the land reform program. Chávez gave the negotiation the
nickname, the "Ch-Az method," abbreviating the last names of himself
and of the estate's owner, Carlos Azpurúa, saying that all large landowners would first be given the opportunity to negotiate. According to
the INTI, it identified 317 latifundios throughout the country, which
will be examined one by one for possible expropriation for the land
reform.

For the opposition, the El Charcote case was emblematic, as the
National Land Institute has, three years after its founding, begun to
systematically examine property titles of estates it suspects to be latifundios. It is entirely possible that the land institute will decide that most
of these not only consist of idle lands, but that their claimed owners do
not have proper documentation. If this happens, it is possible that
violence in the countryside will erupt. Already over 80 peasant leaders
have been killed by assassins in the past three years over land disputes.

For example, in one case that is unusual, mainly because it is one of
the few the media picked upon, a highly respected and well-known
surgeon, Pedro Doria, who was also a leader of the local land committee,
was killed by an assassin on August 25, 2002. The land committee Doria
led was in the process of claiming title to idle lands south of the
Maracaibo Lake. According to government records, the land belongs
to the state and could thus be legally transferred to the fifty peasant
families that had applied for ownership through their land committee.
However, a local large land owner also claimed title to this land, and on
several occasions he refused to let Doria and government representatives
to inspect the land. In the region it is considered to be common
knowledge that this land is actually being held by former Venezuelan
president Carlos Andres Perez, who is said to own over 60,000 hectares
through third parties throughout the country, the vast majority of it idle
land.

Another who escaped an assassination attempt in 2002 was José
Huerta. He was shot in the shoulder, but barely survived the attack.
Huerta was working for a local office of the national land institute at the
time and was in charge of processing the claims of Doria's land
committee. According to Braulio Alvarez, the director of the Agricultural

Coordination Ezequiel Zamora, a coalition of about a dozen peasant organizations, none of the over 80 cases of assassinated peasant leaders has been resolved, mostly due to the collusion that exists between large land owners and the police. For example, in Doria's and Huerta's cases, the land owner suspected to be behind the assassins is Omar Contreras Barboza, a former agriculture minister in Carlos Andres Perez's government and brother of a former governor of the state of Zulia, where the disputed lands are located. In August 2006 Braulio Alvarez, who had just been elected to the National Assembly the previous December, was also the victim of an assassination attempt, which he barely survived.

As such, besides the resistance of large land owners and the violence against peasant leaders, the rural land reform faces a tremendous number of obstacles, such as the inaccurate land registry, corruption, and the logistical and economic problems of making sure the redistributed land actually becomes productive. However, despite these tremendous problems, the Chávez government has made a clear commitment to land reform and even though the process has been slow at times, it is one of the policy areas where a significant amount of progress can be shown.

Urban Land Reform[16]

Another very important social justice measure of the Chávez government is the urban land reform program, which is to provide land titles to the inhabitants of the barrios, the urban slums. The concept is similar to the one Hernando de Soto has promoted in Peru and in other countries,[17] but it incorporates significant additional elements that make this program unique and an example for other countries.

The urban land reform program has the potential to affect a majority of Venezuela's mostly urban (87%)[18] population. Of this predominantly urban population, an estimated 60% live in the barrios, that is, in slums whose homes the inhabitants built themselves, on land that they occupied by means of land invasion or squatting. Many of these barrios are built on unsafe land, on the hillsides that surround the capital city of Caracas, for example, and are at risk of sliding into the valley whenever there are strong rains.[19]

Earlier Venezuelan governments have always argued that the only solution to the squalor and poverty in Venezuela's barrios is to tear down the homes and to relocate the inhabitants to government housing. This policy has, however, practically never been implemented because it is prohibitively expensive and disruptive. Instead, ever since the riots of February 27, 1989, a barrio movement began, known as the *asamblea de barrios* ("Barrio Assembly"). This movement made the issue of legalizing the barrios a central demand of Venezuela's poor. The *asamblea de barrios* eventually merged into Chávez's Bolivarian movement and contributed to Chávez's election as president in late 1998.

The demand that the inhabitants of the barrios should be given legal title to their homes became a nearly forgotten issue early in Chávez's presidency, until February 4, 2002, when Chávez announced, on the 10th anniversary of his failed 1992 attempted coup, that he would turn over title of the barrios to their inhabitants. Part of the motivation for making this announcement was in all likelihood to revisit an old issue, which had been lobbied for and prepared by barrio activists for quite a while, in a time when the government was under intense siege by the opposition. That is, shortly prior to this announcement, on December 10, the main chamber of commerce, Fedecamaras, and the main labor federation, CTV, had joined forces to organize its first work-stoppage. Through the opposition's and the media's constant onslaught, the government was clearly losing popularity and had to do something dramatic.

Another impulse for the urban land reform initiative probably came from the fact that one of the main opposition parties, *Primero Justicia*, was also proposing a Barrio Law. Their law was also supposed to give ownership titles to the barrios' inhabitants. *Primero Justicia's* Barrio Law was directly inspired by Hernando de Soto's work *The Other Path* and *The Mystery of Capital*, rather than by the barrio assemblies of the early 1990s, as the Chavista law is. The *Primero Justicia* law emphasized the sanctity of private property and would punish land invasions with up to five years' imprisonment.[20] The transfer of ownership to barrio inhabitants would primarily apply to cases where either the government owns the property or where the inhabitants have occupied the land for ten or more years (also known as *usucapión*).

When Chávez announced decree 1,666 on February 4, 2002, he laid the groundwork for beginning the transfer of legal ownership of the barrios to its inhabitants. However, the decree can only transfer publicly owned land. Ivan Martinez, the director of the National Technical Office for the Regularization of Urban Land Tenancy estimates that approximately one third of the land that the barrios now occupy belongs to the state, one third is privately owned, and for one third the ownership is undetermined. To transfer privately owned land to barrio inhabitants, a law would have to be passed.

The corresponding law, the "Special Law to Regularize Land Tenancy in Poor Urban Settlements," is being proposed by Chávez's Fifth Republic Movement (MVR) party, and has been held up in the National Assembly for several years. One of the reasons it has taken so long to pass the law, besides the legislative gridlock that existed between 2003 and 2004, is that the decree specifies that the details of the law will be worked out in conjunction with the communities that are to benefit from the law. This has meant that the land committees that are created in every barrio sent representatives to the National Assembly to discuss the law together with the legislators. According to Martinez, the communities have proposed numerous changes to the original draft law, such as making a provision for the creation of communal property. This is one of the first laws in Venezuelan history that is being drafted together with the affected local communities and was scheduled to pass the legislature sometime in late 2006.

Martinez emphasizes that this is a law which will have a significant impact on the lives of more Venezuelan citizens than any other governmental program, except for public education. As many as ten million Venezuelans, or 40% of the population, could eventually benefit from this redistribution program. But, according to Martinez, this is going to be a relatively slow process that could take up to ten years to fully implement.

Martinez says giving title to the barrio inhabitants is "a recognition of the social debt which the state owes the population." After all, while the state constructed merely one million homes in the past fifty years and the private sector constructed about two million homes, the barrio inhabitants constructed over three million homes. Also, considering that it costs about ten times as much to tear down a barrio home and build a new one somewhere else, it becomes clear that, according to Martinez, "the barrios are part of the solution, not the problem."

Andrés Antillano, an organizer in La Vega, one of Venezuela's largest, oldest, and most politicized barrios, who together with Ivan Martinez helped draft the new urban land reform law, adds that this project is "about recognizing the barrio as a subject with legal rights and with profound transformative potentials." In other words, the urban land reform is not just a means for advancing capital accumulation in the barrios, but it is also a means for instituting participatory democratic self-help in the communities.

So as to organize the affected communities for land redistribution, the decree and the proposed law stipulate that "land committees" have to be created. These committees constitute seven to eleven individuals who are elected by a gathering of at least 50% of the families in any given community, representing between 100 and 200 families. These land committees are free to choose the boundaries of the land that they represent.

By mid-2005 there were over 5,600 active land committees (at an average of 147 families per committee, this means that about 800,000 families or just over 4 million individuals are organized in these committees). Through these, 126,000 families, representing 600,000 individuals, had received titles to their homes, in about one third of the country's municipalities.[21] This makes the urban land reform program one of the most far-reaching civil society–governmental programs, along with public education and the *Barrio Adentro* program of community doctors. Also, it is the single largest organized civil society movement in Venezuela.

The land committees have a wide variety of tasks, all of which involve organizing the community in one way or another. Broadly speaking, their tasks can be divided into three areas, according to the community organizer Andres Antillano: 1) participation in the regularization of urban property titles, 2) the self-government of the barrio, and 3) the self-transformation of the barrio. An additional more temporary task is their participation in the formulation of the urban land law.

With regard to their participation in the regularization of urban property titles, the committees are actively involved in measuring the plots of land that each family occupies and in adjudicating disputes over territory. Also, since this measuring and registration process has to be accurate, government officials participate in the measuring and train community members in how to use the measuring equipment. This process can be tricky because barrio homes often have quite irregular shapes. The measuring and cadastre registration also involves designating which parts of barrio land should be communally owned, so as to provide recreational spaces for the families.

Once the land is registered, a family can claim title to it by providing proof of ownership, usually in the form of receipts used to pay the costs of building the home or in the form of utility bills, or other kinds of documentation. The National Technical Office then provides a certificate which, once the property is ready to be transferred and if no-one else claims title to the land within three months, can be exchanged for the actual title to the land.

However, only homes built on safe land, that is, land that does not endanger its inhabitants because of its instability due to being built in a precarious location, is eligible for ownership. Inhabitants of homes built on unsafe terrain have the right to exchange their property claim for a government-built home in a different location. Similarly, people involved in land invasions that occurred after the urban land reform decree of February 4, 2002 cannot participate in the titling program, but would have to be taken care of under the government's public housing program.

With regard to the communal self-government objective, the land committees embody much more manageable units than the current districts, which in Caracas can currently consist of over half a million citizens. The land committees provide direct partners for the city's infrastructure agencies and utility companies, so as to improve services such as water, electricity, waste disposal, and road access. The committees have even begun to form sub-committees that work on these different tasks, including the organization of cultural activities, beautification, and the improvement of security in the barrio.

Finally, in terms of self-transformation, the land committees have the task of drafting a barrio charter, which tells the history of each barrio, defines its territory, identifies ground rules, and elaborates its values. This charter is meant to strengthen the communal identity of the barrio. The idea is that only a strong sense of communal identity will lead to a true sense of community and thus to communal self-transformation.

When asked what they most hoped for from this program, barrio inhabitants regularly mentioned "recognition." Nora, a participant in a land sub-committee said, "We believe in the government here not because of the titles, but because we now have a greater amount of participation in the issues that affect the community." While the full implementation of this program has the potential of increasing Chávez's popularity in the barrios, Nora adds that "People are saying, 'Why has it taken so many years for a government to finally meet this demand?' "

The concept of urban land redistribution thus addresses many issues simultaneously. First, when people acquire title to their own self-built home in the barrio, they have some security for the first time that the home is theirs and will not be repossessed by the original landowner. Second, they can use the home as collateral for a small loan, to either improve their home, to buy a better home, or to invest in a small business. Third, the process of acquiring urban land titles is a collective process, which brings the neighborhood together in the interest of improving the neighborhood's infrastructure, such as roads, access to utilities, security, comfort, etc.

Education Policy

Of all the different sub-areas of social policy, the one that Chávez and his supporters probably highlight the most, as being the government's top priority, is education policy. Chávez often likes to cite Simon Bolivar in this regard, who said, "a people advance in step with their education." As such, the Chávez government has perhaps dedicated the greatest increases in state resources to education, all the way from pre-school, to elementary and high school, and to university level. More recently, Chávez has also focused on improving education for the country's poor, mostly via the missions, which provide financial aid and special programs, such as literacy training.

As mentioned earlier, Venezuela's free public education system gradually excluded larger and larger numbers of the poor, as the school system increased the barriers for poor children's participation. These barriers mostly took the form of registration fees, which were set by each school individually, often to compensate for the lack of resources it was receiving from the central government. By 1996 public spending for education had dropped to \$118 per capita, which was 37% lower than it was in 1990.[22] Another indicator of the worsening situation of public education was that even with a steadily increasing population, the number of students attending public schools stayed almost exactly the same, at 5.5 million between 1992 and 1998.[23]

When the Chávez government came to power, spending on education was one of the areas the government focused on the most. By 2001 it increased public spending on education to 4.3% of GDP (or $220 per capita), twice the level of 1996 and one of the highest levels in twenty years.[24] Much of the new investment in education went towards the building of new schools and the transformation of old ones into "Bolivarian Schools." Also, public school enrollment (primary and secondary) increased from 5.5 million in 1998 to 6.5 million in 2001—an increase of one million (or 18%) in just three years, when in the previous six years there had been no increase at all in public school enrollment.

Educational Philosophy

For the Chávez government and its education minister, Aristobulo Isturiz, the contrast between the educational philosophy of the previous governments and the current one could not be stronger. According to Isturiz, the earlier governments were guided by what he calls a "neo-liberal" educational model, which emphasized competition and individualism, both in terms of its curriculum and its approach for organizing the educational system. "There has been a marked tendency towards privatization and exclusion, as elements that have characterized the education model, as a result of the neo-liberal policies," says Isturiz.[25] As mentioned earlier, over the years access to the educational system became increasingly more expensive and competitive. For Isturiz, this is what makes it a neo-liberal model of education.

In contrast, the Bolivarian model emphasizes cooperation and community in its curricula and universal access and egalitarianism in its organization. The individual educational policies, from pre-school, to elementary and high school, to professional and university education, are supposed to reflect these principles. However, it was not until late 2003, once the state budget began its recovery, that the Chávez government made an additional push to universalize education and make sure that the poor who had been excluded from the educational system in their childhood could also gain access to an education, via the missions.

Pre-School Education: Proyecto Simoncito

As one of its main goals, the Chávez government decided to provide universal pre-schooling to all children in Venezuela (ages 0 to 6). The project for implementing this program is known as "Simoncito," or "little Simon," in allusion to Simon Bolivar. As Aristobulo Isturiz, the minister of education explains, "We in the school do not have the capacity to resolve socio-economic inequalities. But we do have the capacity, independently of the origin of the children, to make the conditions more equal before they enroll in first grade. The function that pre-school carries out is to guarantee the equality."[26] Of course, in addition to equalizing the starting conditions for children entering school for the first time, the pre-school program also provides for daycare for working parents, making it less of a financial burden to place a child in a daycare program or to keep one parent at home to watch the children.

According to Isturiz, in 2004 about 1.38 million children between the ages of 0 and 6 were enrolled in public pre-schools,[27] which is about one third of the population in that age group. The total enrollment in pre-school education, both public and private, for the ages 3 to 5 have shown a steady upwards trend over the past ten years, going from 43.5% of children in that age group in 1993/94, to 52.3% in 2002/03 (an increase of 8.8%). The greatest increases took place during the Chávez presidency (5.7%, compared to 3% during the Caldera presidency).[28] Still, to make pre-school education universal, the government has quite a task ahead.

Bolivarian Elementary Schools

The creation of so-called "Bolivarian schools" represents one of the government's main educational policies. These schools are supposed to address Venezuela's poverty in a variety of ways. First, they are day-long schools, thus freeing up both parents from daytime childcare duties, allowing them to work during the day. Also, the day-long program allows the incorporation of more cultural and sports activities. Second, Bolivarian schools provide breakfast, lunch, and a late afternoon snack, regular meals that many poor children often would not otherwise receive. Third, the schools are supposed to be more closely integrated into the community than traditional public schools.

As of 2004, approximately 3,600 Bolivarian schools had been opened, of which 650 (18%) are newly constructed and the rest are rebuilt traditional schools. These schools now serve about 700,000 children, or 17% of all elementary school children.[29] The goal of the Chávez government is to gradually turn all public schools into Bolivarian schools.

According to the government, Bolivarian schools embody six characteristics:[30]

1. They seek to transform the children into participatory, critical, and integrated individuals who identify with their national identity.
2. They are participatory and democratic, where all members of the school community participate in the decision-making and execution of school activities.
3. They are at the service of the community.
4. They promote social justice and thus seek to ensure that all children complete their schooling.
5. They are examples of permanent pedagogical renovation, where "the school is converted into a space for the dialogue of knowledge and cultural productions."
6. They fight against educational exclusion.

While school enrollment has increased significantly during the six years of the Chávez government, the increases in the most recent period have slowed down, from 7.0% and 5.6% increases in 2000/01 and 2001/02, to an increase of only 1.3% in 2002/03. Part of this deceleration, though, is probably attributable to the government having already reached all those who were easy targets for incorporation in the school system and now the government has to reach out to those who, for various reasons, are more difficult to incorporate. For the school year 2004/05 the elementary school enrollment rate (ages 6 to 11) is practically at the maximum level now, at 99.0%. This represents an increase of 10.5 percentage points, relative to ten years earlier. Nearly all of that growth, in those ten years, took place during the Chávez presidency (1999/2000 to 2004/05).[31] A similar picture exists for junior high school enrollment (ages 12 to 14), where the enrollment rate increased from 47.5% in 1993/94 to 58.7%, again, with this entire growth (11.2%) taking place during the Chávez presidency and not before.

Another serious problem that Venezuela's school system has had to face for a long time is the high drop-out rate. Of the cohort of students that enter first grade in any given year, about half drop out sometime before they reach 9th grade. This statistic seems to have improved slightly from 2000 to 2003, according to the human rights group Provea, from a drop-out rate of 54% in 2000 to 47% in 2003.[32]

As mentioned earlier, one of the main reasons for the increases in school enrollment is directly attributable to the Chávez government's elimination of enrollment fees at public schools. This used to be a common practice among public schools, largely in order to make up for school budget cuts. Venezuela's 1999 constitution, however, explicitly prohibits the charging of fees for public schools. Nonetheless, according to the Ministry of Education, the practice still continues, illegally, in about 10% of public schools. Some of these schools now face having to pay fines.

Mission Robinson I and II—Adult Literacy and Elementary Education

In July 2003, after the government had had some time to recover financially from the devastating economic recession that the coup and the oil industry shutdown had provoked in 2002, Chávez announced the first of what later would become twelve "missions" for fighting poverty.[33] The first mission was Mission Robinson, named after Simon "Robinson" Rodriguez, who was Simon Bolivar's teacher. Mission Robinson is supposed to address illiteracy. While illiteracy is fairly low in Venezuela, only about 7%, compared to the rest of Latin America, where it is 11%, it is certainly one of the most serious contributing factors to poverty.

Thus, via a cooperation agreement with Cuba, Venezuela invited hundreds of Cuban literacy experts to come to Venezuela to train literacy teachers. In the first phase of the program, which was launched July 1, 2003, students were taught to read and write, using a Cuban methodology which is based on numbers, since most people who are illiterate do know numbers. According to government statistics, over 1.3 million Venezuelans benefited from the program by late 2004, with the help of over 100,000 literacy teachers, who work throughout the country.[34] In late 2005 the government announced that Venezuela was now officially "illiteracy free."[35]

The second phase, Mission Robinson II, goes beyond literacy and aims to teach participants everything they need to reach 6th grade. The program is very compressed, so that in two years students would complete the Robinson II program, instead of taking the usual six years for Venezuelan primary education. Mission Robinson II began October 28, 2003, and as of late 2004 had attended to over 1.1 million students since its conception, most of whom had participated in the Robinson I program. Both programs, Robinson I and II, depend on volunteer teachers and the programs are conducted mostly in people's homes, often with the aid of a TV and VCR that the government provides. According to the independent human rights group Provea, "both missions comply with the state's obligation to guarantee the right to education and, within this, to fight illiteracy. The project awakened a popular motivation and participation that is positive from all points of view."[36]

Venezuela's opposition, though, claim that the literacy program is nothing other than a cover for a Cuban indoctrination program. However, even a cursory glance at the materials used (so-called "libraries" of a dozen books, which every household or participant receives for free) and conversations with people who have graduated from the program, show that there is nothing to such accusations.

Bolivarian High Schools

A relatively late innovation of the Chávez government is the Bolivarian High School. One of the main tasks of these Bolivarian high schools is to lower the drop-out rate and to prepare the country's youth to be more effective once they enter the world of work. According to Venezuela's constitution and education laws, the educational process is "strongly connected to work with the aim of harmonizing education with productive activity . . ."[37]

The objectives of the Bolivarian high school are somewhat similar to those of the Bolivarian elementary school, except that the emphasis is on retaining students for the entire duration of the high school and on relating their school work to the real world, through projects, through an emphasis on teaching them to apply the ideas of "endogenous development," and on participating in their communities, such as the local public planning councils.

The pedagogical difference between the old schools and the Bolivarian schools the ministry of education describes as follows. The old high school system:

has perpetuated a type of encyclopedic knowledge that is disciplinary and based on memorization, which is removed from both the mentality of adolescents and youth and from their real-life problems. This scientific knowledge, which is based in a rationalist perspective, is articulated by two basic characteristics: specialization and abstraction. This specialized knowledge is disciplinary in that it delimits a portion of reality and it is abstract in that it eliminates the relations it establishes with other aspects of itself.[38]

In contrast, the Bolivarian high school system is based on the paradigm of the sciences of complexity:

> . . . complementarity in the face of antimonies and dichotomies, and instead of betting on an interdisciplinary conception, on a transdisciplinary or metadisciplinary conception . . . Overcoming curricular fragmentation supposes the adoption of a perspective of integration, assuming that science is a means for making sense of the problems of society and never an end of its own . . . the objects of study do not have to be scientific problems, but rather the problems of society.[39]

This conception for high school pedagogy is largely based on the educational theories of Edgar Morín, a French philosopher of education, who has gained a strong following in Europe and in Latin America in recent years (few of his works have been translated into English).[40]

In practice, the idea is to create a high school curriculum that is oriented more by practical applications, rather than by traditional disciplinary divisions. For example, instead of having separate classes in chemistry, physics, and biology, these would be grouped together in the area of science. Other areas would include social science, humanities, and health, for example. All of these areas are also supposed to focus on practical project work, so as to make the learning as closely related to real-life situations as possible.

As part of a measure to integrate knowledge more and to also overcome the high drop-out rates, students are supposed to interact with fewer teachers during the school day. That is, instead of having twelve different teachers for twelve different subjects, the education ministry wants to limit these to five teachers for five areas: math and natural science, social science and citizenship, language and culture, physical education, and education for endogenous development.

Clearly, such changes represent a fairly radical departure from the traditional ways of organizing a school curriculum. By early 2005 these plans had received little public attention, especially since they had not yet been put into practice. According to the Ministry of Education, though, during the 2004/05 school year, 26 pilot projects were started. The number of schools and students involved in the program will be increased progressively, so that by the end of a three-year test period 259 Bolivarian high schools and 128,000 students will be incorporated into the project. This represents about 7.5% of all high school students.

Mission Ribas—Adult Secondary Education

Parallel to the literacy and primary education programs of Mission Robinson, the government has created Mission Ribas, named after independence hero José Felix Ribas (1775–1815), so that individuals who dropped out of high school can complete their high school education. According to government statistics, there are over five million Venezuelans who dropped out of high school. Mission Ribas is supposed to incorporate these into an educational program that would allow them to graduate in a maximum of two years. In 2003, the year the program was launched, over 430,000 Venezuelans registered and participated in the program, with the help of over 10,000 volunteer facilitators. By 2004 the number of participants increased to over 700,000 and over 27,000 facilitators.

Just like all of the missions, the program is free. However, 100,000 participants receive scholarships, based on financial need. Most of the courses are in the form of "tele-classes," or videos, with the help of a facilitator. Once students complete their studies, the state-owned oil company PDVSA and the electric company CADAFE offer to place students in the mining, oil, and energy sector. The whole program is being primarily coordinated by PDVSA and CADAFE, which are also providing most of the funding for the program.

The primary criticism of the program has been that many of the volunteer facilitators are too inexperienced and often do not know the material they are supposed to teach. Government spokespersons point out, though, that most of the teaching is via books and audio-visual equipment.

Bolivarian University

Just as primary education gradually excluded more and more poor children from the school system in the period from 1978 to 1998, so did higher education. This development accelerated particularly due to the fact that Venezuela's population grew much faster than the university system. While technically anyone with a high school degree ("*bachiller*") is supposed to have access to university, public universities restricted university entrance via entrance examinations. These, as is usually the case, ended up filtering out students coming from poor or working class backgrounds. An important factor in this filtering process is that middle and upper class students can afford to take special classes that prepare them for entrance examinations, while those from poor backgrounds cannot. While in 1984 70% of students from poor backgrounds who applied for entrance to the university were admitted, by 1998 only 19% were admitted.[41] For working class students the admission rate dropped from 67% to 27%. As a result, it is estimated that there are over 400,000 Venezuelans who formally fulfill the requirements and would like to attend the university, but cannot because they did not score well enough in the entrance examinations.

The Bolivarian University of Venezuela (UBV) is supposed to fill the gap that exists between university supply and university demand. More than that, it is supposed to prioritize its admissions towards students from poor backgrounds. Two thousand four hundred students were enrolled in the university's first classes in October 2003, and another 20,000 were pre-registered. The university will have branches throughout the country and is eventually supposed to reach a total enrollment of 100,000.[42] The initial programs of study are Medicine, Journalism, Law, and Environmental and Development Studies. Within a year of its official launch, five campuses of the UBV had been opened, many of them in buildings that used to belong to the state oil company PDVSA. In Falcon State, for example, a large PDVSA building that was meant for training PDVSA staff was turned over to the UBV—a move that symbolizes the turning over of state assets that used to be exclusively for the country's elite to the country's poor.

However, more than just filling the gap between those who would like to attend a university and the university space available, especially for Venezuela's poor, the Bolivarian University is also launching a new concept of university education; one which is again closely modeled on the principles of Edgar Morín. That is, the university is organized on the principle of practical applications rather than abstract disciplines, much of the education is project-oriented, and students are required to work closely with poor communities.[43]

A third and perhaps less often articulated purpose of the Bolivarian University is to provide an educational space for the training of Bolivarian professionals, that is, professionals who share the goals and ideas of the Bolivarian project. Ever since Chávez's election, one of the most serious and chronic problems his government has faced has been a lack of highly trained professionals who support the Bolivarian project or who, at the very least, are not actively interested in subverting and destabilizing the government. The vast majority of the country's professional class clearly identifies itself with the opposition. Having these people ensconced in the state bureaucracy, often simply because no qualified personnel can be found to replace them, has created countless problems for the Chávez government in running the state efficiently. All too often, Chávez replaces skilled and capable opposition sympathizers with unskilled and incapable supporters. This rarely solves the problem. The long-term solution to this problem would thus be the creation of a new professional class. As a result, "The UBV [Bolivarian University of Venezuela] contributes to the change of the Venezuelan state," says the university's founding document.[44]

The clear implication of this last and mostly unarticulated objective is that mainly students who share the goals and ideals of the Bolivarian project are welcome at the university. Already, complaints have emerged from the opposition, accusing the university of political discrimination. University officials, though, deny this. Whether there is an active process of discrimination is difficult to tell. The Venezuelan human rights group Provea does not make any mention of such discrimination, except to say that political discrimination on both sides of Venezuela's political divide is endemic across the educational system, from pre-school to university.[45] To any casual visitor of the university it is obvious that the UBV is a university at which students and professors who believe in the Bolivarian project predominate. It is quite likely, though, that the vast majority of these professors and students are pro-Chávez mainly because of self-selection and not as a result of discrimination on the part of university authorities.

Mission Sucre—Higher Education Scholarships

For the poor, one of the greatest hindrances to a university education is their lack of financial resources. They generally have to work on the side, often supporting family members at the same time, making studies nearly impossible. Mission Sucre, named after another independence hero, Antonio José de Sucre (1795–1830), is meant to bring a university education to the country's poor. It is essentially a preparation, insertion, and scholarship program for a university education.

A census conducted by the Ministry of Higher Education in 2003 found that there are slightly over 500,000 Venezuelans who have completed the requirements for a university education, but who were not admitted to a university. According to the ministry, these will be incorporated into a university education in phases. In the first phase, as of November 2003, 72,144 poor Venezuelans signed up. Thirty thousand of these received a scholarship of the Venezuelan equivalent of $100 per month for their university education. By July 2004 another 90,193 students had joined the program, with 40,000 of these receiving scholarships.

These students are all either involved in a university initiation program (*Programa de Iniciación Universitaria*), in the Bolivarian University of Venezuela, in one of the regular public universities, or in new "University Villages." The University Village represents another educational innovation of the Chávez government, which aims to bring a university education to the areas of the country where these are needed. That is, rather than having students come to the capital or one of the other urban centers with a university, where students often end up staying, the idea is to "municipalize" the university. These will be small universities that attend to the specific needs of the community, offering a limited selection of courses of study. As of 2005 there were three pilot projects, with plans to begin another 40 throughout the country soon thereafter.

Already by September 2003 over 420,000 Venezuelans had indicated an interest in Mission Sucre. Guiseppe Gianetto, the then rector of Venezuela's largest public university, the Universidad Central de Venezuela, who is also an outspoken critic of the Chávez government, said, though, that Mission Sucre is a "demagogic" program because the government will never be able to accommodate the 400,000 students who want to enter the university system, but for whom there is no place. The existing public universities cannot possibly accommodate these students, according to Gianetto. The government, however, says that most of these will eventually find a place through the UBV, expanded capacity at the old universities, or through the university villages. In the medium term the success of *Misión Sucre* depends on whether Venezuela's educational spending and the oil income that supports it can maintain this significant expansion of the university system.

A perhaps more serious criticism of *Misión Sucre* is raised by Provea, which points out that this mission, just like many of the other educational missions, suffers from political patronage and from the creation of parallel state structures. That is, with respect to patronage, the mission all too often benefits only those who support the Chávez government. Provea cites a campaign manual of the pro-Chávez coalition, which states, "All of the Bolivarian elements (missions, political parties and social movements, student and youth organizations, community groups, etc.) will form part" of the electoral battle units, which campaigned for Chávez during the 2004 presidential recall referendum. As Provea correctly points out, state programs should not be incorporated into political campaigns.

With regard to the creation of parallel structures, this is a problem insofar as it undermines existing democratic structures, such as the legislature's ability to approve budgets for programs such as these. That is, the educational missions are all funded directly by PDVSA and, at first at least, were not part of the regular state budget. Also, many existing state institutions, whether the universities or the education ministry, are largely being bypassed by the missions. Education Minister Aristobulo Isturiz, though, says that the missions were run outside of the existing state institutions only in their initial phase, when they were pilot programs. Now, however, they will be gradually integrated into the existing state structures.

Health Care Policy

Just as with all other areas of social policy, Venezuelan health care in the two decades prior to Chávez suffered from the long economic downturn and the implementation of neo-liberalism. For example, the percentage of GDP that the state spent on health care declined dramatically, from 1.8% of GDP in 1992 to 0.8% in 1996[46]—a decline of over 50% in a four-year period. It recovered slightly in the following two years, reaching 1.3% of GDP in 1998, the year before Chávez became president.[47]

In addition to this decline in public funding for health care, Venezuela's system for providing health care has become quite confusing and fragmented. There are four main national public institutions that manage health care, each with their own insurance and hospital system.[48] In addition to these national institutions, there are numerous state and municipal hospitals, which further complicate the bureaucracy and funding of health care in Venezuela. An effort to decentralize the hospital system took place in the late '90s, in order to make the hospitals more accountable to community needs and to reduce bureaucracy, but after some initial successes, it did not go very far.

Venezuela's health indicators show that the population's health also did not do too well during the 1990s. While the trend in the previous three decades had been that life expectancy and infant mortality steadily improved, during the 1990s there was little or no improvement. Life expectancy averaged 71.9 years during this time and infant mortality hovered around 24 deaths per 1,000 live births between 1990 and 1996.

It is fair to say that with the beginning of the Chávez government health indicators and public health expenditures increased or improved steadily for the first time since the early 1980s. For example, health care expenditures as a percentage of GDP increased from 1.3% of GDP in 1998 to 1.61% in 2004. In absolute terms, per capita public health expenditures went from 66.8% of the 1990 level in 1998 ($61.47/person), to 111% of the 1990 level in 2005 ($102.64/person).

Overall health indicators show a similar trend, in that life expectancy increased almost a full year between 1998 and 2005, going from 72.4 years to 73.2 years. This represents the largest average annual increase since 1988. Similarly, infant mortality dropped from 21.4 deaths per 1,000 live births in 1998 to 17.7 in 2001 (increasing, though, due to the economic crisis, to 18.2 in 2002 and dropping to 17.1 by 2004).[49] Again, this represents the greatest average annual lowering of the infant mortality rate since the late 1980s. What did the Chávez government do, though, to bring about these changes?

The Universalization of Health Care

The primary objective of the Chávez government's health care policy was to universalize health care, to make it accessible to all Venezuelans, regardless of income. Actually, this had been the goal of previous governments and to some extent the governments of the oil boom years (1958–1978) were able to fulfill this objective. However, as stated before, the health care system, just as the education system, had become increasingly exclusionary during the two lost decades. Thus, the universalization of health care had to be put on the public policy-making agenda once again.

One of the first measures the Chávez government thus undertook was to pass a decree stating that all Venezuelans had the right to be treated at public hospitals, regardless of whether they were insured. With formal sector employment reaching 50–55%, ever larger numbers of Venezuelans were no longer covered by the public health insurance system, IVSS.[50] Making IVSS and other public hospitals available to the uninsured literally opened the hospital doors to millions who over the years had come to be excluded from Venezuela's public health care system. While this certainly benefited many, the change was rather small, relative to the extent of Venezuela's health care problems.

Hospitals were still very under-funded for much of Chávez's presidency (1999–2005). Stories abounded of people lying or even dying in hospital hallways and of patients having to bring their own syringes and other equipment for treatment in hospital. Also, in many cases doctors and other hospital staff went months without pay. As a result, hospital strikes became quite common. In 2003 and 2004 there were a total of 27 health care strikes, which represented a 24% decrease compared to the previous two-year period.[51] Thus, despite the fact that hospital doors were opened to the general population, what patients found behind these doors left a lot to be desired.

Venezuela's health care system and the universalization of health care did not really make a qualitative and quantitative leap for the better until the introduction of the *Barrio Adentro* (Inside the Barrio) program in mid-2003. Another important program that improved health care significantly was the vaccination program, which was introduced early in the Chávez presidency. In the year 2000 the Chávez government decided to reach the goal of covering all children with vaccinations. This goal, according to the human rights group Provea, has still not yet been reached, though. Depending on the type of disease, coverage now oscillates between 17% and 90%.[52] However, when compared with previous governments, the average annual vaccination rate during the Chávez government for different diseases tends to be higher. For example, the measles vaccination rate oscillated at around 45% in the 1980s and around 65% in the 1990s. During the Chávez government, though, the annual vaccination rate (1999–2003) was 76%.[53] Similar trends of a 10% jump in immunization coverage can be seen for most other types of vaccinations as well.

Misión Barrio Adentro

By November 2004, Mission Barrio Adentro (Inside the Barrio) existed in 320 of Venezuela's 335 municipalities, employing 13,000 Cuban and 29 Venezuelan general practitioners, working in 8,500 "popular" (home-based) clinics. Also, the program was expanded to include dentists, employing 3,054 Cubans and 543 Venezuelans. According to the Ministry of Health and Social Development, Barrio Adentro has provided over 45 million doctor's consultations since its inception and annually saves the lives of 25,000 children.[54]

The program, while immensely popular among the country's poor, has outraged Venezuela's medical establishment. According to the Venezuelan Medical Federation (FMV), the program is costing Venezuelan doctors' jobs, and is undercutting the quality of health care, since Cuban doctors are supposedly not as well trained as Venezuelan doctors, and are indoctrinating the country's poor with Marxist ideology. The FMV, which has 55,000 doctors, is one of Venezuela's more powerful lobby groups and has been opposed to Chávez from the beginning. Their opposition, though, has gone far beyond dealing with merely professional concerns. In June 2003 the FMV filed a suit against the Cuban doctors, challenging their ability to practice medicine in Venezuela, saying that they had not passed the proper licensing procedures. The court that took the case was the First Administrative Dispute Court, which at the time was known for being in the hands of the opposition. In August 2003 the court ruled in favor of the FMV, saying that the Cuban doctors were not allowed to practice medicine in Venezuela without being licensed by a Venezuelan medical university. However, the government decided to appeal the ruling to the Supreme Court and to ignore the lower court's ruling with the argument that the human and constitutional right to health care preceded the court's bureaucratic ruling. By late 2005, the Supreme Court had still not ruled on the matter.

In the long run, though, Barrio Adentro cannot survive without Venezuelan doctors. However, Venezuelan doctors have proven to be quite unwilling to participate in the program, since most of them come from middle class backgrounds or higher and share the prejudices that middle class Venezuelans have against the barrios, believing that they are far too dangerous and dirty for them to live or work in. So, to solve this problem, the government has begun recruiting medical students from the barrios, who study medicine either in Cuba or in the Bolivarian University of Venezuela. The first class of 250 Venezuelan medical students graduated in late 2004, with another 1,000 still studying in Cuba.

The other problem that the program could face is financing. Currently, with the price of oil at its highest level in twenty years, the Venezuelan government is experiencing a revenue boom that has allowed it to spend generously on programs such as Barrio Adentro. Should those revenues decline suddenly, the program, which is estimated at costing around $1.5 billion per year, would probably dry up quickly. On the other hand, since Barrio Adentro is providing primary and preventive care, it could be saving large amounts of money for Venezuela's medical system in the long run, lowering the need for people to be hospitalized or their need for more expensive treatment. Also, start-up costs for such programs are higher than their operating costs, so that once the "popular" community clinics are built, maintaining these will become much cheaper.

The tasks for the Chávez government in health care, despite recent advances, remain numerous and challenging. First, to make Barrio Adentro a stable and effective program, it has to finish building 9,500 community health centers (only 280 were constructed as of mid-2005). Second, it has to gradually replace the Cuban doctors with Venezuelan ones. Next, with regard to the larger health care system, it must find a way to both unify and decentralize the existing fragmented hospital network. An "organic" law (a law based on the constitution) of health care is in the works, which would address this issue. Finally, it must properly equip and expand the existing hospitals and pay doctors their back salaries.

Only in mid-2005 did Chávez address this latter point, when he announced two new programs, Barrio Adentro II and III. Barrio Adentro II involves the construction of brand new community clinics in the barrios, where no clinics had ever existed before. Barrio Adentro III, in contrast, involves the full funding, after more than a decade of neglect, of Venezuela's existing hospital system. $2.5 billion was to be allocated from the country's foreign currency reserves (from the Fonden fund) to purchase medical equipment abroad. This represented one of the largest allocations of Fonden monies.[55]

Housing Policy

Of all the areas of the Chávez government's social policies, its accomplishments with regard to housing have perhaps been the weakest (followed by public hospitals). Early on in Chávez's presidency, in 2000, it was celebrated as a major accomplishment that per capita spending on public housing had reached its highest level in over a decade, amounting to 104.5% of the spending level in 1990. However, after that per capita spending on public housing declined precipitously every year, reaching an all-time low in 2004 of only 39.8% of the level it was in 1990.[56] Similarly, in terms of actual homes that were built by the government, these reached a peak in 2000 with 70,000, dropping to 11,000 in 2003.[57] In terms of the square meters constructed, this reached 4,635,000m^2 in 2001, dropping to 1,770,000m^2 in 2003. The Chávez government constructed fewer public homes per year in its first four years in office (1999–2002) than the government of Carlos Andrés Perez (1989–1993) and only slightly more than the government of Rafael Caldera (1994–1998). That is, the annual average for the Chávez government was 34,228, compared to 37,018 for the Perez government and 33,754 for the Caldera government.[58]

The problem with the housing sector is that Venezuela suffers from a severe housing shortage. The combination of rapid urbanization, strong population growth (doubling between 1976 and 2004), and the widespread increase in poverty made it impossible for the private sector to provide sufficient homes for everyone that needed one. It is estimated that at least 135,000 new homes are needed per year, just to satisfy the new annual demand. In 2004 the total housing deficit in Venezuela was a need for a staggering 982,000 new homes and the improvement of over 1.4 million existing ones. However, if one adds together the homes that both the public and the private sector built between 1990 and 2000, only 63,500 were built per year.[59] It thus becomes clear that at the current rate of home construction the housing shortage will only worsen over time.

The problems the Chávez government faced and so far have been unable to overcome in this sector are manifold. First of all, the government's procedures for constructing homes are extremely bureaucratic. That is, there are currently at least five different state agencies responsible for the construction of public housing, which makes coordination quite complicated. Also, Chávez, often out of frustration with the relative lack of results of his ministers, has named new ones responsible for public housing on a continuous basis, making it practically impossible for a recently appointed minister to get used to his new job, find his way around the complicated bureaucracy, and to produce results. In the five years of government from 1999 to 2004, Chávez had seven ministers who were responsible for public housing (the first five as minister of infrastructure and as of 2004 as minister of housing and habitat). Every time there is a change of minister, they tend to change all of the next level of management at the ministry, which produces tremendous upheavals in the entire institution. Third, in addition to the relatively large number of national institutions responsible for public housing, there are state-wide and local agencies, which further add to the general confusion in the sector. Finally, fourth, just as in all other social policy areas, the government had to initiate large public spending cutbacks in 2002 and 2003, due to the political and economic crisis during those two years.

In mid-2004 the Chávez government announced two new major policy initiatives that were supposed to turn around this rather poor record in the housing sector. The first was the creation of a new ministry that would unify all of the existing public housing-related institutions, which would be placed under the overall guidance of a "Mission Habitat." The second was the passing of a new law governing mortgages and state support for home purchasing.

Chávez announced in early 2005 that the new housing ministry and the Mission Habitat would build or reconstruct enough homes for all Venezuelans, so that the country's housing crisis would be solved by the year 2021, the year Chávez has announced his Bolivarian revolution will be completed. An important change in the new housing policy would be that the focus is no longer solely on the state building homes for Venezuelans who need them, but also on involving ordinary Venezuelans in the construction or reconstruction of their own homes, with the help of the state. Recognizing that nearly one million new homes would have to be built and 1.5 million homes would have to be reconstructed, the government's goal was to build at least 120,000 new homes in 2005 and another 200,000 in 2006, according to an announcement Chávez made on one of his weekly television programs, *Aló Presidente.*[60] A majority of these new homes (mostly apartments) would be built under a cooperation agreement with China, which would consult on technical aspects of building so many homes in such a relatively short period of time.[61] However, by mid-2005, Chávez had to admit that the program was still not running properly. "I am supremely unhappy with myself and with my government on this issue [of housing] and the first one responsible is myself. I have given much time to see results, but the signs are bad," said Chávez during the July 30, 2005 broadcast of *Aló Presidente*. Despite this admission and the installment of another two housing ministers by mid-2006, the government was able to construct only 42,000 of the 120,000 homes planned for 2005 and, at most, another 78,000 instead of 200,000 by the end of 2006.[62]

The second measure, of passing a law on mortgages, regulates the interest rates and subsidies provided to homebuyers. Currently, unregulated mortgage rates are at 38%, but according to the new law, individuals can get interest rates of between 5.7% and 10.7%, depending on their income. Also, all banks are required to make 10% of their mortgage loans available at these low-interest rates. Finally, everyone with an income of less than 588,000 bolivars ($273) per month can receive a subsidy of 19 million bolivars ($8,837) for the purchase of a home.

Another measure for promoting home buying and construction includes the publication of a book on how to build your own home. For decades Venezuelans have been building their own homes in the barrios and many barrio inhabitants have become experienced in "popular architecture," the skills and knowledge for building homes in the barrios. The Chávez government argues that the private and public sectors cannot possibly fill the enormous housing gap on their own. What is also needed is the initiative of the barrio inhabitants themselves, who have generally taken this in the past, but never with the support or blessing of the government. The hope is that with some government support the building initiatives of private citizens could perhaps be directed towards less dangerous and more functional constructions. Henry Rangel, the director of the National Housing Institute (INAVI, *Instituto Nacional de Vivienda*), says, "the national government will favor self-construction and for this will organize training workshops for popular builders and will distribute 500,000 copies of the *Popular Construction Manual*, which will serve as an orientation for those who want to build their own homes, but who often do not have the technical know-how for doing so."[63] It is precisely this willingness to involve the community that the human rights group Provea highlights as one of the positive aspects of an otherwise poor housing record: "In contrast to the deficient management that characterized public housing policy in the last four years [1999–2003], the growing and organized community participation stands out."[64]

Social Security

Social security in Venezuela refers to a whole variety of means for providing enduring financial security in cases of disability, sickness, unemployment, maternity, etc. The Venezuelan social security system was first set up in the 1940s and was basically an insurance system for health and disability that covered only salaried employees. Over the years, and especially during the oil boom, the insurance system was expanded to cover more people and a wider variety of circumstances. Also, the system became increasingly complex as more types of insurance systems were introduced, particularly for retirement, so that today there are over 400 systems.

In addition to the problem of increasing complexity, by the 1990s it became obvious to most politicians that the existing system had to be modified. The contributions were too low to cover the ever expanding pool of beneficiaries, especially as the proportion of retirees increased and the proportion of contributing employees shrank. One of the main reasons for the shrinking pool of participating employees was the steadily increasing informal employment, which reached over 50% by 2000. Several reform efforts were made in the early 1990s to privatize the social security system, at least partially. However, none of the efforts were successful. It was not until the very end of Rafael Caldera's presidency, in 1998, that a new social security law was passed, which completely phased out the old system, known as IVSS (Venezuelan Institute of Social

Security) and replaced it with a privatized system of social security. Another very important change in the new labor law, on which the social security reform was based, specified that severance pay, which essentially represents a form of unemployment insurance in Venezuela, would be cut dramatically.

However, before the new law could enter into effect, Chávez became president and, in keeping with a campaign promise, he passed a law-decree that nullified Caldera's social security reform with the legislature's permission. The 1999 constitution that passed shortly thereafter specified in unusual detail that Venezuela's social security system had to be state-run and that it had to cover all aspects of social security. It even stated that housewives' labor in the home must be counted as paid labor for social security purposes. The main catch in this approach towards social security was that in order for the constitution's mandate to take effect a whole variety of new laws would have to be passed that would detail the functioning of this new system.

It was not until three full years later, in late 2002, that the Organic Law of the Social Security System (LOSSS)[65] was passed. The social security law specified that only those who were economically capable of contributing to the social security system were required to do so, but that everyone would have a right to the system's benefits. However, exactly how these benefits would be paid, given the relatively small contributor base, was left open for additional laws that still had to be passed. As of late 2005, some of these additional laws, with which the new system would go into effect, had still not been passed.[66] Through this delay, the legislature violated the LOSSS, which stated that the deadline for passing the additional laws that were required for the social security system was one year after passing the LOSSS.[67]

The Chávez government did make some important changes in the social security system that did not require legislative action. The most important of these was to raise the retirement benefits of retirees. Previously, retirees received, on average, a mere 60,000 Bolivars ($37.50 in 2003) per month. As of May 2003, though, Chávez decreed that retirement benefits had to be directly tied to the minimum salary, which at the time was at 247,000 Bolivars ($154) per month, thus effectively quadrupling retirement benefits. Also, over the years the social security system incurred a massive debt with its beneficiaries, which the Chávez government started to pay down. Another factor is that as more and more Venezuelans retire, more of them have a right to receive retirement benefits. As a result of these factors, the expenditures for social security, as a percentage of GDP, have more than tripled during the Chávez administration. Between 1990 and 1995 social security expenditures never exceeded 1% of GDP. The year before Chávez came into office the figure was at 1.3%. It climbed steadily thereafter, reaching 3.2% in 2004.[68]

During this same period, though, the number of people paying into the social security system has decreased, as there were fewer and fewer full-time formally employed Venezuelans. While in 1994 12.4% of the total population were insured in the social security system IVSS, by 2003 this number had dropped down to 9%. Meanwhile, the percentage of Venezuelans over the age of 60 who receive pension benefits increased from 14.2% in 1997 to 27.3% in 2004.[69]

Other Social Assistance

A common consequence of any increase in poverty is malnutrition. In Venezuela, with the economic crisis of 2002 and 2003, not only did poverty increase (from 39% to 54%), but so did malnutrition and low birth weight. According to Venezuela's System for Alimentary Vigilance (Sisvan), malnutrition, largely as a result of the economic crisis, rose from 24.4% to 26.8% between 2000 and 2004 for children between 7 and 15.[70] Similarly, low birth weight statistics showed a similar trend, increasing from 8.5% of newborns in 2002 to 8.8% of newborns in 2004.[71]

Acute malnutrition is something that points to serious problems in a society that is normally not associated with what otherwise appears to be a relatively rich country, such as Venezuela. Early in the Chávez presidency the main program to combat this type of problem was the *Plan Bolivar 2000*, which distributed thousands of tons of food, often free of charge, to the country's poor, between 1999 and 2001. However, no general food assistance programs existed in 2002 and 2003, mostly due to the government's preoccupation with the economic and political crisis and also due to the acute shortage of government funds that this crisis provoked. This lack of government attention, as well as the dramatic increase in unemployment and in inflation probably explains why malnutrition increased and meat consumption declined during this time period.

Just like most Third World countries, Venezuela does not have a general welfare program that guarantees financial assistance to the poor. The poor have almost always been left either to fend for themselves or to rely on charity. One of the Chávez government's most important anti-poverty programs is *Misión Mercal.* Mercal stands for *Mercado de Alimentos* (Food Market).

The program was started on a relatively small scale in early 2003, shortly after it appeared that the country's food distribution network might break down as a result of the December 2002 to January 2003 oil industry shutdown. About a year later, in early 2004, the program was upgraded to be a mission. The mission's main purpose was to provide food to poor Venezuelans at heavily discounted prices. In the beginning of the project, Mission Mercal sold about 880 tons of food per day to 1.2 million persons. A year later, by early 2005, it sold 4,700 tons of food per day to 11 million Venezuelans. It is thus estimated that as of mid-2005 the mission provides 43% of Venezuela's population with food. The government's goal is to increase this figure to 60% of the population by the end of 2005, providing 6,000 tons of food to 15 million Venezuelans.[72] This food is being sold in over 3,800 stores of a wide variety of sizes, from large supermarkets to medium-sized food markets, to very small corner "bodegas."

More and more Venezuelans have taken advantage of the Mercal supermarkets and food stores because inflation is chronic and at Mercal the prices have not only consistently remained the same, but they are also well below the level found in regular supermarkets. The discounts provided are between 25% and 50% below market rates, making it a good bargain for shoppers. In other words, the government subsidizes the Mercal mission, to the tune of $24 million per month or $288 million per year (in early 2005).

A perhaps more important program than the *Misión Mercal* in the effort to fight malnutrition is the *Casas de Alimentación* (Houses of Food), which provide food at half price to the country's poorest. About 2 million Venezuelans receive their food through this program. Associated with this program is also a network of Popular Bolivarian Cafeterias (*Comedores Populares Bolivarianos*), which provide free meals, shelter, educational programs, and basic health care to about 600,000 Venezuelans suffering from extreme poverty.

As another measure to ensure that poor Venezuelans receive an adequate diet, the government has controlled the prices of basic food staples, such as flour, eggs, beef, poultry, cheese, fruit, beans, etc. Of course, Venezuela's opposition, particularly the Chambers of Commerce, such as Fedecamaras and Confagan (the association of farmers and cattle ranchers) have complained bitterly that the price controls undermine the proper functioning of the market and make it very difficult for private industry to supply the market with alimentary products. The government, though, says that the price controls still allow private producers to make a profit as the controls are set below production cost. Nonetheless, shortages of various products, usually of powdered milk and also of some meat products, have been reported periodically since the introduction of the price controls.[73]

Realizing that all of the above-named programs still weren't solving the problem of extreme poverty, the government introduced yet another program in January 2006, called "Mission Negra Hipolita," named after Simon Bolivar's wet nurse. This program is supposed to identify homeless people and families in critical poverty and provide them with a variety of programs, such as health care, shelter, food, and drug addiction rehabilitation. An important aspect of the program is to actively seek out those in critical poverty instead of relying on them finding the program. For example, in its initial phase, program organizers went to garbage dumps, where many families were found that live off these dumps. They then made sure that the children were enrolled in schools and gave some of the adults grants for educational programs. Another important aspect of the program is the launch of numerous drug rehabilitation centers throughout the country—a project that has never existed before just for the country's poor.[74]

Finally, in March 2006, Chávez launched the country's newest mission, "Mothers of the Barrio." This mission provides poor women who have children and no full-time job with a stipend of 60–80% of the minimum wage (around $176) per month. The basic idea of the program is based on article 88 of the constitution, which states that the state recognizes women's work at home as economic activity. Initially the program started with 100,000 women and in August was expanded to include 200,000, selected by neighborhood committees according to needs-based criteria. While critics decry the program as a crude pre-election patronage program, the government assures that beneficiaries are selected purely on a needs basis and, so that more people might benefit from it, there will be a rotation of who receives the stipend. While the stipend is relatively small, since it does not even cover the basic food expenses of a family of four, and covers only a relatively small fraction of poor mothers (about 8%), it does not look like it will have much of an impact in alleviating poverty. However, the organizational model, of working with communities in implementing it, and the example it sets, of affirming household labor as economic labor, have a political effect that exceeds the size of the program.

Poverty Rates Revisited—During the Chávez Presidency

Crucial, of course, for the success of the foregoing policies and for the objective of attaining social justice is the elimination of poverty. Also, its elimination was one of Chávez's primary campaign promises, back in 1998. Much confusion, though, has surrounded the issue of whether poverty has decreased or increased during the Chávez presidency. In late 2005 a myth began to circulate in Venezuela's oppositional media and in the international media that poverty had risen during Chávez's presidency. Countless Venezuelan and international editorials and news articles referred to statistics from the Venezuelan government's own National Statistics Institute (INE) that showed that poverty in Venezuela had risen from 43.9% in the second half of 1998 to 53.1% in the first half of 2004. While this data is accurate, it failed to take into account more recent data (which was available when most of these editorials were written) that by the end of 2005 poverty had dropped to 37.9%[75] and by the end of 2006 to 32%.[76] Since poverty is a crucial issue for evaluating the Chávez government's performance with regard to its effort to eliminate social injustice, we'll now take a closer look at how Venezuela's poverty has evolved, before and during the Chávez presidency.

There are several different measures of poverty and general well-being in Venezuela, one of which is the Human Development Index (HDI), created by the United Nations Development Program (UNDP). The HDI measures not only the per capita income of a country, but also factors in health and education statistics, such as mortality, schooling, literacy and other rates. Venezuela's HDI, however, does not reflect the dramatic growth of poverty in Venezuela in the 1980s and 1990s. Between 1970 and 2004 Venezuela's HDI rose more or less steadily from

0.689 to 0.799, with occasional dips occurring in 1998, 2002, and 2003.[77]

There are at least two plausible explanations for why the HDI increased even though the poverty rate also increased throughout this period. First, since the HDI is an aggregate indicator that does not differentiate between classes, one possibility is that the increasing HDI of the wealthier portions of the population raised the country's total HDI because their HDI improved disproportionately with regard to the HDI of the poor. Second, it is possible that even though the proportion of the population that is poor increased, their HDI, just as that of the population in general, improved because government measures strengthened the country's social safety net. While lacking concrete data to make the argument conclusive, I would suggest that an examination of the poverty policies during the Chávez presidency shows that the improvement in the HDI during this period mostly traceable to public policies that are focused on the country's poor.

Ignoring the HDI trends, Venezuela's opposition has focused instead very strongly on the poverty statistics during the Chávez presidency. Since Chávez was elected with the specific mandate of alleviating poverty in Venezuela, the opposition argues that in this signature area, for his electoral base, Chávez has failed. They make this argument by pointing out that even according to the government's own poverty data, poverty has increased during the Chávez presidency, from 43.9% of the population in 1998 to 54% in 2003. Also, the rate of extreme poverty (included in the previous figure), which measures the percentage of the poor with insufficient means to cover their basic needs, increased from 16.7% to 25% in that same time period.

Here, just as with all economic debates between opposition and government supporters, the debate falls back upon what happened during the years of 2002 and 2003. If one looks at the poverty statistics for 1998 to 2001, poverty declined slightly, from 46.5% to 39%. However, during the recession years 2002 and 2003, it climbed dramatically, to the aforementioned 54%, with the sharpest increases happening between the first semester of 2001 and the first semester of 2003, exactly the time period between the April 2002 coup and the end of the 2003 oil industry shutdown. Non-governmental statistics, while generally higher, show similar trends. Thus, the question of who is to be held responsible for the increase in poverty all boils down to who was responsible for the crisis years 2002 and 2003: the Chávez government or the opposition?

Once the economy recovered, in 2004, the poverty statistics also reflected this recovery, in that poverty declined, from 54% to 37.9% in the second half of 2005, according to the government's statistics.[78] It should be noted that this poverty statistic measures only income poverty. However, many government programs have increased the population's quality of life indirectly, such as via the new educational, health, and food programs, the "missions." If one takes just the benefit of the health care program into account, some calculations say that poverty dropped down to 35.3% in the second half of 2005. This is a decrease of an additional two full points in the poverty rate.[79] In short, there is no doubt that poverty has decreased during the Chávez presidency (from 44% to 38%), despite the truly massive recession of 2002 and 2003, which had temporarily reduced Venezuela's GDP by an unprecedented 16%.[80] That is, poverty decreased both because of the economic recovery and because of the numerous new social programs, most of which were introduced in 2004 and after.

Conclusion

The Chávez government's social policies are characterized by two main elements. First, they are redistributive in the sense that programs such as the land reform or the Missions are designed to provide state resources, such as land or oil revenues, first and foremost to the country's poor. Second, they tend to incorporate participatory elements in that the land reform and the missions actively seek out the participation of the affected communities in their implementation. These two general characteristics have their roots in Venezuela's 1999 constitution, which states that the Venezuelan state is one based on a participatory democracy and that it guarantees certain social rights, such as health and education, in addition to the usual political rights. As such, the government's social policies represent a significant advance with respect to those of previous governments, where social rights were not recognized and social policy was based more on charity. Also, the implementation of social policies rarely involved community participation.

The redistributive aspect of the social programs and policies is actually not something particularly anti-capitalist or even socialist, both in comparison to earlier Venezuelan governments and in comparison to other governments around the world. Earlier Venezuelan governments, particularly in the 1960s and 1970s, gradually built up a significant welfare state in Venezuela along social democratic lines that incorporated free health care, free education, and broad social security coverage. That Chávez is re-introducing such programs now, following the dismantling of Venezuela's welfare state in the 1980s and 1990s, makes the policies appear radical to younger poor Venezuelans, who did not experience the country's boom years.

The truly innovative and indeed radical aspect of the social programs, which are all known as "missions" now, is not merely their existence, but the way they are being implemented. That is, rather than being instigated in a top-down fashion through the extremely bureaucratic ministries, they are being implemented with the close participation of the beneficiary communities. Land reform, educational missions, the health care mission, and the mothers of the barrio mission are all being implemented in conjunction with committees from the communities that have a substantial say over exactly how and where the missions should be organized. This means that in many cases the missions are creating a parallel structure alongside the ministries, that either complement (as in the case of the educational programs) or practically supplant (as in the case of the housing mission and the health care mission) the ministries' work. Eventually these missions will have to be integrated more closely with the existing state structure and then it will be an open question as to whether the missions end up transforming the ministries into a participatory public administration or whether the ministries end up bureaucratizing and alienating the missions from the communities.

However, until this merger of ministries and missions is completed, there are two serious limitations to the implementation of the government's social policies. First, social policies, while guaranteed by the constitution, are generally not guaranteed by law. That is, many social policies, such as the educational missions, the Bolivarian University, *Misión Mercal*, and the urban land reform are not guaranteed by laws, but only by presidential decree. This means that they can easily disappear from one day to the next, as has been the case with past social policies whenever the oil revenues suddenly dried up, or they can be implemented capriciously, as part of a political patronage system. The practical implication of such a lack of entitlement (other than in the form of the general formulations in the constitution) is that the programs could disappear at any time and those who are selectively excluded from certain social policies have a difficult time challenging their exclusion in court.

This problem of lacking legal guarantees (or entitlement) is closely related to the second problem, which is precisely that often these programs appear to be related to partisan or patronage interests. That is, for some of the educational programs, the land reform, and for some of the micro-loan programs, accusations have become numerous and in many cases quite credible—that many programs benefit primarily Chávez supporters. Certainly, his supporters are more likely to seek participation in these programs, since they come mostly from the country's poor majority. However, as long as vocal opponents have difficulty participating, these programs will not lose their patronage aspect.

Between the August 2004 referendum and early 2005 the oppositional private media began to focus on publicizing numerous cases where Venezuelans who had signed the December 2003 petition in favor of holding a recall referendum were later excluded from government services, such as obtaining a passport, or were either denied or fired from a government job. The list of petition-signers had become public via the National Assembly deputy Luis Tascon, who posted the petition signer list on his personal website in early 2004. Tascon said that his intention was to allow people who did not sign the petition to check if their name appeared on it even though they did not sign it. Tascon removed the list from his website shortly after the referendum, but apparently it had been downloaded and was then used to exclude opposition supporters from government jobs and services.[81] Once the story about the list's misuse began to appear more and more frequently in the news in April 2005, Chávez declared that government officials had to stop using this list. For the opposition, though, his declaration was too little and too late. Also, another list surfaced around this time, the "Maisanta List," which included not only the signers of the referendum petition, but also all of the participants in the missions, identifying them as Chávez supporters, by virtue of their participation. According to Chavistas, though, this list was intended to identify Chávez supporters for the recall referendum campaign, not as a means for blacklisting opposition supporters.

The part of the story that the opposition and the private media regularly leave out, is that there are credible reports that the list is used just as often the other way around, for private companies to give preferential treatment to opposition supporters who signed the petition. Also, when the opposition was in power, membership in the former governing parties, AD or Copei, was a requirement for government positions and services. That is not to say that their past government patronage or current opposition patronage makes patronage under Chávez all right. However, it points to just how ingrained patronage culture is in Venezuela and that it will require a concerted effort to overcome it.

5

Foreign Policy: Latin America, Cuba, Colombia, the USA, and a Multi-Polar World

Of all of the policy areas of the Chávez government, foreign policy is probably the one that has received the most attention by the international media and by international analysts. This should come as no surprise because for most analysts, Chávez's foreign policy has the most direct impact on other societies and, unlike many other policy areas, Chávez is at his most outspoken, if not outrageous, when he makes foreign policy statements. This is unfortunate, though, for both Venezuela's and for Chávez's image because it creates the impression that Chávez's policies as a whole, both foreign and domestic, are characterized by an outrageousness that is generally not reflected in the actual policies.

To analyze Chávez's foreign policy one thus has to do an unusual amount of separating fact from fiction and rational policy from outrageous statement. In addition, an analysis that seeks to identify what policies would lead towards the fulfillment of the ideals of twenty-first century socialism also has to be clear about what kind of foreign policy could lead in this direction.

Twenty-first Century Socialist Foreign Policy

What kinds of foreign policies fulfill the ideals of twenty-first century socialism? One way to simplify this rather complex question is to look at what kinds of relations a country should have with other countries and what kinds of relations a country should have with inter-governmental organizations (such as the UN). Regarding inter-country relations, whether political or economic, these ought to transcend the "realist" paradigm of international relations, where countries seek only to maximize their own country's self-interested gain, because such a policy approach only means that the strong will always dominate and the weaker will always lose out. Rather, countries that truly seek social justice, both nationally and internationally, need to cooperate with one another in the pursuit of liberty, equality, social justice, and sustainability.

A complicating factor for such a simple principle is that while other countries might happily agree to cooperate in the name of achieving greater social justice internationally, perhaps purely for their own gain, these same countries might be extremely repressive and pursuing the opposite of liberty, equality, and social justice domestically. How should a foreign policy guided by the principle named here respond to such a situation? There is no hard and fast answer to this question, except, that all alliances should be oriented not just towards achieving greater social justice between countries, but also contribute towards greater social justice within the cooperating countries. In other words, cooperation that achieves greater social justice internationally, but that ends up strengthening social injustice or repression in one or more of the cooperating countries serves no positive purpose. As we will see, this general foreign policy principle has important implications for the evaluation of the Chávez government's foreign policy.

The Objectives of Chávez's Foreign Policy

The Chávez government's six-year development[1] plan lists five main objectives for its foreign policy:

1. Promote multi-polarity
2. Promote Latin American integration
3. Consolidate and diversify Venezuela's international relations
4. Strengthen Venezuela's position in the international economy
5. Promote a new regime of hemispheric security.

Exactly what does each of these mean and how have they been actioned? Also, if these objectives are achieved, do they contribute towards the objectives of twenty-first century socialism?

Promote Multi-Polarity

According to the Chávez government's analysis of contemporary international relations, the world is dominated by a sole super-power, the United States, which is subordinating the world to its geo-strategic interests. Chávez has repeatedly criticized the US government for its unilateralism with regard to the wars against Afghanistan and Iraq and also regularly points out how the world's international financial and trade institutions, such as the IMF, World Bank, and WTO are generally operating in the interests of the developed North, and in the interests of the US government in particular. In short, the US is pursuing imperialist aims.

The best way to oppose such a "uni-polar" world, according to Chávez, is to create a "multi-polar" world, in which there are many centers of power instead of one. For this purpose, Chávez supports the strengthening of supra-national bodies, particularly the UN, and of multilateral initiatives. However, just strengthening these bodies is not good enough; they must also be democratized, so that the more populous Third World has a greater say in how they are run. In this context Chávez has supported the development of China, India, the European Union, and Latin America as competing centers of political and economic power in the world. In practical terms, this has meant that Chávez supports the restructuring of the United Nations Security Council, so that developing countries, such as Brazil and India, have a permanent seat on the council. Also part of this strategy is to strengthen the role of multilateral groups, such as the G–15 and the G–77.

Promote Latin American Integration

The second main objective, to promote Latin American integration, is based on the recognition that Venezuela and Latin America will be in a better position to succeed in their development if Latin America integrates economically, politically, and socially. That is, the Chávez government does not believe, as its predecessors did, that Venezuela could forge its own path towards development independently of the rest of Latin America. According to the development plan, "it is important to highlight that the challenges that human development, social inequality, and the high levels of poverty represent can be tackled with greater efficiency to the extent that the countries of Latin America and the Caribbean deepen and effectively promote their regional integration, both in dialogue and in South–South as well as South–North cooperation."[2] This Latin American integration is supposed to replace any free trade agreement involving the US, such as the FTAA (Free Trade Area of the Americas) because the US is too powerful and would overwhelm and thus exploit its weaker southern partners.

Integration, though, is not just part of the Chávez government's platform, it is also in the 1999 constitution, which mandates that Venezuela will work towards the economic and political integration of Latin America.[3] The constitution also says that the Republic may transfer to supra-national bodies powers that otherwise normally belong to the Venezuelan state. That Latin American integration was adopted as part of the constitution and is a major foreign policy goal of the Chávez government is, of course, also directly related to one of the ideals of Simon Bolivar, who sought to unify all of Latin America after its independence from Spain and Portugal.

One of the main ways Chávez has proposed to move toward Latin American integration is by having Venezuela join the Common Market of the South (Mercosur), whose principal members are Argentina, Brazil, Paraguay, and Uruguay. Venezuela's move in this direction achieved its objective in July 2006 when Venezuela officially joined Mercosur as a full member. The move was a major diplomatic triumph for Chávez and provides a stronger institutional framework for the already existing bilateral agreements Venezuela has with Brazil and with Argentina.

The second element in the effort to advance Latin American integration is to push for closer ties between the Andean Community of Nations (CAN—Venezuela, Colombia, Ecuador, Peru, and Bolivia) and Mercosur. In December 2003, with the Chávez government pushing particularly hard, an agreement was struck between the two regional associations to form a CAN-Mercosur trade agreement, whose goal is to establish a free trade zone in all of South America over the next 12 years, that is, by 2015. In terms of population, with over 350 million inhabitants, such a common market would rival that of NAFTA and of the European Union. Another mandate of the agreement was that within a few years, at least 60% of the components of all products traded within this zone must come from the CAN-Mercosur region. The tentative name of this new regional block would be "South American Community of Nations" (CSN in its Spanish initials). In early 2007 this was changed to UNASUR, "Union of Nations of the South."

According to Venezuela's chief trade negotiator in this agreement, "The CAN-Mercosur integration is a very concrete manifestation of the birth of the Bolivarian Alternative for the Americas and the Caribbean (ALBA), which is the first priority for the Venezuelan government."[4] That is, the concrete proposal for integration is something that the Chávez government calls ALBA.[5] The basic idea of ALBA is modeled to some extent after the European Union. One of its key elements is the "Compensation Fund for Structural Convergence," which would redistribute wealth between member nations, just as exists in the European Union. Poorer countries would receive development aid from the fund, while wealthier ones would have to contribute to this fund. Such a compensation fund would benefit all countries because economic development in the poorer regions would mean expanding markets for the wealthier, more productive countries. In Europe, this type of compensation has significantly contributed to the development of formerly poorer countries within the European Union, such as Ireland, Spain, and Portugal.

Another important element of ALBA would be to protect Latin America's agriculture. The creators of ALBA say that it is practically impossible for Latin American agricultural products to compete with those of the United States, as long as the US subsidizes its agriculture as much as it does. But even if the subsidies were eliminated, US productivity is too high for Latin American agricultural products to be competitive. The solution is thus to "level the playing field" by protecting Latin American products, all the while maintaining competition (hence free trade) within the regional trade block, so that there is an incentive to improve Latin American productivity.

With regard to the protection of intellectual property rights, as proposed by the World Trade Organization (WTO), ALBA would be opposed to this regime. Here the critique is the same one that has come from Third World activists around the globe, who argue that such an intellectual property regime does nothing more than solidify the intellectual property piracy that has already occurred. That is, according to critics of the WTO intellectual property rights regime, much of the patented genetic material originally comes from Third World countries and giving ownership over this material to a corporation, which could then sell or license this genetic material back to Third World countries is terrifically unjust. Also, critics say that even when such material did not originate in a Third World country, it is often essential for these countries in order to prevent or cure deadly diseases. If corporations have the right to charge exorbitant prices for their products, long after they have recouped their investment costs, then this is simply another form of exploitation and extortion. The Chávez government has thus been vehemently opposed to this form of intellectual property rights protection.[6]

Finally, a third key element of ALBA is that, in contrast to the FTAA, it does not advocate liberalization and privatization of state services. Under the FTAA state services, such as communications, water utilities, electricity, education, health care, etc., are to be privatized and/or opened up to competition. The Chávez government, though, argues that "public services are for satisfying the needs of people, not for commerce and economic profit. Therefore, its benefit cannot be governed by the criteria of profit but by social interest."[7] Part of this rejection of privatization and liberalization of state services also has its roots in the effort to maintain the nation's sovereignty. According to FTAA rules, a government would not be allowed to treat some companies better than others, even if the company it wants to favor is offering to transfer technology or to employ more people as a result of its investment. Also, it would not be able to favor domestic businesses over foreign ones.

Whether Venezuela will succeed in building a Union of Latin American countries is an open question, of course, especially considering the history of unification attempts. The first such attempt—that of Simon Bolivar—failed miserably.[8] Ever since then governments all across Latin America have said that they wanted Latin American unification. Numerous agreements have been signed in the past to cement the intention to integrate Latin America, such as the Latin American Free Trade Association (ALALC) in 1960, the Andean Pact of 1969, the Latin American Economic System (SELA) of 1975, the Amazon Cooperation Treaty of 1978, and the Latin American Association of Integration of 1980, to name just a few of the older efforts. However, none of these ever amounted to anything. Part of the problem, prior to the 1980s, was that the military dictatorships in most of Latin America tended to not be particularly interested in integration if it meant abdicating some element of their dictatorial power. Also, the lack of a Latin American infrastructure, such as continent-wide highway and rail systems, made integration difficult. Another important factor has been the dominance of the US, where different governments, but especially the earlier governments of Venezuela and the Latin American dictatorships, tended to prioritize close political and economic ties to the US instead of to its Latin American neighbors.

The perhaps most serious obstacle to Latin American integration was the one mentioned last, of lack of interest. While the governments of the region gave vocal support for integration, as long as more conservative governments were in power, they believed that their countries' development could better be advanced by their ties to the US than with each other. Leftist governments, though, such as now govern in Venezuela, Brazil, Argentina, Uruguay, and Chile, tend to believe that Third World and Latin American solidarity and integration is more likely to promote their countries' development. The fact that most major Latin American countries are governed by left-leaning governments now is why Latin American integration will probably advance more now than it ever did in the past. The recent moves towards uniting CAN and Mercosur and the defeat of the FTAA appear to bear this out.

Consolidate and Diversify Venezuela's Foreign Relations

As mentioned earlier, in the past Venezuela focused most of its foreign relations energy on the United States. Consolidating and diversifying its foreign relations means for the Chávez government, primarily, to increase South—South cooperation with the rest of the world outside of Latin America. In this context the Chávez government has particularly pushed for closer relations with India and China. Chávez signed several cooperation agreements with both China and India in 2004, 2005, and 2006. The agreements with China were especially important because they opened the door for oil exports to China. Such exports are currently not very economical because of the transportation distance, but if Venezuela manages to expand an oil pipeline across Panama and if the price of oil further increases, along with the expanding energy needs in China and possible lower oil output in the Middle East, then China would become a crucial and lucrative oil market for Venezuela. Going the other way, though, China has agreed to help Venezuela solve its housing shortage by constructing 20,000 new homes in 2006.

Another country with which Venezuela has strengthened ties, much to the chagrin of the US, is Iran. Iran has agreed to provide engineers and other technical help for Venezuela's oil industry, which, following the 2002/03 oil industry shutdown, lost a tremendous number of its professional staff. Another important Iranian project is the construction of an Iranian tractor factory in Venezuela, which will help advance the government's land reform program and its efforts to increase agricultural production, among other joint projects. In return, Venezuela has provided Iran with political support in its efforts to expand its nuclear power generating capability.

Finally, as part of the effort to strengthen South–South relations, Chávez has been very active in trying to strengthen the multilateral groups of the Third World, such as the G–15, the G–77, the Rio Group, and the Non-Aligned Movement.

Strengthen Venezuela's Position in the International Economy

The main elements to strengthening Venezuela's position in the international economy are the strengthening of OPEC, the diversification and internationalization of the Venezuelan economy, and expanding Venezuela's state-owned companies, such as Citgo and PDVSA, into other countries of Latin America. The first of these, strengthening OPEC, was one of Chávez's first foreign policy tasks after he assumed the presidency in 1999. It is fair to say that Chávez's effort to bring OPEC back together and to exercise more self-discipline with respect to member countries' adherence to their oil production quotas was a success. Chávez visited all OPEC countries and several non-OPEC oil producing countries, such as Mexico and Russia, and managed to get commitments from all of them to restrain their oil production so that the price of oil would once again reach a "fairer" level.

The main drawback of Chávez's travels to OPEC countries was that he visited Libya and Iraq. In Iraq, Chávez was the first head of state to visit Saddam Hussein since the 1991 Gulf War and the visit gave his opponents a key weapon for a long time afterwards, who accused him of being "friends" with Hussein, which to many proved the evil nature of Chávez. After those visits, the international media, in their boilerplate descriptions of Chávez, never failed to omit his supposed friendship with Saddam Hussein of Iraq and Muammar Qaddafi of Libya.

There have been more mixed results in the case of the second objective strengthening Venezuela's international economic position, the diversification and internationalization of the economy. Non-traditional exports (that is, mostly those that are non oil-related) remained pretty much the same between 1998 and 2003, at about $5.2 billion per year. For 2004 and 2005, though, exports jumped significantly, by 31%, to $6.8 billion and another 8.7%, to $7.4 billion, respectively—one of the highest levels in Venezuela's history. Imports, however, increased as well, from $14.2 billion in 1998 to $15.9 billion in 2004 and to $22.5 billion in 2005,[9] which means that the government's effort to wean itself from imports via the diversification of its economy failed.

With regard to the third objective, of expanding Venezuela's state-owned enterprises into Latin American countries, only in late 2004 and early 2005 did the Chávez government begin to pursue this seriously. Part of this strategy was—although it was not really conceived as such in 2001, when the government formulated its strategic plan—the creation of Petroamerica, the Latin America-wide integration of state-owned oil companies. That is, Chávez proposed that all of Latin America's state-owned oil companies, such as Petrobras of Brazil, Petroecuador of Ecuador, Pemex of Mexico, to name three of the most important, unite so that these might be in a better position to compete with the large transnational oil companies, such as ExxonMobil or ChevronTexaco, and to advance the continent's economic development. The first tentative steps towards creating Petroamerica were taken with regard to one of the smallest state-owned oil companies, when PDVSA formed a joint company with Argentina's Enarsa.[10] Later, in mid-2005, Venezuela launched Petrocaribe (for Caribbean countries) and Petroandina (for Colombia, Ecuador, Peru, and Bolivia), which, together with Petrosur (Argentina, Brazil, and Uruguay) are the three sub-projects that together make up Petroamerica.[11]

So far Venezuela had always only focused on selling gasoline to US consumers, via its Citgo refineries and gas station chain. In addition, PDVSA announced in early 2005 that it would construct several refineries in other Latin American countries, such as in northern Brazil. All of this is a clear change in direction, away from Venezuela's formerly almost exclusive US-orientation, towards Latin America.

Such moves away from focusing on the US market have repeatedly provoked speculation that perhaps Venezuela is interested in withdrawing from the US market entirely. Announcements by the PDVSA president that Venezuela is looking to sell two of its six Citgo refineries in the US have further inflamed speculation about the Chávez government's plans to supposedly withdraw from the US and to sell oil to Latin America and Asia instead. However, PDVSA's presidents Ali Rodriguez (2002–2004) and Rafael Ramirez (2004–2006) repeatedly insisted that Venezuela has absolutely no interest in abandoning the US market. Rather, what PDVSA is doing is rationalizing its US operations and getting rid of unprofitable refineries, which do not refine Venezuelan oil. As for focusing on Asian and Latin American markets, PDVSA's presidents have repeatedly stated that the Chávez government is looking for new markets for its expanded oil production, which is to increase from 3.3 million barrels per day (bpd) to 5.5 million bpd by 2012. Any expansion to other markets would come from this increased production and not from supplies to the US market. In other words, unlike speculation from anti-Chávez forces both in the US and in Venezuela, Venezuela's interest in ridding itself of some Citgo assets and in selling to Latin America and Asia is not politically motivated, but is economically motivated. As stated before, it is the Chávez government's conviction that Venezuelan development is more likely to succeed if Latin American and the Southern economies in general are integrated than if Venezuela seeks its fortune solely through its linkage with the wealthy North, as previous governments generally believed.

Promote a New Regime of Hemispheric Security

The promotion of a new regime of hemispheric security is perhaps the least developed objective of the Chávez government's foreign policy. The 2001–2007 Economic and Social Development Plan mentions only two sub-points in its elaboration, which are the encouragement of citizen participation in the military, that is, in the strengthening of the civilian— military unity, and the promotion of peaceful dialogue between countries. While there is relatively little of a concrete nature to point to with regard to the latter point, the former received much attention in early 2005, when Chávez announced that he would form a 2 million-strong reserve army and that Venezuela would purchase 100,000 AK–103 and 104 rifles, 30 helicopters, and 24 Sukhoi–30 fighter jets from Russia, several Brazilian Super-Tucano propeller planes, and several Spanish patrol boats. All of these measures caused Bush administration officials, such as Defense Secretary Donald Rumsfeld and Secretary of State Condoleezza Rice to claim that Venezuela was engaging in an arms race, that some of its weapons, such as the assault rifles, would end up in the arsenals of Colombia's FARC guerilla group, and that Venezuela was destabilizing the region.

Of course, the Chávez government denied this and argued that it was merely re-equipping its weapons arsenal, which had become very dated in the past 20 years and that it needed to prepare itself for a possible US invasion. Also, it needed the weapons so that it could better patrol the Venezuelan—Colombian border, which is a task the Bush administration repeatedly criticized Venezuela for not doing properly,[12] even though Venezuela has three times the number of soldiers along its 1,400-mile border as Colombia does. Venezuela, which spends about 1.5% of its GNP in 2004 on the military, ranks towards the bottom in terms of military expenditures, compared to the 3.3% the US or the 3.4% Colombia spends, which both rank towards the top.[13] Thus, during 2005 and 2006 Venezuela went on an arms spending spree, to renew its ageing arsenal.[14]

With regard to the military reserve force that Venezuela began organizing in 2005, here too the justification is that Venezuela needs this because the government is concerned that the US could be preparing for some sort of military action against Venezuela. The opposition to Chávez makes fun of such expressions of concern, saying that this is merely an excuse to arm its supporters along the lines of Cuba's Committees in Defense of the Revolution and that these supporters will be used to turn Venezuela into a "Castro-Communist" dictatorship once and for all. Also, the opposition argues that it is a campaign tactic of Chávez's to rally his supporters by generating fear of an invasion.

A US invasion might seem far-fetched to even those who are convinced of the aggressive nature of US foreign policy, mainly because the US cannot afford another invasion force the size of the one in Iraq, both in terms of material and political resources—especially against a popular government. However, anyone who has closely observed the thinking of Chávez, his supporters, and of people in the upper levels of the Chávez government, knows that many, if not most, are genuinely concerned about the possibility of a US invasion.

In summary, with regard to promoting a "regime of hemispheric security" that is based on a civilian—military union, the Chávez government has certainly advanced this objective, not just through mobilizing a reserve military force, but also by involving the military in many civilian tasks, such as the various anti-poverty missions. However, with regard to promoting a new hemispheric security regime via peaceful dialogue, much remains to be done. Chávez is known for his rather incendiary rhetoric, which, when applied to his opponents, such as the opposition or the Bush administration, never fails to provoke. While both of these opponents are experts at provocation themselves, Chávez has usually only added fuel to the rhetorical fires between himself and his opponents.

Cuba–Venezuela Relations

There are three countries whose relationship to Venezuela deserves to be analyzed more carefully: Cuba, Colombia, and the United States. The Cuba–Venezuela relationship has developed into one that is characterized by extremely close cooperation and solidarity. The perhaps three most important reasons for this are the close personal relationship between Presidents Chávez and Castro, the ideological affinity between the two governments, and the defense against a shared opponent or enemy, the United States.

Chávez already established a personal relationship with Castro shortly after he was released from prison for his 1992 coup attempt. Ever since then Chávez has deepened this friendship, so that Castro has become a mentor or even father-figure of sorts. When in late 2004 Castro tripped and fell, breaking a knee-cap, Chávez immediately made sure that on his next foreign trip he made a detour to Havana to visit Castro in the hospital and see how he was doing. Chávez, who at first considered himself more of a "Bolivarian" than a socialist, could have felt that the two of them are not that close ideologically. However, Castro too started out as an anti-imperialist nationalist and only once in power did he move towards socialism. Also, in both cases their brother was the socialist, who exercised an influence on the future president in his move towards socialism (Raul Castro in the case of Fidel and Adán Chávez in the case of Hugo). Chávez now says to Castro, "What you call socialism in Cuba, we call Bolivarianism in Venezuela."[15] Finally, besides the personal friendship and ideological affinity, there is also a mutual hostility with the US. Both countries are now targets of US subversion, mostly in the form of overt and covert financial support that the Bush administration provides to the opposition in both countries.

Cuba–Venezuela Cooperation Agreements

The close cooperation between the two countries covers a wide variety of areas, such as oil, health care, education, sports, and the arts. The first agreement, signed October 30, 2000, already dealt with a whole variety of issues, the most important of which was that Cuba would be included in the "Energy Accords of Caracas"[16] and would receive 53,000 barrels of oil per day. Another part of this agreement was that Cuba would send doctors, sports trainers, and experts in the sugar industry, in tourism, in agriculture, in medical equipment, and education to Venezuela. Altogether, the number of Cubans going to Venezuela as part of this program began with several thousand and eventually reached around 20,000 in 2005. Also, part of the agreement was that Venezuelans could go to Cuba for either free medical treatment or to become trained as doctors. By 2006 about 13,000 Venezuelans had been treated in Cuban hospitals for everything from cardiovascular surgery, ophthalmology, orthopedics, to organ transplants.[17]

This 2000 agreement was further deepened in December 2004 and again in April 2005. The 2004 agreement eliminated all tariff barriers for Cuban imports and provided Cuba with technical assistance to explore for oil off the Cuban coast. Also, grants would be provided to 2,000 Venezuelans per year to study at Cuban universities. Next, the total number of Cuban doctors, who participate in the Barrio Adentro program, was raised to 15,000 and would also include a wider variety of specialists, such as ophthalmologists and dentists. The April 2005 agreements further intensified the cooperation in the health care sector, so that now 10,000 Venezuelan students would be trained in medicine in Cuba and 30,000 Cuban doctors and support staff would come to Venezuela. Also, the two countries would cooperate to create a continent-wide plan for eliminating illiteracy in Latin America, using the Cuban *Yo si puedo* (Yes I can) method. Furthermore, oil exports to Cuba under the Caracas Accords were raised from 53,000 to 90,000 barrels per day.

As part of these intensified cooperation agreements, Venezuela's PDVSA opened up a branch office in Havana, which would serve as the PDVSA headquarters for its Caribbean operations. Also, the state-owned bank, *Banco Industrial de Venezuela* (BIV—Industrial Bank of Venezuela) opened up a branch office in Havana. Similarly, it was agreed that Cuba's state bank, the Foreign Bank of Cuba, would open an office in Caracas. Altogether forty-nine agreements were signed with Cuba in 2005 that included the lowering of tariffs, mutual support for the creation or improvement of the rail infrastructure in both countries, and the promotion of ALBA in international forums, among many other issues.

Venezuela, Cuba, and Bolivia formalized and solidified the creation of ALBA with yet another treaty, known as the "People's Trade Agreement," which was signed on April 29, 2006.[18] The agreement added Bolivia to the treaty that Cuba and Venezuela had already signed in December 2004. Second, it committed the countries to develop a "strategic plan" "to guarantee complementary products that can be mutually beneficial based on the rational exploitation of the countries' existing assets, the preservation of resources, the expansion of employment, market access and other aspects inspired in the true solidarity fostered by our peoples." The treaty goes on to stipulate exchanges in the areas of technology, literacy training, investment, and cultural projects, that exchanges can take place with in-kind payments instead of cash, that communication infrastructure between the three countries will be strengthened, and that Cuba will provide free eye surgery to Bolivians and Venezuelans and that Cuba would give medical training to students from these countries. Also, Venezuela committed itself to provide Bolivia with technical support in its effort to develop its natural energy resources.

Colombia–Venezuela Relations

Colombia is the country that most resembles Venezuela in terms of the history, culture, and interconnections between the two peoples. It is thus no surprise that Venezuelans should see Colombia as a "brother country" (*país hermano*). However, at the same time, there are many tensions between Colombia and Venezuela, ranging from border disputes and access to natural resources along the border, to the tension generated by border crossings of various Colombian regular and irregular armed forces, such as the Revolutionary Armed Forces of Colombia (FARC), the National Liberation Army (ELN), Colombia's military forces, and the United Self-Defense Forces of Colombia (AUC).

The border disputes between the two countries date back to the very founding of each, when what used to be one country, *La Gran Colombia*, was divided in 1833. Over the years, in various border disputes, Venezuela has lost territory to Colombia. The border issue has always been very sensitive for the two countries, because much oil and mineral wealth is located in this border region. Also, given the geography, some of the border region is an ideal transit area for Colombian products and contraband to be transported into the Caribbean. The position of Latin America's largest lake, Lake Maracaibo, in Venezuela, which opens to the Caribbean, and the Andes on the Colombian side, make it much easier to transport goods through Venezuela than through Colombia.

For these reasons, there are powerful interests in Colombia that would like to displace Venezuelans and Colombians in Venezuela, who live along the border, so that they can exploit natural resources and transport drugs and other goods to US markets without interference from local residents. Pro-Chávez inhabitants of the area report[19] that Colombian paramilitary forces regularly cross the border to Venezuela to terrorize Venezuelan villages in the border region and force them to move someplace else. Partly in reaction to such incursions and the relative inability of Venezuelan security forces to keep the conflict under control, a new guerilla force seems to have emerged along the border, known as the "Bolivarian Liberation Forces" (FBL—*Fuerzas Bolivarianas de Liberación*). The FBL not only wants to defend Venezuelans against incursions from Colombia, but they say that they support Chávez and are preparing for the possibility that he might be removed from office, either by external or internal forces, and that Venezuelans should therefore be ready to wage a guerilla war against those who would topple Chávez.[20] As a result of all these developments, the border region has become something like a "Wild West" where lawlessness predominates, due to the mixture of corrupt Venezuelan police and military, drug traffickers, and Colombian regular and irregular forces (which include both rebels and paramilitary forces), all of whom interact and clash.

Chávez's Relationship to the FARC and the ELN

One of the main bones of contention between Venezuela and Colombia is that Colombian government officials and conservative senators often claim that Chávez is covertly supporting one or both of Colombia's guerilla groups, the FARC and the ELN. These accusations, although never substantiated with concrete proof and always denied by Chávez, frequently receive additional support from US government officials, who repeat the accusations, but also fail to provide anything resembling proof. US government officials have made contradictory statements about Venezuela's supposed support of Colombian rebels. The US government's 2004 report on terrorism refers to this issue because the US considers the FARC and the ELN to be terrorist groups, but only suggests that Chávez might be providing support.[21] The report does claim, though, that Venezuela provides only "limited" counter-terrorism support to Colombia.

Despite these accusations, Venezuela has 20,000 soldiers, three times as many as Colombia, which has a far larger military, stationed along its 1,400 mile border. According to some analysts, Colombia is in a much weaker position with regard to securing its border with Venezuela because it cannot afford to withdraw its soldiers from the interior of the country and to station them along the border, lest it risk exposing the capital and other key areas to attacks from the guerilla forces.

US government officials have repeatedly complained that Venezuela has not declared the FARC and the ELN to be terrorist groups. Although, what this would mean if Venezuela did so is unclear, since Venezuelan law does not provide for such designations in its criminal justice code. In any case, the official policy of the Chávez government is that it takes a neutral stance with regard to the Colombian conflict. Chávez has stated that his government would not support one side or the other in any way. This position of official neutrality makes sense because Venezuela is profoundly affected by the conflict and if it were to take one side or the other, it would have to treat the other side as an enemy, which would then easily lead to Venezuela being drawn deep into the conflict. Instead, Chávez says that his government supports all peaceful efforts to resolve the conflict and has offered himself as a negotiator between the Colombian government and the rebels on several occasions.

Also, part of the Chávez government's official policy with regard to the Colombian conflict is that Venezuela will try to prevent border incursions and encampments on its side of the border, no matter which party of the conflict is involved. This policy has seen several practical applications in 2004 and 2005, as, for example, in September 2004 the FARC engaged in a gun battle with Venezuelan National Guard troops, where six of these were killed. There have been several other similar incidents, some involving Colombian paramilitary forces (AUC), some the ELN, and some even the Colombian army.[22]

Despite numerous incidents in which Chávez opponents in Venezuela, Colombia, and the United States repeatedly tried to essentially frame Chávez and make it look like his government supports Colombia's rebel groups and despite the fact that Venezuela's Chávez and Colombia's Uribe come from opposite ends of the political spectrum, the relationship between the two countries has been surprisingly good. That is, Presidents Chávez and Uribe appear to get along quite well. In November 2004 Chávez and Uribe signed a series of agreements, including a plan to build a gas pipeline from Venezuela across Colombia, to the Pacific, so that Venezuela can supply gas to Asia or to countries along the North and South American west coast. Colombia and Venezuela clearly have a mutual interest in preserving a good relationship that is much stronger than the damage the efforts to sabotage the relationship has caused. Both sides know that it is to their mutual advantage to maintain good relations and both sides would lose tremendously, in economic terms, because of the large volume of trade between the countries, should the relationship sour.[23]

US–Venezuela Relations

In contrast to the Colombia-Venezuela relationship, where neither side has anything to gain from bad relations, the situation is much more ambivalent where the US is concerned. That is, the Bush administration has strong interests that contradict those of the Chávez administration. Bush is interested in promoting the Free Trade Area of the Americas (FTAA) and desperately needs allies in his "war on terrorism." Chávez, on the other hand, is emphatically opposed to these policy agendas and is pursuing an agenda diametrically opposed to that of the Bush administration, by seeking to promote a multi-polar world and the establishment of the Bolivarian Alternative for the Americas. It is thus no wonder that Bush would like to see Chávez disappear and vice-versa.

Of course, in addition to these conflicting interests, the US and Venezuela share strong economic interests, such as an interest in maintaining Venezuela's sale of oil to the US. With sales of 1.5 million barrels per day to the US, Venezuela is the 4th largest oil supplier to the

US and the US is by far Venezuela's largest oil customer. Also, there are long-standing cultural connections, such as a shared passion for baseball and countless other US entertainment exports. As a result, there is a constant back and forth in the relationship, between mutual hostility and efforts to make up and to improve relations between the two countries.

The antagonism expresses itself in that both countries are actively lobbying leaders in Latin America and in the rest of the world for support. The difference between the approaches of the two, though, is that Chávez's efforts to counteract Bush are mostly on the level of lobbying and "microphone diplomacy." The Bush administration, on the other hand, has been actively undermining Chávez when it supported the April 2002 coup attempt and by financing the opposition to Chávez. Also, there is reason to believe that the US is engaged in psychological warfare, such as the planting of damaging rumors in the media about the Chávez government.

Chávez and Clinton

Relations between Chávez and the US president weren't always this tense. When Chávez first became president, he attempted to maintain a cordial relationship with Clinton, even though in his speeches Chávez often used harsh words to criticize US imperialism. When Chávez was scheduled to visit President Clinton shortly after his election, he was asked not to come to the US via Cuba, one of the other stops on his trip. Chávez angrily dismissed the notion and visited Cuba first anyway. When he arrived in Washington, fresh from his visit to Castro in Havana, he was given a cool welcome. Clinton met with him, but only in the most unofficial manner possible, for only 15 minutes, with no press allowed and with Clinton dressed in jeans.[24]

Relations took a turn for the worse when the December 1999 mudslides happened. In the course of the rescue effort, the Clinton administration offered to send US navy ships and helicopters to help. Chávez, though, rejected the offer, saying that Venezuela did not need these, but needed money instead. Also, in mid-2000, when Chávez visited Saddam Hussein as part of his tour to visit all OPEC countries, the US State Department reacted angrily, saying that Chávez was violating UN sanctions against Iraq.

Bush and Chávez 1: Increasing Tensions

Chávez's first action to annoy the new in-coming president was to criticize the FTAA at the April 2001 Summit of the Americas in Quebec, Canada. Chávez was the only president to sign the closing document "with reservations," mainly because he argued that the document should also mention the importance of participatory democracy and not just representative democracy.

Then, in September 2001, just before the attack on the World Trade Center, Chávez announced that Venezuela would cancel its 50-year military cooperation agreement with the US. Apparently, the training program (International Military Education and Training—IMET) was much more than just a training program; it was also designed to increase the influence of the US military in the Venezuelan military.[25] The US government required Venezuela to place IMET graduates in "key positions" in its military. The Bush administration did not react much to the cancellation of the program at first, probably because it was not actually canceled until much later.

What the Bush administration did react to, though, were Chávez's comments in October 2001, when Chávez went on television to denounce the US attacks on Afghanistan. Chávez held up pictures of Afghani children who were killed by the attack and said, "Terror cannot be fought with more terror . . . This has no justification, just like the attacks in New York didn't either." The US ambassador to Venezuela, Donna Hrinak, was immediately recalled to Washington "for consultation" and, upon her return, she asked Chávez, in the name of the US government, to retract his remarks. Chávez, of course, did no such thing and instead angrily told her to leave his office.

Bush and Chávez 2: Funding the Opposition

Even though tensions between the US and Venezuela were publicly gradually increasing, Chávez did not express his displeasure with the Bush administration all that often. Actually, it was not until early 2004 that Chávez attacked Bush verbally as being the world's most dangerous political leader, who is trying to maintain the US "empire."

Despite the relative low key nature of Chávez's opposition to Bush until then, the Bush administration was actively working behind the scenes to undermine Chávez since the year 2000. Exactly how far this effort went is still unknown, but many documents have surfaced that show that at least on the level of funding it went much further than most people were aware.[26] Between the year 2000 and 2001 US government funds for Venezuelan opposition groups increased nearly four-fold, from $232,831 to $877,435. They increased almost four-fold again in the next year, from $877,435 in 2001 to $3.9 million in 2002. For 2003 the funds reached an all-time high of $10 million—an increase by a factor of 2.5 compared to the previous year.[27] Altogether, from 2002 to 2005, the US government provided over $26 million to Venezuelan NGOs,[28] with at least $9 million in the pipeline for 2006.[29] How much of this money is directed specifically to opposition groups and activities is unknown because the US government refuses to release the names of most of the beneficiary groups.

All of these funds were channeled through the National Endowment for Democracy (NED) and the US Agency for International Development (USAID). The NED, which was founded in 1983, is formally a non-governmental foundation that receives all of its funds from the US Congress. It is supposed to fund civil society projects that help strengthen democracy in different countries all around the world. The NED did not come into its own really until the Nicaraguan elections of 1990, when it provided over $10 million to Nicaraguan opposition groups to defeat the Sandinistas.[30] Most of the NED's funds go first to one of four organizations, which then distribute the money to local groups: the International Republican Institute (IRI), which is run by the Republican party, the National Democratic Institute, run by the Democratic party, the Center for International Private Enterprise (CIPE), which is controlled by the US Chamber of Commerce, and the American Center for International Labor Solidarity (ACILS), which is run by the AFL-CIO.

The second main funder is USAID, which was originally not intended for the purpose of funding the political work of civil society organizations. Rather, it was meant to fund traditionally conceived development projects in the Third World, such as building bridges, schools, and hospitals. However, shortly after its founding in 1961, it began funding political organizations, often via the AFL-CIO's American Institute for Free Labor Development (AIFLD, the predecessor to the ACILS), which at that time was largely under the control of the CIA.[31]

NED funds, which are a bit better known that those of USAID, went and are continuing to flow to a wide variety of civil society groups in Venezuela, including political parties, such as *Primero Justicia* (Justice First), the union federation CTV, *Asamblea de Educación* (Education Assembly)—an opposition group that lobbies against the government's education policies—and numerous other types of groups. The list of groups is very long and it is quite probable that some of them are front groups for channeling funds for more explicitly political purposes, as they are largely unknown within Venezuela.

USAID channels all of its funding through a private company called Development Alternatives, Inc. (DAI). As a result, the funds are well hidden from public view. In its publicly available information about its activities in Venezuela, DAI posts on its website about its Venezuela program, "The project supports democratic institutions and processes to ease social tensions and maintain democratic balance. The grants support projects that emphasize conflict mitigation, civic education, confidence building, dialogue, and efforts to bring people together around common goals for the future of Venezuela."[32] Most of DAI's projects in Latin America are of the traditional development project sort or are designed to promote free market reforms, but Venezuela's projects appear to be the only ones targeted explicitly at the country's political institutions.

DAI and USAID sign contracts to create "Offices of Transition Initiatives," (OTI) which, officially, are meant to help countries either master a transition to democracy or prevent it from moving away from democracy. Curiously, the USAID website that lists all of its projects around the world, prominently lists almost all countries in the world, except Venezuela, the information for which is hidden deeply within the site.[33]

Venezuela's OTI, which operates out of the US embassy in Venezuela, was at first supposed to be a limited two-year project, from August 2002 to August 2004. However, following the August 2004 recall referendum that Chávez won, Venezuela's OTI project was extended indefinitely. USAID's first contract with DAI for setting up the OTI says that total funding for the project's first two years was $10 million. For 2005, USAID allocated another $5 million for Venezuela's OTI.[34] The US embassy's and USAID's control over DAI and OTI is nearly complete. According to the USAID-DAI contract, USAID would designate all top-level staff and closely supervise its work. Exactly what the OTI and DAI are doing in Venezuela is quite difficult to determine. Golinger and

Bigwood's FOIA requests uncovered countless documents, but the US government blacked-out nearly all organizational names (supposedly to protect these against persecution). Only by inference is it possible to figure out who some of the funds went to. There are three projects that stand out, though: a publicity campaign during the oil industry shutdown, Sumate, and the development of a political program for the opposition.

Among the more suspicious projects was a USAID/DAI-funded media campaign for nearly $10,000 exactly during the national oil industry shutdown (the agreement states 12/9/02 to 2/7/03, which is a few days after the shutdown began until a few days after it ended). The grant's description states that it is for "Social Dialogue and Citizen Formation, use of the mass media to promote the values of a modern and democratic society breaking with the patterns of paternalism and populism . . . create commercials for radio and television . . . in collaboration with Carlos Fernandez."[35] During this time no advertisements could be seen that fit this description. However, countless television advertisements could be seen that promoted the national strike and demonized the Chávez government. Since Carlos Fernandez, the then-president of Fedecamaras, was one of the strike's main leaders, it is safe to assume that the money went towards the advertisements of the *Coordinadora Democrática* (CD) and not what the grant's description claimed. Certainly, $10,000 would never have been enough relative to the number of TV advertisements that were broadcast, if the CD had to pay for them. It was public knowledge, though, that it did not have to pay for the TV air time because the country's main television stations (RCTV, Globovisión, Venevisión, and Televen) had donated the air time. Rather, what the money was probably used for was to pay for the production of these advertisements.

The funding of the opposition NGO Súmate ("Join-up") received much attention when it was discovered that it had received $53,000 from the NED and another $84,840 from USAID. Súmate was the main organization behind the effort to organize the February 2003 consultative referendum petition that asked for Chávez's resignation, the December 2003 petition drive for a presidential recall referendum, and the August 15, 2004 presidential recall referendum. According to the grant documents Súmate was to receive these funds only for "elections education," where it would produce election materials and "consolidate its national network of volunteers." Even though it was obvious to anyone familiar with Venezuela that this was an organization dedicated to removing Chávez from the presidency via electoral means, the organization itself always kept a neutral non-partisan façade. When it became public, in early 2004, that Súmate had received funds from the US government, the Attorney General decided to investigate whether Súmate had violated Venezuela's election laws. Súmate's directors, Maria Corina Machado and Alejandro Plaz, were indicted by the National Prosecutor Luisa Ortega Diaz in May of that year.[36]

The National Endowment for Democracy immediately went into damage control mode, sending its president Carl Gershman, on November 8, 2004, to Venezuela to meet with President Chávez to convince him to drop the case against Súmate. Chávez, however, did not meet with Gershman and so Gershman only met with the Supreme Court President, Ivan Rincon, and the Attorney General, Isaias Rodriguez. In his meeting with Rincon, Gershman threatened that if the case against the Súmate directors was not withdrawn, he would make sure that the World Bank would stop all of its funding for the overhaul of a judicial reform program. Rincon refused to intervene and soon thereafter the World Bank cut the project's funding. Gershman's meeting with Attorney General Rodriguez did not fare any better. Rodriguez insisted that his office had proof that Súmate did not use its funds as it claimed it did and that this use violated campaign law, since the funding came from a foreign government. Immediately following Gershman's visit, an open letter appeared, signed by 70 political dignitaries from around the world, demanding that the president stop the case against Súmate. The large majority of the letter's signers were either on the NED's board of directors or beneficiaries of NED grants.[37] Venezuelan officials reacted by pointing out that in Venezuela the Attorney General's office and the Office of the President are two different and independent branches of government, an interference on the part of the president in the case would have been completely unconstitutional.

The third US-funded project that caught the Venezuelan public's attention was a project called *Plan Consenso País* (Country Consensus Plan), which the NED funded via CIPE's (Center for International Private Enterprise) partner in Venezuela, CEDICE (Center for the Dissemination of Economic Knowledge). The $33,000 grant was to bring opposition groups together. According to the project description,

The business and labor sectors, the media, the church, and other non-profit groups will gather to discuss and develop a broad consensus on a National Agenda—the specific economic policies that Venezuela should adopt in order to resolve the urgent crisis that the country currently faces in the economic as well as political and social arenas.[38]

The project involved almost all opposition parties, the largest chamber of commerce (Fedecamaras), the union federation (CTV), media organizations, the Church, and various NGOs. Although one cannot say for certain, it is quite likely that a USAID/DAI grant for Bs. 378 million ($200,000), under the title "The Country We Want" and "Developing a Five Year Plan for the Country," also contributed towards the CEDICE project.[39]

Shortly before the August 2004 recall referendum the plan was ready and presented to the media with a great fanfare. Finally the opposition had a political program and could no longer be criticized for lacking one or being too vague about what it intended to do in a post-Chávez Venezuela. The Country Consensus Plan, which Chávez nicknamed "Consensus Plan for Bush," was nonetheless somewhat vague and proposed a more market-driven approach to the economy than the one Chávez had been taking. When it was revealed that the plan was developed with US funding its organizers at first denied this and eventually it was quietly shelved.

Bush and Chávez 3: Escalating Tensions

The most serious aspects of US intervention in Venezuela have mostly consisted of the Bush administration's support for the April 2002 coup attempt and its funding of opposition activity. However, these are the aspects that the Venezuelan and the international media rarely pay attention to. Rather, most attention has been focused on the war of words between the two countries and the occasional measure that limited cooperation. Since Chávez is generally much more outspoken than Bush and his spokespersons, the media easily create the image that it is Chávez's fault that relations between the two countries are so bad, completely omitting the Bush administration's actions in undermining Chávez.

A few months after the April 2002 coup, relations between Venezuela and the US seemed to improve, even though Chávez clearly blamed Bush for much of what had happened. It appeared that a secret deal had been struck between Chávez and Bush, where Bush promised to leave Chávez alone and, in return, Chávez would tune down his anti-imperialist rhetoric and allow US military drug interdiction flights through Venezuelan airspace. The Bush administration limited itself to promoting a conflict resolution approach to Venezuela by supporting the activity of the Carter Center, the UNDP, and the OAS in facilitating discussions between the Chávez government and the opposition. Also, in early 2003, Bush supported the creation of a "Group of Friends of the Secretary General of the OAS,"[40] to which belonged Brazil, Chile, Mexico, Spain, Portugal and the United States, which was supposed to observe and accompany (and possibly pressure) the negotiation process.

The Bush administration had its hands full preparing for war with Iraq and so it is quite probable that it was not interested in any more instability in Venezuela, which might cause additional upward pressure on international oil prices. In other words, Bush probably did not support the December 2002 to January 2003 shutdown of the oil industry because it happened during the lead-up to the Iraq war. Also, Bush's man in Caracas, Secretary General Cesar Gaviria, who was heading the facilitation effort between Chávez and the opposition, was visibly disturbed when the opposition announced its intent to launch the strike, in the first week of December, just as he was waiting for a major response from the Chávez government about a new proposal for tuning down the conflict.

Nonetheless, on December 13, 2002, the Bush administration did attempt to put pressure on Chávez to call for early presidential elections, something that would have been completely unconstitutional in Venezuela. The White House statement said, "The United States is convinced that the only peaceful and politically viable path to moving out of the crisis is through the holding of early elections."[41] Chávez and his supporters rebuffed the idea, pointing out that only someone ignorant of the Venezuelan constitution could have made such a recommendation.

After this, for most of 2003 the Bush White House and State Department seemed to be too preoccupied by Iraq to pay much public attention to Venezuela. It was not until October 2003 that it seemed that a new publicity campaign had been launched, via the US media, which was designed to discredit the Chávez government by associating it with terrorism. This is when the *US News and World Report* article, "Terror Close to Home," and a variety of anti-Chávez articles in UPI and editorials appeared in the US media. It appeared that the temporary truce was off again. At the same time, pro-Chávez National Assembly members Nicolas Maduro and Juan Barreto presented a videotape that they said showed CIA operatives giving a training course to Venezuelan police officers. According to Maduro and Barreto, the person in the video was a known CIA agent who is talking about how to shadow someone and about creating "security rings." The most revealing moment in the video was when one of the students says, in reference to problems that might come up in the field, "We are doing a job and [I trust] he will not be childish, Mr. 'Corey,' and that he will be on the corner saying, 'I am from the CIA, I am from the CIA.'"

The US embassy in Venezuela immediately responded by saying that the video was a training session organized by the US security firm Wackenhut, to which the embassy subcontracts its security services. While this seemed plausible, given the discussions on the tape, it did raise the question of what else, exactly, Wackenhut is doing in Venezuela. Investigative reporter Greg Palast says that the US government has "privatized" its espionage and "black ops" to mercenaries and outfits such as Wackenhut.[42] That is, the CIA itself is now, in the post-Cold War era, more devoted to actual intelligence gathering, while the secret operations of overthrowing governments are "outsourced" to private companies, so as to evade the stricter reporting requirements of the US Congress and to maintain "plausible deniability," should anyone be caught in the midst of an operation. What the Maduro-Barreto video tape suggests is that this is precisely what has happened in Venezuela.

It was around this time, in October 2003, that Chávez began a new rhetorical offensive against the US, just as it became increasingly clear to him that the US government was involved in more clandestine activity in Venezuela than he had previously known. By early 2004 the FOIA documents had been made public and it was clearer than ever that the US government was quite involved in getting rid of Chávez. At the same time, the electoral council was counting the signatures of the petition for the presidential recall referendum. In a rally against US intervention, on February 29, 2004, Chávez called Bush a "pendejo" (gullible fool) for believing that he, Chávez, could be toppled on April 11, 2002. He further lambasted US imperialism, saying, "Mister Bush, you and your cronies have been supporting the putschists here, who have supported political destabilization, who have supported economic destabilization, who have violated our sovereignty, who have done everything to topple the legitimate government of Venezuela." "The United States has installed in America its empire and all governments, that in one way or another oppose themselves to imperialism, begin to be attacked, to be satanized, to be battered . . ."[43] added Chávez.

A few days before the speech, on February 26, Vice-President José Vicente Rangel announced that all training of Venezuelan military at the so-called "School of the Americas" (now known as, "Western Hemisphere Institute for Security Cooperation") would be suspended. The program has long been notorious among Latin America solidarity activists for being the school at which Latin American officers were taught to torture and to violate human rights. Several participants in the April 2002 coup against Chávez were graduates of the school, such as General Efrain Vasquez Velasco. Rangel made the announcement of the suspension of Venezuela's participation shortly after Father Roy Bourgois, a Catholic priest who had been organizing against the school for many years, made a visit to Venezuela and personally asked Chávez to stop sending officers there.

US—Venezuela relations appeared to improve again briefly in the period leading up to and immediately following the August 15 recall referendum against Chávez. US government spokespersons said that they would accept whatever results the OAS and the Carter Center endorsed. When the results were announced and the Carter Center and OAS accepted them a day later, State Department spokesperson Adam Ereli said on August 17 that, "We will join . . . in acknowledging the preliminary results of the referendum and noting that they show that President Chávez received the support of the majority of voters."

While official Bush administration statements were sparse during this time, numerous newspaper editorials began encouraging Bush to take a harder line against Chávez, especially following his re-election. However, it was not until the confirmation hearings of Condoleezza Rice as Secretary of State that Bush administration officials began taking a hard line against Chávez. During her confirmation hearings, Rice referred to Chávez as "a negative force" in Latin America because he was supposedly contributing to the destabilization of its neighbors. Following Rice's lead, numerous other spokespersons continued along these lines.

Further complicating matters for the Bush administration was an initiative the Chávez government launched in mid-2005 to provide discounted heating oil to poor communities in the US. The US department of energy had sent a request to all major oil companies that year, asking them to help out with the heating oil cost explosion. The only company to respond positively to the request was Citgo, the wholly owned subsidiary of Venezuela's PDVSA. Chávez announced the program during a visit to New York, where he met with community leaders in the Bronx. The basic idea was to cut out intermediaries in the supply of heating oil, so that Citgo could provide heating oil at a 40% discount. Chávez said that up to 10% of Citgo's oil production could be used for this purpose. The rationale for the program was that the Venezuelan government, at a time when it was receiving high oil revenues, was acting in solidarity with the world's poor, whether in Venezuela, the Caribbean, or the US.

The program began in Boston, with the help of US Representative William Delahunt, where Citgo was to provide 12 million gallons of discounted heating oil. Later, the program was expanded to the Bronx, Connecticut, Maine, Rhode Island, Pennsylvania, Vermont, and Delaware, for the provision of a total of about 40 million gallons of heating oil to poor communities during the winter of 2005/06.

Critics argued of course that Chávez was merely trying to buy support in the US with the program. Others, mostly US liberals and progressives, though, praised the effort as a real show of solidarity. An important side-effect of the program, though, was to undermine the argument of Chávez opponents in Venezuela and the US that Chávez is anti-US.

Conclusion

As stated at the outset, the relationship between Venezuela and the US is full of contradictions because on the one hand the two countries need each other. Venezuela needs the US as a market for its oil and the US needs Venezuelan oil. On the other hand, the two countries could hardly be further apart in terms of their foreign policy agendas. The US wants a Venezuela that is subservient to its interests and that will quietly integrate itself into a Free Trade Area of the Americas. Venezuela, though, is one of the few countries in the world today that is fundamentally opposed to US hegemony and imperialism. As long as these contradictory interests co-exist, it is no wonder that the relationship between the two countries should be one of constant frictions and reconciliation, as has been generally the case since Chávez became president in 1999.

What does this mean, then, for the incomparably smaller and weaker country that Venezuela is? The US under a President Bush will, of course, always be tempted to get rid of the annoyance that President Chávez represents. An outright US invasion of Venezuela, as many Chávez supporters are convinced will happen sooner or later, is quite unlikely for several reasons. First, the US would make all of Latin America its enemy. And, second, the US does not have sufficient military resources as long as its troops are tied up in Iraq and Afghanistan. To most analysts of US foreign policy it might seem silly to make this point, but the conviction among many Chávez supporters that the US will invade is very strong.[44]

A much more likely scenario for US government efforts is that it will continue and intensify its existing strategy of undermining Chávez by supporting the opposition, financially and logistically in the domestic arena and morally in the international arena. Surely the Bush administration will pull out all the stops to try and defeat Chávez in 2006, mostly by bringing the opposition together under a slick campaign and by the spreading of harmful rumors that have to do with corruption, human rights abuses, and the supposed destabilization of Venezuela's neighbors. Those in charge of such a strategy appear to have learned how to better confront Chávez electorally, since they have lost so many electoral contests to Chávez between 2000 and 2004.

However, one of the US's largest obstacles remains one of the Chávez government's largest foreign policy successes, which is Chávez's tremendous popularity around the world. Despite the efforts to tar Chávez as a supporter of terrorism, of destabilization, and of autocracy, Chávez is currently regarded as one of the world's foremost leaders of the left. Perhaps less so by elected leftist leaders, practically all of whom tend to be more moderate than Chávez, than by mass movements of the left around the world. Whenever Chávez is invited to speak in India, Mexico, Brazil, or even the US, he is greeted by enthusiastic standing-room only crowds.

A Twenty-first Century Socialist Foreign Policy?

Chávez's long-term success at challenging the US and global social injustice, though, depends on whether Venezuela's foreign policy is actually promoting his socialist ideals. We can examine the extent to which Venezuela does so in the two spheres of the economy and of the polity. Also, we can then examine whether Venezuela's foreign policy promotes economic and political social justice between countries and whether it does so within the countries to which it relates.

Venezuela's highly critical stance towards US interventionism and the US promotion of neo-liberalism certainly contributes towards social justice because Chávez manages to call the world's attention to global social injustice in a way that few world leaders (other than Fidel Castro) do on an international stage. Also, Chávez does more than just criticize the US in numerous international forums, but has been actively organizing international coalitions, such as in support for Venezuela's bid for one of the rotating two-year UN Security Council seats in 2006, and seeks to strengthen the G–15, G–77, and the Non-Aligned Movement. Politically, these efforts can contribute towards weakening US political power on the international stage.

Venezuela's efforts to build a united Latin America, currently via Mercosur, and an economically stronger Third World, via bilateral economic alliances with China, India, Iran, and numerous other countries, no doubt contribute towards greater economic social justice. As Chávez's foreign policy program states (cited earlier), Third World countries are generally worse off if they trade with the First World from a position of weakness. While both might benefit from such trade, most of the benefit, though, goes towards the economically more powerful. It thus makes more sense for Third World countries to first unite economically, so that they are in a better position to then negotiate better terms of trade with the First World. OPEC is perhaps the world's most successful example of how unity can lead towards greater benefits for those uniting.

The situation with respect to social justice within countries, as a result of Venezuela's foreign policy, is a lot less clear, though. First, Chávez and his foreign ministers until now appear to have paid little to no attention whatsoever to the political and economic conditions within the countries that they are dealing with.[45] For example, Venezuela is forging close economic and political ties with many countries that most human rights groups condemn as chronic human rights violators. Examples of such countries are Belorussia, Iran, Syria, China, Zimbabwe, and Russia, among others—all of which Venezuela has forged much closer ties with in recent years. It is understandable that Chávez is possibly very skeptical about accusations of human rights abuses against these countries, given the seriously distorted accusations of human rights abuses against Venezuela. Nonetheless, there should be little doubt about the seriousness of the accusations against these countries because of their notoriety.[46] Chávez does the peoples of these countries no favor by publicly praising their leaders and strengthening their positions while these same leaders trample on the rights of their people. By supporting these leaders, Chávez makes it more difficult for activists in these countries to fight for social justice.

Chávez thus finds himself in a slightly contradictory situation, where the fight for social justice between countries appears to contradict the fight for social justice within repressive countries. On the one hand Venezuela, China, and Russia need each other to counteract the political and economic dominance of the United States. On the other hand, neither Russia nor China nor most of the other countries mentioned above can in any way be considered to have a government that works towards social justice within their borders. That is, Venezuela's foreign policy ought to involve a delicate balancing act between these two important goals, but, unfortunately, Chávez appears to be ignoring the social justice situations in the countries that he is building close relations with.

6

Opportunities, Obstacles, and Prospects

Nosotros, hagamos la historia
y otros la escriban
en un mundo mejor
Buscar, buscar la lucha adentro
por transformar el mundo
significa amor[1]
—Alí Primera,
El Despertar de la Historia

Opportunities for the Creation of
Twenty-first Century Socialism in Venezuela

There are six distinct opportunities in recent Venezuelan history that favor the creation of an anti-capitalist project. Three of these—the failure and collapse of neo-liberalism and of Venezuela's old regime, the emergence of Chávez and the Bolivarian movement, and Chávez's charisma—pre-date Chávez's election as president. The other three— the hubris of the opposition, the new oil boom, and the radicalization of Chávez and his movement—developed in the course of Chávez's presidency.

The Collapse of the Old Regime

For better or worse, Venezuela, at the end of the twentieth century, found itself in a historically unique situation. One of the richest countries in Latin America, in terms of natural resources, it had suffered the largest decline in per capita income and the largest increase in poverty of any

Latin American country in the last two decades of the century. In short, Venezuela's old regime, now known as the "Fourth Republic," failed miserably in turning the country's natural wealth into well-being for the majority of its citizens. Twice Venezuelan presidents (Perez and Caldera) tried to apply the recipes of neo-liberalism in an effort to reverse the decline, which only ended up making things worse.

At the same time, Venezuela was also Latin America's longest-running democracy, which, according to many, was actually a fairly repressive democracy. While more and more Venezuelans were sliding into poverty, the regime avoided calls for social change using a variety of mechanisms that kept challengers out of the political system. However, just as the economic system was falling apart at the seams by the late 1980s and early 1990s, so was the political system, mainly because it needed a functioning oil-based economic system in order to survive.

The Growth of Resistance

Parallel to this economic and political decline, a resistance movement was growing, both within the Venezuelan military and within civil society. The first spontaneous outburst of the civilian resistance was the *Caracazo* riot of February 27, 1989. The subsequent brutal repression of the riot radicalized and mobilized a progressive sector within Venezuela's military, which proceeded to organize a coup (together with leftist civilians) that would bring "real" democracy to Venezuela. That coup, although it failed, catapulted coup leader Hugo Chávez onto the national scene. Also, the coup, together with the *Caracazo*, provided new organizing impetus for social movements. By the time Chávez was ready to launch his candidacy for the presidency, in 1998, Venezuela's political system and neo-liberal economics had been so thoroughly discredited and the mechanisms for keeping outsiders out had completely fallen apart, that Chávez was able to take advantage of this opportunity and win the presidency with a landslide.

The Hubris of the Old Elite

All of these events would not have amounted to much, though, if Chávez had continued on the moderate "third way" political path that he originally seemed to intend to go down. Chávez's initial policies, such as the Plan Bolivar 2000 and the Constitutional Reform, clearly put him on the side of the country's poor majority, but it was not a radical program. In other words, it was not his policies that caused the country's old elite to oppose him with a vehemence rarely seen in Venezuelan politics. Rather, the country's old elite opposed Chávez because he thoroughly removed them from their accustomed role in politics. It was this deposing, rather than his—at first—rather moderate economic and social policies, combined with the old elite's deeply ingrained racism and classism, that gave rise to their vehement opposition. Eventually, their campaign against him radicalized Chávez's rhetoric and policies, which then caused more sectors, particularly the middle class and the moderate left, to turn against him.

Every failed attempt of the opposition to depose Chávez ended up giving Chávez and his movement more power and thus more leeway to pursue more radical policies. The April 2002 coup attempt caused the opposition to lose its foothold in the military, the December 2002 oil industry shutdown caused it to lose its foothold in the oil industry, the August 2004 presidential recall referendum caused it to lose its foothold in the general population, and the December 2005 boycott of the National Assembly elections caused it to lose its foothold in the legislature. Meanwhile, as the opposition was progressively losing more and more power, Chávez deepened his studies of socialism and in January 2005 declared himself to be a committed anti-capitalist and socialist.

The New Oil Boom

Another crucial opportunity that opened itself to Chávez and his movement was the rise in the price of oil. The initial higher oil prices were probably caused by Chávez, following his tour of oil producing countries and his effort to convince these to reduce oil production. However, as prices rose ever higher in the wake of the Iraq war and the rising demand for oil, Venezuelan oil revenues doubled between 2002 and 2004 and handed Chávez yet another opportunity, to fund new social programs and to cut ties to private domestic and international capital, giving his government greater freedom to encroach on their interests, in the form of nationalizations and tax increases.

Chávez's Charisma and Radicalization

All of the foregoing was further enabled by Chávez's personal ability to bring together a previously very fragmented movement of progressive civilians and military officers. Chávez was able to do this largely because of his charismatic ability to appeal to the country's disenfranchised. Max Weber, one of the founding fathers of sociology, argued that charismatic leaders are individuals who change the history of nations and even of the world because they can break through the old ossified institutions and create something new. That is, their ability to rally a large segment of the population behind them can create new belief systems and discourses and thereby, eventually, new institutions that break with old institutions that have become dysfunctional.

Chávez is that type of leader. The attachment that his more dedicated followers feel for him is a very strong emotional bond and reaches a significantly large segment of the population. According to most polls, about one third of Venezuela's population, almost all of them coming from the underprivileged segment of Venezuelan society, belong to "*Chavismo duro*" or hard-line Chávez supporters. It is with the help of this dedicated following that Chávez was able to rally a movement behind him, to win the presidency, and to reform the constitution. It is thanks to his ability to rally the poor that the poor have broken with their traditional apathy for politics and their pragmatic support for the democratic system of the past. Instead, they have become very interested in politics and in becoming involved in politics. Their support for democracy is no longer pragmatic, but has become filled with the hope that true democracy can transform the country into a more egalitarian and just one. This is, among other things, why, according to the Latinobarometer, support for democracy has grown more in Venezuela than in any other country in Latin America over the past five years.[2]

The Popular Movements

Crucial in this process is what is known in Venezuela as the "popular movement": the grassroots community organizations, the community media, and the labor movement. These too have been pushing for more changes and for more radical changes in recent years. Whether it is the urban land reform, the rural land reform, the worker takeovers of factories, the lack of public housing, the outcry against corruption, or the need to improve the country's basic infrastructure, community groups and the pro-Chávez labor movement have been supportive of the Chávez government, but have also put pressure on it to deepen the changes. Meanwhile, the community media, which have been sprouting up throughout the country in recent years, are acting as a catalyst, spreading the word about what changes are still needed and also educating people in the poor neighborhoods about what changes are being made and how they can get involved.

There is no census or national organization of community groups in Venezuela, which could give one a good idea of just how many there are or how well organized they are. Instead, there are fragmented community groups throughout the country that pre-date Chávez's election, plus countless committees dedicated to various missions and government programs, such as the committees dedicated to improving the water supply, electricity supply, health care, and urban land distribution, among others. Only as of early 2006 has the government been promoting their self-organization, via communal councils of 200 to 400 families that communities are supposed to create throughout the entire country. It is this wide diversity of groups that has been the most vocal about the failures of local, regional, and national government, keeping issues of corruption, crime, and the slowness of reform at the top of the government's agenda.

The other main impetus for radical social change has been the labor movement. Up until the 2002 coup attempt the labor movement was a conservative force in Venezuela. However, when the country's old labor union federation, the CTV, sided with the right-wing coup, progressives in the labor movement split off from the CTV and formed a new union federation, the National Union of Venezuelan Labor (UNT), in mid-2003. Since then, the UNT has grown significantly and as of 2006 encompasses more workers than the CTV. Also, it is far more radical than the CTV, supporting takeovers of idle factories, pushing the Chávez government to expropriate more of them and to turn these over to worker self-management or co-management. Despite this, the UNT is still a weak organization, with many factional fights over just how far it should go in pushing Chávez or in supporting him.[3] Its leaders realize on the one hand that their movement would be a lot worse off without Chávez and that criticizing the government too much would play into the opposition's hands. On the other hand, they also realize that Chávez needs to be pushed and criticized because without such criticism their movement would not advance much. The level of unionization is still quite low in Venezuela (13% of those formally employed), which means that the movement is not as strong as it could be. Still, it is one of the main forces pushing from below for radical change.

Thus, while community groups, labor movement, and community media push from below, Chávez is pushing from above for "deepening the revolution." In the middle are the old state bureaucracy, old mentalities, and the contradictoriness of the process itself. In short, while many opportunities have opened up for radical change in Venezuela, many obstacles still persist.

Assessment of the Effort to Build Twenty-first Century Socialism

Before we turn to the obstacles to the creation of twenty-first century socialism in Venezuela, let's briefly review to what extent the policies and institutions that Chávez and his supporters are creating might deserve this label. It is not good enough to look at the stated values of a government or movement to determine whether it is socialist or worth supporting. Too many movements in world history proclaimed wonderful values and then proceeded to create institutions that ended up completely contradicting these values. Despite this, values are a good place to start, before examining whether the institutions and policies actually work towards the fulfillment of these values.

The main values of twenty-first century socialism, according to Chávez, ought to be liberty, equality, social justice, and sustainability. According to most anti-capitalists, for these values to become a reality we would need to replace the political and economic institutions of the private ownership of the means of production, of the market system, and of the pro-capitalist state. However, exactly how Chávez and his supporters propose to replace these institutions is not entirely clear yet; we only have some indications as to what alternate institutions they propose.[4] The following will briefly summarize the extent to which the Chávez government's governance, economic, social, and foreign policies fulfill or fail to fulfill the ideals of twenty-first century socialism. As we will see, the policies and institutions that fulfill the ideals are all too often partly undermined by countervailing policies or cultural tendencies.

Governance Policies

With regard to governance policies, Chávez's three most important policy innovations involve, first, the effort to create a participatory democracy, not just a representative one. The introduction of participatory democracy is being tried mostly via communal councils, referenda, social oversight (*contraloria social*), and the involvement of civil society organizations in the implementation of social programs (such as the missions and the land reform), and in governmental appointments. These efforts, some of which are still only at an early stage of implementation (especially the communal councils, which are arguably the most important manifestation of participatory democracy), clearly represent an effort to create a polity that overcomes the shortcomings of traditional representative democracy. As such, these policies represent a very important step in creating a state that is not beholden to private interests, as is generally the case in capitalist democracies.

The second policy area that affects governance is the effort to include those who had traditionally been excluded, such as women and the indigenous population. This policy objective is being pursued via affirmative action programs in the areas of education, micro-credits, and land reform. Also, the inclusion of women and the indigenous population in the constitution, by assuring them a wide variety of rights and by making the constitution itself a gender-neutral document moved Venezuelan society a great deal closer towards being more inclusive. These policies of inclusion live up to the ideal of Venezuela's constitution, of creating a state "with equality and justice," that is, of making sure that not only is everyone treated equally, but that everyone also has a more or less equal chance in life.

The effort to create a civilian—military unity (*union civico-militar*) is the third key policy area to transform the Venezuelan polity. The Chávez government has tried to promote this unity mainly by encouraging civilians to become involved in the military reserves and by involving the military in what normally are civilian tasks, such as the various social programs of the missions. The logic behind this is to redefine the concept of national defense to include defending the country not just from physical attack, but also from social problems, such as hunger, disease, and poverty.

For most progressives it is difficult to relate to the concept and existence of the military, no matter what their concrete functions. Too often has it been used to repress progressive movements in the Third World and too often has it been used to implement colonialist rule by the First World. However, if one agrees that there is a need for a country's self-defense, then the question is, how should such self-defense be organized? The Chávez government's answer to this question appears to be such that it precisely attempts to create a military that does not employ the repressive functions of the past, but is rather truly used purely for (broadly defined) national self-defense, by breaking down the boundary between civilians and military. In the end, it appears that Venezuela is moving towards the type of defense that has made Switzerland famous, where national self-defense is everyone's responsibility, without creating a militarized society in the process and which thus contributes towards creating a society with liberty, equality, and social justice.

However, the policies for creating a participatory democracy are undermined by the creation of a strong presidency and the persistence of an old public administration that operates according to very hierarchical principles. Despite the participatory nature of the social programs known as missions, practically all other areas of the government operate in a very top-down manner, where the president is the foremost commander in chief and everyone else has their place in the hierarchy and is expected to obey uncritically. The inability to distinguish loyalty from uncritical obedience makes the implementation of policies not only non-participatory, but also resistant to the correction of mistakes in accordance with criticism from below.

The Economy

With regard to the economy, here too there are three main policy areas, which are also affected by contradictions in their implementation. The first area is the effort to create a social economy, by which is meant the support for cooperatives, worker—state co-managed large enterprises, self-managed micro-enterprises, and democratized rural and urban land ownership. This is a fairly complex set of policies, whose objective is to move the country's economy beyond oil dependence and capitalism. So far, the government has made a fairly consistent effort to pursue the creation of a social economy, but given the power and size of the conventional capitalist economy and of the oil industry, the social economy still remains small in comparison. Still, there are plans to greatly expand the size of the social economy in Chávez's second full term.

The creation of a social economy clearly represents one of the Chávez government's most dramatic efforts to move away from capitalism and towards self-management and overcome one of capitalism's greatest causes of social injustice, the private ownership of the means of production. Also, very importantly, it is not a frontal assault against capitalism, as socialist parties used to advocate, but a much subtler assault, where self-managed enterprises co-exist with traditional capitalist enterprises and with, so far, a minimal number of expropriations. The much slower substitution of the capitalist economy by the social economy reduces the level of resistance from domestic and transnational capital (in contrast to the old elites), thus making the success of such a transition much greater.

The second policy area within economic policy is the oil industry reform, which involves regaining government control over the industry and asserting Venezuela's sovereignty over its oil reserves by increasing taxation and royalties for transnational oil companies in Venezuela. Also, part of the government's strategy is to use oil as a means for furthering Latin American integration, by creating Petroamerica. Asserting sovereignty over one's own natural resources is a form of self-management on a national scale and thus roughly fits within the institutional framework proposed here for creating a better society.

The third economic policy area developed relatively late in the Chávez presidency and involved the creation of a variety of new state-owned enterprises, which were either the result of the expropriation of bankrupt private companies, as in the case of the paper company Invepal and the valve company Inveval, or the result of the government's own direct investment, such as with the continental television channel TeleSur, the airline Conviasa, the petrochemical company Corporación Petroqimica de Venezuela (CPV), or the new telecommunications company. None of these companies constitute a monopoly in their area of business, so they compete against private businesses. State management and co-management in some of these enterprises represent a move away from private capital accumulation and potentially towards greater social justice. However, as long as the oil industry and other state-owned enterprises are run as typical corporations, as they currently are, self-management is being prevented in some of the country's most important industries.

All of these economic policies represent a clear divergence from neo-liberal economics and an emphasis on state intervention and worker's self-management in the economy. In this sense, the policies are an effort to democratize the economy, both in terms of the distribution of capital (urban and rural land reform) and in terms of control over capital (cooperatives, co-management, and better state control over the oil industry).

Undermining these efforts, though, is the continuing predominance of the oil industry, which enables the changes in the economy and many social programs and, as a result, calls into question the long-term sustainability of the Bolivarian project. That is, were oil prices to suddenly collapse or Venezuela's oil production to drop off for some reason, many of the government's projects, such as subsidies for cooperatives or the expropriation (with compensation) of private enterprises would no longer be possible. More importantly, though, the high oil revenue perpetuates the typical "Dutch Disease" problem, which contributes to chronic inflation and makes domestic agricultural and industrial products un-competitive, thus requiring continuing subsidies.

Society

The social policies of the Chávez government have three characteristics that distinguish them from the social policies of previous Venezuelan governments. First, relative to the previously reigning paradigm of neo-liberalism, they involve a significant increase in social spending, which increased from about 8% of GDP in 1998 to over 12% in 2004. Similarly, per capita social spending increased by over 30% in this period, in real terms, compared to the previous presidency.[5] This is a tremendous increase by any measure, even taking into consideration that oil revenues rose significantly during 2004. However, one should be clear that these programs are redistributive policies, such as free education and health care, subsidized food and housing, and rural and urban land reform. As such, they are typically social democratic policies in the sense that they represent social spending in areas that governments around the world normally focus on and do not fundamentally alter the economic structure of capitalism.

Second, in contrast to social policies of previous Venezuelan governments, Chávez decided to avoid the existing state apparatus with many of his social programs. That is, the state proved to be so ossified and difficult to use for the implementation of new social programs that many social programs were "outsourced"—not to private companies, but to newly created state institutions, the "missions." While this proved to be an effective way to get state resources and services to the population, it is creating a longer-term problem in terms of parallel budgets and institutions, which will eventually have to be integrated either into the existing state structures or into a completely reformed state.

Third, the Chávez government's social policies represent an important innovation in the ways that they involve local communities, such as via land committees, community health committees, water committees, and citizen participation in educational programs. This citizen participation has proved to contribute significantly to mobilizing the population both in defense of the social programs and in defense of the government and has generally contributed to an activation of civil society that has never been seen previously in Venezuela.

It is this last point, of citizen participation, that represents a significantly new way of implementing social policies that is in line with the ideals of creating twenty-first century socialism in Venezuela. However, large parts of the public administration still operate outside of this innovative principle and, depending on whether the integration of the missions into existing state structures transforms the old public administration and not vice-versa, it is unclear whether the Bolivarian project will advance in creating a public administration that is in tune with twenty-first century socialism.

Foreign Relations

Finally, in terms of foreign policy, Chávez's main policy innovations revolve around the aforementioned regaining of sovereignty over its natural resources, its resistance to US imperialism and to neo-liberalism, and its emphasis on Third World solidarity and integration. There is little doubt that this is one area where one can say that the Chávez government's policies contribute towards strengthening social justice between nations. The main issue here is that Chávez has developed strong relations with many countries that are outright repressive and/or reactionary, such as the governments of Iran, China, Zimbabwe, Belorussia, and North Korea. Chávez justifies such a foreign policy approach mainly on the basis of respecting every country's sovereignty and by arguing that many of these countries' leaders are actually as progressive as he is.[6] However, by lending legitimacy to these governments Chávez ends up promoting greater social injustice within these countries.

Bringing it Together

In short, Chávez is clearly pursuing an anti-capitalist strategy that is replacing two of the three key institutions of capitalism. First, he is gradually supplanting private ownership/control of the means of production with a mix of worker and state ownership/control. Second, the defeats of the insurrectionary opposition, the implementation of more participatory forms of governance, and the freedom that large oil revenues have provided, have broken the state free from the control of powerful private or capitalist interests.

However, the third key institution of capitalism, the market system, is still firmly in place for allocating most of the country's products and wealth. As of yet, the recognition that the market fundamentally works against social justice is not very strong in Venezuela. There are initial efforts, though, to gradually replace market mechanisms, such as via the state's redistributive function (which is nothing new) and via the barter trade with various countries, such as Cuba and Argentina. The potentially most interesting innovation in this direction, though, would be the "communities of production and consumption" that Chávez has talked about, in connection with the work of István Mészáros. If the social production enterprises (EPS) whose formation the government is encouraging, become truly integrated with communities and with the communal councils, then something like participatory democratic planning could be the result. That is, consumers, via the communal councils, could voice their needs and requests to councils of EPS workers and EPS workers could outline their production plans to communal councils. A third instance—a pricing board[7]—could adjust prices in accordance with supply and demand, and let each side revise their consumption or production plans until the two plans balanced. The end result would be a participatory planning process, where the economy is based on the principle of cooperation instead of competition. The participatory nature of the social programs and the governance system would, if substantially strengthened, complement the transition towards a society that fulfills the ideals of liberty, equality, social justice, and sustainability.

The Chávez government is complementing the transformation of Venezuela's economy with transformations in the political sphere, such as the communal councils and the participatory nature of many social programs. However, the slow pace of the political and economic transformation, along with the countervailing factors of presidentialism, the economy's resurgent Dutch Disease, the persistence of powerful domestic and transnational capital interests, and the parallelism and poor efficiency in the public administration (missions and ministries) place significant brakes on the transformation of Venezuela. These brakes, though, are merely the internal contradictions of the policies themselves. In addition to these, there are obstacles that originate from within the Bolivarian movement and from outside of it.

Obstacles

The internal obstacles are internal in two senses, in that they are internal to the Bolivarian movement and in that they tend to be in people's heads, in their ways of thinking and making sense of the world. The external obstacles, on the other hand, are both external to the Bolivarian movement and external in that they have an objective manifestation, that is, they have to do with the concrete actions and dynamics of people and systems.

The internal obstacles include the persistence of patronage-clientelism and corruption, of a top-down management style, and personalistic politics. These constitute internal obstacles in that they are part of the thinking within the Bolivarian movement. They represent obstacles in the sense that these tendencies undermine the Bolivarian project from within and unnecessarily exacerbate external obstacles, such as the opposition to the government. The external obstacles include US intervention in Venezuela, international and domestic capital interests, and Venezuela's old elite that continues to refuse to accept Chávez as the country's democratically elected president. Internal and external obstacles tend to reinforce each other, potentially creating a vicious cycle that could undermine the Bolivarian project altogether.

Internal Obstacles

In a book called *Reflections on the Revolution in France*, the conservative British political theorist Edmund Burke argued in 1790 that revolutions, such as the French Revolution, are bound to fail. According to Burke, societies have their own developmental logic, their own organic growth, which cannot be intentionally re-organized in accordance with the will of revolutionary leaders. Societies develop traditions and ways of doing things for a reason that, if disrupted, is likely to cause more harm than good.

The reference to Edmund Burke is not meant to suggest an argument for why revolution in Venezuela (or anywhere) is wrong or impossible, as Burke argued. Rather, it is supposed to call attention to Burke's arguments for why revolutions are so difficult to institute and to maintain. Certainly, as a founder of conservative ideology, Burke was intent on preventing revolution, but he and more recent theorists have something important to say about the problems any radical transformation of society faces. Later, in the early 20th century radical social and political theorists, such as Lenin, Lukacs, and Gramsci, also recognized the problem of how belief systems, ideology, and culture could present severe obstacles to social transformations.[8]

In essence, the cultural critique of revolution argues that societies cannot be reorganized at will by the state or by individual leaders because societies are the result of centuries of complex gradual development, in which traditions, habits, attitudes, customary ways of doing things, and belief systems develop in ways that make structural changes from above very difficult or impossible to implement without a corresponding change in people's ways of thinking.

A common objection to this line of argument is that a revolution is only a true revolution when the "masses" are behind it, which already embody the cultural changes that the revolution merely implements in the political and economic sphere. In other words, a "true" revolution brings about political and economic changes that have already taken hold in the larger culture. The dispute between cultural critique of and social-structural justification for revolution thus ends up centering around which comes first, cultural revolution or social-structural revolution?

The Venezuelan experience during the Chávez presidency at least partially confirms the cultural critique of social transformation; that ways of thinking change much more slowly than policy-makers would like. In other words, Bolivarian revolutionaries need to pay attention to the ways in which culture is very resistant to change. More specifically, Venezuelan cultural tendencies towards patronage and preferences for strong leaders stand in direct contradiction with efforts to establish a participatory democratic revolution. In other words, for the Bolivarian project to succeed, it has to be conscious of these tendencies and must find ways of overcoming them. Originally, part of Chávez's objective was precisely to eradicate what he called "Fourth Republic" patronage systems. While Chávez did manage to introduce constitutional changes that were intended to undermine Fourth Republic patronage systems, many of his supporters and officials within the government simultaneously went about reestablishing their own patronage systems.

Chávez himself has begun to call attention to the internal obstacles the Bolivarian project faces. During the November 2004 strategy workshop Chávez quoted from Victor Hugo's *Les Miserables*, "the work is incomplete, I admit this. We have demolished the old regime in deeds, but we have not been able to overcome it completely in ideas. It is not enough to destroy the abuses and it is necessary to modify habits—the windmill no longer exists, but the wind that moved it still continues to blow." Chávez then said, "We must demolish the old regime on the ideological level."[9]

While Chávez recognizes the internal problem that threatens the Bolivarian project, he is often not that clear as to what these old beliefs consist of or how they could be overcome. That is, Chávez and government officials often talk about the need to disseminate the "Bolivarian ideology" and to educate the nation's children in Bolivarian values and morals, but what this means is often left at relatively general themes, such as the need to emphasize cooperation over competition, solidarity over self-interest, and pursuit of the collective good over individualism.

Internal Obstacles 1: Patronage-Clientelism and Corruption

Part of the problem with all of the above named values that the Bolivarian project proposes to emphasize is that they all signal a shift from individual to collective without specifying which collective is to be favored. That is, it is of course safe to assume that one's own collective is what is supposed to be emphasized—in this case presumably Venezuelan society as a whole. However, collective could also refer to one's family, to one's network of friends, to one's ethnic, class, religious, or political group, to one's nation, or to all of humanity. The question of which collective is supposed to be preferred is an important one because all too often the collective that people give preference to is that of their network of friends and family or their particular political grouping. In other words, placing collectivity above self-interest can all too easily turn into patronage-clientelism, where only those who are members of that particular group help each other out, with the tacit understanding that everyone will benefit from such mutual help in the long run.

The concrete manifestation of such forms of patronage-clientelism in Chávez's Venezuela have been those instances where only those who support the Bolivarian project get a particular job or government service, such as a micro-credit loan or education spot in one of the missions. Unfortunately, there is no concrete data on how widespread this practice is, but anecdotal evidence suggests that it is fairly common. One must keep in mind, though, that this is not a practice that the Chávez government invented. It is well known among Venezuelans that patronage was well established in the Fourth Republic, where it was essential to be a member of one of the two dominant parties, AD or Copei, in order to get a government job or service. Also, the practice exists within the sectors opposed to Chávez, who often also base decisions on who to hire for private sector jobs (or even public sector jobs, in cases where the institution is still controlled by opposition sympathizers), based on their support of the opposition. The bottom line, though, is that Chávez promised to do away with such practices, but so far they have often been reproduced.

One reason such patronage-clientelism practices undermine the Bolivarian project, aside from being a violation of one of the project's main objectives, of creating greater inclusion, freedom, equality, and social justice, is that they strengthen the opposition. The opposition movement becomes ever more intransigent, the more it feels excluded from government and its benefits and services. Also, more importantly, the patronage-clientelism mentality prevents rational, just, and efficient administration. A third reason why patronage-clientelism undermines the Bolivarian project is that it easily leads to corruption, which significantly contributes to the loss of political legitimacy. It is just a few small steps from providing small special favors in return for political support to providing larger favors in return for larger sums of cash.

One should note here, though, that while corruption in Venezuela is indeed a serious problem, it is probably overestimated. Venezuela ranks very low on Transparency International's Corruption Perception Index (CPI),[10] meaning that the level of corruption the foreign business community perceives in Venezuela is quite high. Part of the reason for this perception can be found in the fact that the international business community generally receives its news about Venezuela from the oppositional private media and otherwise communicates with opposition supporters in Venezuela. Another reason for the high perception of corruption is that Venezuelans appear to have a completely false idea of how rich Venezuela is, according to some surveys, which tends to make them believe that the gap between the country's immense wealth and their personal poverty is the result of corruption.[11] This national perception of widespread corruption is generally pervasive in the culture, so that national analysts and international business people pick up on it and end up reflecting the overestimate of corruption in Transparency International's CPI.

However, there also is evidence that corruption in Venezuela is not as bad as the CPI would lead one to believe. The 2005 Latinobarometro survey found that Venezuela ranks third in Latin America, after Colombia and Uruguay, in terms of people who say that the country has made much progress in fighting corruption in the previous two years (42%). In nearly all other Latin American countries citizens agree with that statement 34% of the time or less. Also, the perception that the fight against corruption has been progressing has increased from 2004, when only 33% of Venezuelans agreed. The percentage of Venezuelans who say they personally know of an act of corruption declined from 27% in 2001 to 16% in 2005 (average in Latin America is 20% for 2005). Only the estimate of the percentage of Venezuelan civil servants who are corrupt is fairly high, at 65% (with the average estimate being 68%).[12]

Whether Venezuela's government is more corrupt or less corrupt than other governments is not the point here. Rather, the Chávez government must find ways to truly eradicate patronage and corruption if its project is to succeed in the long term. The reason it threatens the project is that the continued perception of the persistence of patronage and corruption will eat away at the government's popular support and legitimacy and it undermines the efficiency and fairness of the state. While the government recognizes this problem, it does not seem to have a strategy to combat patronage and corruption, other than better ethics education and increased transparency and policing. In other words, the government seems to lack a clear analysis of what causes patronage and corruption and how these root causes might be addressed, other than to say that laws are not enforced well enough (which is true, but only part of a comprehensive analysis).

Actually, the government indirectly contributes to patronage and, by extension, to corruption, in at least three ways. First, the emphasis on collective responsibility over individual responsibility contributes to the typical patronage notion of "we help each other out," where the ones who are being helped are members of one's own political group. Second, the constant reminder that the Bolivarian project is under attack further strengthens the perceived need to "hold together" and to help each other out and to keep the "enemies" (such as agents of the opposition or of the US government) at bay—all of which are ideas that further strengthen patronage. Third, there is a low-level personality cult around the figure of Chávez, which binds people to him and creates a clear distinction between those who are with the Bolivarian project and those who are against it, thus further strengthening the patronage system.

Internal Obstacles 2: Personalism

Venezuela does not have a full-fledged personality cult around President Chávez, in the sense that Chávez is worshipped and adulated in all government literature and in all public appearances of government officials. However, there is a very clear persistence of personalistic politics in Chávez's Venezuela. That is, there is a tendency to celebrate and adore Chávez in ways that exceed what one would see in most European or North or South American capitalist democracies. To a large extent this should not be surprising because Chávez is, after all, a very charismatic figure and it is largely thanks to his charisma and political skill that Venezuela's left has united in the form of a Bolivarian movement and that it has been able to win as many elections as it has. Still, the low-level personality cult that exists around Chávez is an obstacle to the full implementation of the Bolivarian project.

Chávez and the government have issued contradictory messages as far as the development of a personality cult is concerned. On the one hand Chávez has often tried to understate his role in recent Venezuelan history, saying things such as "I am merely a leaf in the winds of history." Also, the government has issued executive orders that the ministries cannot use Chávez's image for their publications without prior approval from the president's office. On the other hand, though, Chávez has reinforced the notion of his indispensability by saying things like, "Those who are with me are with me, those who are not with me are against me . . . I will not accept gray areas: that one would have one foot here and another there . . ."[13] While this was probably meant as a demand for absolute loyalty, which fits with the premium Chávez places on loyalty, it can be easily interpreted as a demand for uncritical obedience. That is, as long as Chávez does not clarify the difference between uncritical obedience and absolute loyalty, where the latter allows for constructive critique and the former does not, he gives the impression of being indispensable and unquestionable. More than that, it is well known in Venezuela that, all too often, die-hard Chavistas will immediately pigeonhole as "escualidos" (squalids, as Chavistas like to call opposition supporters) those who are critical of some aspect of Chávez or his government, even if the critic is otherwise a supporter.

Also, campaign slogans used to reflect this, saying, "Those who are against Chávez are against the people" and "With Chávez the people rule." A popular graffiti slogan during the oil industry shutdown was, "With Chávez everything, without Chávez nothing." More recently, in the run-up to the 2006 presidential election all government posters carried the slogan, "With Chávez we all govern."[14]

There are several consequences of this personalism. First, it makes the entire Bolivarian project extremely vulnerable. That is, having all of the attention focused on Chávez and his ability to rally and mobilize the movement means that the movement depends on him. Should he be assassinated it is very likely that the movement will fall apart into at least three factions: a radical wing, a moderate wing, and a military wing. Recognizing the benefit of his disappearance for the opposition, this is almost certainly the reason why so many plots to assassinate Chávez have been hatched.

Second, personalism further strengthens the boundaries between those who belong to the in-group, that is, those who benefit from political patronage and those who do not: either one supports Chávez or one is opposed to him—gray areas are not allowed. This makes it more easy to define who is to benefit from patronage systems than a more ambiguous yardstick would allow, such as adherence to a set of ideas, to an ideology (although, party membership, as was used in the past, would also be an easy yardstick).

Finally, personalism undermines the legitimacy of the government for those who are opposed to this way of thinking. That is, for the above named and other reasons, a significant sector of the population is inherently opposed to personalism and personality cults of any kind and would almost instinctively reject any government in which there was a personality cult around the president.

Internal Obstacles 3: Top-Down Management

Just as with the personality cult, there is no outright authoritarianism or *caudillismo* (strongman rule) in Venezuela. As a matter of fact, many Chávez supporters make a strong argument that the Venezuelan state under Chávez is far too permissive, in that very few individuals have been held responsible for the April 2002 coup or the December 2002 to January 2003 oil industry shutdown or any number of other politically motivated incidents that have caused severe damage to the state or to individuals. While this is accurate, at the same time, pro-Chávez legislators in Venezuela's National Assembly have passed or have considered laws that from a civil liberties perspective could be called authoritarian. For example, the reform of the penal code in early 2005 stiffened prison penalties for insulting government officials, for intimidating them with *cacerolazos* (pot-banging), and for blocking roads.[15] While the Chávez government or, more accurately, the Attorney General's office never applied the penal code's provision for prosecuting people on these infractions, the fact that this law is on the books and that the penalty was stiffened is not good for civil liberties.

Similarly, a new anti-terrorism law that the MVR introduced into the National Assembly in 2001, but did not revive until shortly after the assassination of a state prosecutor in November 2004, would criminalize anyone who directly or indirectly spreads information that terrorizes or threatens people with the purpose of causing alarm in the population or a sector of the population. Also, it would be illegal to use "means that are capable of altering or devastating the economic system of the republic."

Critics point out here that "altering" is so vague, it could end up being applied to a wide variety of situations. While this law appears to have been put on hold indefinitely, the very fact it was proposed shows that some in the pro-Chávez coalition have authoritarian instincts.

Finally, besides some authoritarian tendencies in laws that the National Assembly has passed or is considering passing, there is Chávez's personality, which, it is said, is autocratic. That is, Chávez's management style seems to be completely top-down, rather than bottom-up or team-oriented. He seems to consider it perfectly normal and acceptable to issue orders, much like a general in the battlefield, to his ministers on the spur of the moment, with little regard for their existing work plans or duties. Former ministers have told of how Chávez sometimes called them up in the middle of the night, telling them to take care of a particular task. Combined with this tendency to issue orders as a military general would, Chávez does not seem to take lightly to criticism or to the questioning of these orders. Sometimes, when faced with criticism, Chávez's reaction has been, "I remind you, you are speaking to the president."[16] While this reflects a deeply ingrained Venezuelan cultural pattern of demanding absolute respect and loyalty from one's subordinates, it makes constructive criticism extremely difficult, if not impossible.

The danger that top-down management represents, along with an inability to accept criticism, is that, within the state, it fosters inefficiency and the perpetuation of mistakes. That is, the government, from Chávez on down, often suffers from inefficiency because bosses order their employees around without regard for their work plans or pre-existing commitments, forcing them to constantly re-adjust to changing orders from above and to discard plans. The inability to criticize this state of affairs merely perpetuates the problem, thus making improvements in organizational management practically impossible, despite persistent calls for improving the functioning of the state apparatus.

The authoritarianism of some of the new laws, such as the penal code and the anti-terrorism law presents a different type of problem, in that these strengthen opposition arguments that the Chávez government is seeking to stifle freedom of expression and to repress the opposition. It seems unlikely, though, that the opposition is correct in its analysis because so far, if anything, impunity in the face of gross violations of the law, such as the coup and the oil industry shutdown, has been the norm. Rather, it seems more likely that if certain sectors of the opposition were to regain control over the executive or the Attorney General's office (which is an independent branch of the state), then they would use these laws to persecute Chavistas. The reason this scenario seems more likely is that this is precisely what has happened in the past. During the 47-hour Carmona coup presidency, for example, opposition mayors had no compunction in raiding Chavista homes or in arresting Chavista government officials without a warrant or due process of any kind. If these opposition leaders reach higher positions of power and have ambiguous laws with repressive potential at their disposal, such as the reformed penal code and the anti-terrorism law, then these leaders would have an even easier time in repressing their traditional adversaries. The existence of these laws thus present a greater threat, in the long run, to the Bolivarian project than their absence ever would.

External Obstacles

However, in addition to the internal obstacles, the Bolivarian project must also contend with formidable external obstacles, which can be grouped into three types. The first is the old Venezuelan elite, such as the former ruling political parties like AD and Copei and their spin-offs (*Proyecto Venezuela, Convergencia, Alianza Bravo Pueblo*) and the network of institutions with which they governed, such as the Church, the CTV, Fedecamaras, the private mass media, and the former oil industry management, all of which seek to regain their lost power. The second type of obstacle includes national and transnational capital interests, which seek to maximize profits. Third, there is the US government under Bush, which is, in essence, pursuing old-fashioned imperial interests of gaining or maintaining territorial control. All of these obstacles overlap with each other to varying degrees.

External Obstacles 1: The Old Elite

Venezuela's old elite, which lost control over the government and its associated institutions, has been trying to regain control ever since Chávez was first elected. On several occasions this former ruling class has proven its willingness to undermine democratic institutions in the name of saving Venezuela from the supposed Chávez dictatorship. However, in its campaign to regain control over Venezuela it has suffered numerous defeats, losing more and more of its power. The only solid base of power that it still has, as of late 2006, is the private mass media, which, as a result of the recent experiences, has become less willing to risk everything in the name of toppling Chávez.

Each assault on the Chávez government, while ultimately unsuccessful, strengthened the internal obstacles of the Bolivarian project by providing a stronger justification for supporters of the project to argue that they had to protect themselves from infiltrators and traitors. This would be achieved by excluding opposition supporters from the public administration and in some cases even from government services. That is, the constant feeling of being under siege heightened the in-group mentality that fosters patronage. This dynamic was on display at its most clearly with the so-called "Tascon List."

In turn, the closing of Chavista ranks and the exclusion of opposition supporters from some government jobs strengthened the sense of justification and urgency of the opposition desire to get rid of Chávez. In other words, the internal and external obstacles created a positive feedback loop. Also part of this feedback loop was the support for Chávez, potentially strengthening the personality cult around him, as he came to be perceived more and more indispensable to the revolution and, at the same time, for the opposition, as the one and only obstacle to their regaining power. At various points in the conflict, newspaper editorials and the commentaries of opposition leaders verged on the absurd as they appeared to blame Chávez for just about every problem in Venezuela, from the Vargas mudslides to the coup.

Ultimately, though, Chávez and his supporters managed to largely neutralize this obstacle, mainly by taking advantage of the opposition's weaknesses, such as its internal disunity, its lack of leadership, and its complete misperception of Venezuelan reality. The only way the opposition is going to be able to build a real challenge to Chávez in the long run is if it manages to unite, if it plays by the rules of the democratic game, and if it takes strategic advantage of the government's weaknesses in the areas of insecurity, corruption, and inefficient public administration. Another, less democratic, option for the opposition is to build on its alliance with the Bush administration and international opinion-makers to portray the Chávez government as a "rogue regime" and to discredit it internationally, so as to at some point justify international intervention in Venezuela.

In the run-up to the 2006 election and in its immediate aftermath it looked like the opposition had learned from its past errors and was following the more moderate strategy outlined here. It united behind Zulia state governor Manuel Rosales as the main opposition presidential candidate, and focused on insecurity and poor public administration. As for building its alliance with the Bush administration, it is clear that many opposition organizations continue to receive advice and millions of dollars in aid.

External Obstacles 2: Domestic and International Capital

Of course, Venezuela's domestic capital interests overlap to a large extent with the aforementioned category of old elites. However, there is an important difference. The main interest of the old elites is to pursue power so that they might restore the status quo ante. The main interest of both domestic and international capital, though, is their ability to make a profit; whether this involves restoring the status quo ante or living with Chávez is relatively irrelevant.

This relative lack of interest in who occupies the presidency is illustrated by the fact that when Chávez was first running for president he was supported by some sectors of Venezuelan capital, such as the newspaper El Nacional and the media mogul Gustavo Cisneros. Also, Luis Miquilena, Chávez's campaign manager, managed to find financing for Chávez's campaign from Venezuelan businesses. Many had hoped, as had always been Venezuelan tradition, that key big business supporters of the president would be named to important ministerial posts. Chávez, however, made a definitive break from Venezuelan political tradition in this case and did not name any of these types of supporters to ministerial posts.

It was thus only a matter of time for these former supporters from the business sector to turn against Chávez. But of course it was not just the slight of their traditional rights that bothered Venezuelan big business; they also had to contend with a number of programs that directly touched upon their privileges. Three policy areas enraged the Venezuelan business class.

First, right after Chávez became president, he rescinded a law that stated that Venezuelan business would no longer have to pay generous severance payments to laid-off workers. Second, Chávez moved forward in enforcing Venezuela's tax code. Third, and perhaps most importantly, Chávez introduced the so-called 49 law-decrees, which included land reform, banking reform, and oil industry reform and touched on a wide variety of business sector interests.

Most domestic capital, as represented by the chamber of commerce Fedecamaras, thus joined Venezuela's old elite in taking a hard-line opposition course to Chávez. Following the recall referendum, though, many of these groups and individuals appear to have realized that the leadership of this opposition led them down a dead end and have, since then, taken a more conciliatory approach towards the Chávez government. For example, immediately after the referendum, Fedecamaras agreed to meet with Chávez and to discuss how the two might cooperate better.

With regard to international capital, unlike Chile in 1973, where large US corporations such as ITT had a major role in overthrowing the Allende government, international capital appears to show much less interest in influencing Venezuelan politics. Part of the reason probably has to do with the fact that Chávez hardly touched international big business interests—at least, not until late 2004. Venezuela's oil was nationalized several decades earlier and until 2006 Chávez showed little interest in nationalizing any other property of transnational capital. The only two areas where Chávez has affected transnational capital is taxation[17] and by forcing oil companies to form joint ventures with PDVSA.

In the case of oil related businesses, though, taxes are not merely being enforced, but have also been raised several times. For strategic associations, which extract extra-heavy crude form the Orinoco Oil Belt, the royalty rate was raised from 1% to 16% in 2005 and then to 30% in 2006. Similarly, in the case of operating agreements, where international oil companies extract regular crude as subcontractors of PDVSA, the government required these to change their arrangement with PDVSA into joint ventures. This way foreign oil companies share costs and revenues with PDVSA and can thus no longer inflate the operating charges (that they previously charged to PDVSA as subcontractors).

In other words, despite the assorted tax increases, so far Chávez has affected international capital interests much less than he has affected the country's old elite, which has lost much more. As a result, insofar as these capital interests are separate from the former elite, they have, while annoyed with Chávez, done relatively little to actively oppose him. There is much speculation that foreign companies might be financing opposition groups, but as yet no evidence has emerged that this is the case. The role that international capital might play in opposing Chávez would probably increase, though, if Chávez radicalizes his economic program.

Normally transnational capital has much more effective means at its disposal than engaging in an active political opposition, such as through the financing or organizing of opposition groups. That is, in most countries around the world transnational capital can force governments to do their bidding by merely engaging in an investment strike.[18] This method, which has been used over and over again around the world, with the active help of the International Monetary Fund, the World Bank, and the World Trade Organization, is much less effective in Venezuela. The reason an investment strike would be less effective in Venezuela than in other countries is because Venezuela has oil, which is interesting to foreign direct investment because even when heavily taxed, it can still provide enormous profits. Also, as long as the price of oil is high, Venezuela can finance much of its non-oil related investment domestically rather than having to rely on foreign sources of investment, as most other countries have to. In the end, while domestic and international capital is opposed to Chávez, their opposition is much more subdued and pragmatic than that of the old elites.

External Obstacles 3: US Imperialism

All too often analysts confuse transnational capital interests with US imperial interests. Such confusion is very understandable because often the two coincide, such as during the Clinton presidency, which was a presidency based on unifying US imperial interests with those of transnational capital.[19] As such, Clinton and Chávez were able to establish a *modus vivendi*, especially since Chávez did not attack any US capital interests. This changed, however, when Bush came to power in 2000, with an administration to which the pursuit of its conservative and imperial ideology was more important than the pursuit of US capital interests.

Chávez has been much more openly opposed to Bush's foreign policy than he was to that of the Clinton administration because Bush is pursuing a more imperial foreign policy. Chávez rarely misses an opportunity to strongly condemn US policy in Iraq and in Afghanistan, for example. Chávez has also been a consistent opponent of US trade policy, strongly fighting against the Free Trade Area of the Americas (FTAA) and favoring Latin American economic integration before making any trade agreements with the US. Another issue that probably has the Bush administration concerned about Venezuela is Chávez's efforts to provide oil to the Chinese market, in case that oil is being provided at the expense of the United States.

US interference in Venezuela on an overt level thus quickly became an issue with the Bush administration, with its constant unfounded accusations that Chávez was supporting Colombian guerrillas, allowing Muslim radicals to move about freely in Venezuela, and that Chávez was funding opposition movements throughout Latin America. The interference in Venezuelan affairs came to a head with the April 2002 coup, in which the US was one of the few countries in the world to welcome the two-day coup regime (El Salvador and Colombia being the other two). Also, much evidence points to the possibility that the US was more actively involved in supporting the coup organizers.

While the Bush administration denied any covert interference in Venezuela, the overt interference continued throughout 2002 and 2003, mostly via spokespersons such as Roger Noriega, Otto Reich, or the head of the US Southern Command, General James Hill, who would all make various accusations against the Chávez government. More recently, ever since early 2004, activists in the US have uncovered documents that show in great detail how the US, via the National Endowment for Democracy, USAID, and Development Alternatives, Inc., are funding Venezuela's opposition, at the rate of five million dollars per year or more.

According to the US government, such funding, which the US engages in countries all around the world, is perfectly legitimate in the name of "democracy promotion." To Chávez supporters such democracy promotion has no legitimacy because Venezuela is, after all, a functioning democracy, which is at least as democratic, if not more so, as the US. The US and Venezuela's opposition deny this of course. However, the US government practice (and also of other governments and NGOs) is also being questioned because what democracy promotion does is to create a civil society in the image of its international funders.[20] This foreign-funded civil society might then act more in the interests of its funders than of the national citizenry, casting serious doubts on this civil society's legitimacy.

Civil Society and Democracy Promotion

Events in Venezuela and in other countries like it, where the US government and international foundations are funding civil society groups, raise serious issues as to how democracy is supposed to function and be funded. In the past two decades political scientists and theorists have argued that civil society is a crucial counterweight and corrective to the power of private enterprise and the power of the state.[21] In the wake of the "democratic revolutions" of Eastern Europe and of Latin America in the 1980s and late 1990s, which to a large extent were driven by the civil societies of the different countries, and the anti-globalization movement of the late 1990s, it seemed all too plausible that civil society (or social movements or the "Multitude," in the case of Hardt and Negri) was the new revolutionary subject, which would bring about a better society.

However, mostly hidden from public view, while political theorists were waxing poetic about civil society, the US government, multilateral organizations, and large foundations became major players in the world of civil society organizations. That is, although civil society organizations certainly played a crucial role in bringing about dramatic change in many countries, groups considered to be part of civil society, NGOs, were gradually brought into the orbit of US and European-dominated international foundations, via large grants. The grants to these NGOs played an important role in helping these groups bring about positive social change, in everything from women's rights, civil rights, the protection of indigenous populations, environmental protection, health care, education, etc.

The question the Venezuelan example raises, though, is whether the support of civil society—to a large extent through foreign funding—does not alter that civil society to reflect the interests and priorities of the funders. In other words, how legitimate is it for civil society to be funded and thus shaped by outside interests? That is not to say that such funding is necessarily illegitimate. However, political scientists, activists, and politicians ought to examine the question of just how far such support should be able to go. Would it be legitimate if foreign funders completely funded all civil society organizations of a country from scratch and thereby controlled every aspect of these organizations? One could say that as long as this funding comes from a variety of sources, the diversity of support will support a diverse civil society. But what if that is not the case? Where does one draw the line and how could one draw any lines in the first place? If 100% outside funding from just one political tendency is unacceptable, would 75% funding from two political tendencies be all right? Also, this is not to say that domestic funding of civil society groups is necessarily better (which the Chávez government does provide). Such funds also could predominantly come from one source that pursues one political interest.

Venezuela has not reached these extreme case scenarios. However, international funding of civil society organizations has gone quite far; with for example the estimate that from the US government alone comes at least $5 million per year, via NED and USAID. One ought to add to this the funds that come from other international foundations, such as the conservative German Konrad Adenauer foundation, which is said to have played an important role in supporting various opposition groups in Venezuela.

The Bush administration tried, unsuccessfully, to take its covert influence over Latin American countries a step further during the 35th General Assembly of the Organization of American States, which took place in June 2005, in Ft. Lauderdale. At this meeting the Bush administration proposed a "democracy monitoring" system, which would at follow how democratic the governments of OAS member countries were. This monitoring system would have the input of civil society organizations, which would also become associate members of the OAS. This proposal was roundly rejected, however, because most governments saw the threat this idea posed to their sovereignty and many believed that it was merely an attempt of the Bush administration to isolate the Chávez government in Venezuela.

Despite this setback for the Bush administration in trying to "promote democracy," an open debate needs to be launched in Venezuela (and in countries around the globe) as to if and how civil society funding should be regulated.[22] The bottom line, though, is that if funds from the US government build up a strong Venezuelan opposition, then such funding represents a clear external obstacle to the Bolivarian project. Whether this obstacle is legitimate is a separate question.

Coping with Internal and External Obstacles and Opportunities

Although the Bolivarian project has both obstacles and opportunities, it is very possible that the obstacles outweigh the opportunities. The main reason for this is that the obstacles form a vicious cycle, while the opportunities do not. That is, the external obstacles of US intervention and reckless opposition tend to strengthen Chavista siege-mentality, the political personalism around Chávez, and exclusionary patronage systems. These internal reactions, in turn, strengthen the opposition's desire to get rid of the government by any means necessary, thus completing the vicious cycle's positive feedback loop.

The opportunities, however, do not form a positive feedback loop, a virtuous cycle in this case, because Chávez's charisma and the delegitimation of the old regime do not strengthen the opposition's fragmentation or increase oil revenues. Actually, if anything, Chávez's charisma has the opposite effect from the effect it has on his supporters, causing his opponents to hate him with a similar passion as his supporters love him. In other words, his charisma serves as one of the main factors in unifying the opposition, thus diminishing the opportunity that the opposition's fragmentation represents to the Bolivarian project. The Bolivarian project will thus have to devise a conscious strategy for overcoming its internal and external obstacles because the existing opportunities will not eliminate the obstacles on their own.

Let us take a brief look at how the Chávez government might defuse the internal and external obstacles, so that it might break out of the vicious cycle it finds itself in every time there is a crisis.

Overcoming Patronage, Corruption, and State Inefficiency

The perhaps largest and most serious internal obstacle is the complex of issues surrounding clientelism, patronage, corruption, the weak rule of law, and inefficient public administration in Venezuela. These issues should be treated as a complex because they are so closely related to one another and a solution to any one of these will also help address the others. As mentioned earlier, the Chávez government has recognized that corruption (if not patronage) is a problem in the current government, but it does not have a clear and comprehensive conception of how to fight it. Rather, there are repeated admonishments that government officials should not engage in corruption and that the law should be strengthened or enforced better, but these admonishments and the lack of concrete action have been too weak to truly deal with the issue.

Instead, what the government needs to do is to recognize the magnitude of the problem and its multi-dimensionality and announce a major re-orientation in the fight against clientelism-patronage and corruption. One way to do this would be to appoint a multi-disciplinary task force, which would study the problem from all its angles and would be authorized to make policy recommendations, to whose implementation the government would commit itself before the recommendations are known. In other words, the Chávez government must recognize that the problem of corruption is not just an issue of lack of enforcement, but that it involves at least the following four problem areas: insufficient individual moral consciousness, fulfillment of needs, insufficient collective structures, and insufficient collective ethical culture.

By individual moral consciousness I mean to say that it is an issue that involves the moral development of individuals; whether they are mature enough to recognize that patronage or even corruption is wrong and whether they are able to resist the temptation to engage in such practices, even when presented with opportunities, material needs, or social pressures to do so. Generally, such moral consciousness is developed through education and so addressing this dimension means including education against patronage and corruption in all educational settings, from elementary school to university.

The dimension of fulfillment of needs means to address the fact that all too often corruption is the result of actual material needs, combined with the opportunity to fulfill that need. That is, many government officials in Venezuela are paid far below their corresponding level of responsibility and what the surrounding culture says they should be paid. As a result, there often is a tremendous gap between expectations and the means to fulfill these. Recently the government has increased salaries of public officials, but it is still quite common, for example, that police officers are paid barely more than the minimum wage and then engage in numerous corrupt activities in order to supplement their income. Even officials working at the highest levels of government such as advisors to the president, often earn little more than $1,000 per month, when the rent for a small apartment in a middle class Caracas neighborhood costs at least $500 per month. It should thus not be in the least surprising that if a government official who makes so little, but who might manage a budget of millions of dollars, is tempted to skim some of this off for him or herself.

The third dimension, of insufficient collective structures, is the one that is most talked about but is nonetheless terribly dysfunctional in Venezuela. It is well-known that Venezuela's judicial system, which has improved in recent years, still functions poorly. There are countless cases that seem to be swept under the carpet and never get resolved. The opposition in Venezuela complains that the only cases that are vigorously prosecuted are those involving individuals allied with the opposition. While this is not always the case, there seem to be many cases involving Chávez supporters that seem to have got lost, such as the case of the $1.5 million that came from a Spanish bank for Chávez's 1998 presidential campaign. On the other hand, the over 100 cases of assassinated pro-Chávez peasant leaders are all practically unresolved. In other words, the government must commit itself to a merciless and politically blind enforcement of the law. One has to recognize, though, that in Venezuela this is not the executive's area of responsibility, in that the Attorney General and the judiciary are independent of the executive. Still, insofar as there is cooperation between the National Assembly and the president, in terms of drawing up the country's budget, the president ought, first, to make sure that the judiciary and the Attorney General receive all the funds they need to prosecute all cases of corruption and political favoritism. Second, the president could also improve enforcement by improving the transparency of the financial accounting of the public administration.[23]

Finally, with regard to the fourth dimension of collective ethical culture, all too often it is not the individual actor whose moral restraint is lacking, but that of the surrounding culture, which encourages people to engage in political favoritism (patronage and clientelism) or corruption. Some areas of government provide strong encouragement for wrong-doing, so that no-one can be found blameless and so that no-one can accuse anyone else of wrongdoing. Also, certain circumstances, such as sabotage from political opponents within the public administration, make public employees more circumspect and careful with regard to the political affiliations of others, so that they see an objective need for political favoritism, as a means of avoiding sabotage. One way of dealing with such a collective ethical culture that encourages patronage and corruption is to engage in a public media campaign against it, so that the message of one's peers might be drowned out by a more compelling message.

Such a possible multi-pronged approach to the complex of patronage-clientelism, corruption, and the weak rule of law would go a long way in overcoming one of the Bolivarian project's greatest obstacles. In essence, it would involve nothing less than a complete overhaul of Venezuela's public administration. Many earlier governments have attempted such an overhaul, but they all failed, partly because they simply did not go far enough and partly because entrenched interests prevented reform.[24] The Chávez government would thus also need to engage in a careful study of these earlier efforts, to see what might be learnt from them.[25]

Overcoming Personalism and Top-Down Management

However, Chávez and his movement also need to address the other obstacles, personalistic politics and the tendencies towards top-down management. Eliminating these is crucial so as to make sure that there is no contradiction between the Bolivarian project's stated goal of creating a more participatory and more democratic society and the actual implementation of this goal. There are at least two ways this could be done.

First, Chávez needs to make sure that other leaders have the space to emerge beside him and are encouraged to do so. Chávez's constant rotation of ministers (though less so recently than in the earlier part of his presidency) and his recent consideration of changing the constitution to allow for an indefinite number of re-elections have only strengthened the dependency of the Bolivarian movement on Chávez. This is very unfortunate and the best way that Chávez, if he truly believes that a "revolution cannot depend on one man" (Chávez), could reverse this dependency is to strengthen the autonomy of his ministers, Governors, and leaders of the National Assembly and to completely renounce any aspirations to a third term in office.

Second, and perhaps more importantly, the Bolivarian movement needs a solid national and thoroughly democratic organization. While Chávez does have his MVR party, this is nothing more than an electoral machine for getting people to vote for MVR candidates and for turning people out to pro-Chávez demonstrations. Also, even though the party leadership insists that it is one of the few that is democratically legitimated by party members, this democratic legitimation process leaves much to be desired. For example, candidates for elected office are rarely chosen in a democratic nomination process. The only time a party nomination vote took place, for the 7 August 2005 local city council elections, fights broke out within the party over alleged irregularities.[26] No internal party vote ever took place for nominating candidates for the October 2004 governors' and mayoral vote, nor for the December 2005 National Assembly deputy vote.

Aside from the relative lack of nomination processes for elected office, the MVR does not hold party debates about its political program. In this, though, the MVR is no different from any other political party in Venezuela (or most of Latin America, for that matter). It is practically impossible to find the political programs of any political parties in Venezuela, whether opposition or pro-Chávez. Rather, Chávez's program is practically entirely dictated from above, decided upon mainly within a small circle of Chávez's advisors. Having a national political party that actively debates political issues would greatly contribute to increasing the participatory nature of the Bolivarian movement. Also, it would encourage constructive criticism from within the movement and would thus counter tendencies towards personalism and top-down management. Strengthening the MVR as an organized political movement, with democracy and internal debate would also make the movement far less vulnerable to either the eventual or the sudden departure of Chávez as the party's and the movement's leader.

Overcoming External Obstacles

While the internal obstacles are formidable, so are the external ones, particularly of US government interference and of the former ruling elite's continuing (though much weakened) refusal to recognize Chávez as the legitimate president. Here, though, given the Chávez government's success both in terms of its foreign policy and in terms of its defeat of opposition challenges, there is not much the government could do differently that would allow it to overcome these obstacles better than it has so far. The only suggestion would be that Chávez's rhetoric, which plays well among his supporters, often undermines his successful strategies because it alienates important allies that have already been won over. Chávez would thus be well advised to moderate his rhetoric on occasion, so as not to undo earlier achievements.

Changing Venezuela by Taking Power

The Chávez presidency and the Bolivarian project are unique in recent world history. The Chávez government is the first, anywhere in the world, at least since the 1980 Sandinista revolution in Nicaragua, that is explicitly anti-capitalist. This does not mean that it has found a way to overcome capitalism, but in its intent it is trying to find a way to do so. In the process, the Bolivarian project has put the issue of state power back onto the agenda of progressive or leftist politics.[27] This, by itself, is very significant because ever since the fall of state socialism in Eastern Europe, state power has become something almost taboo for the left. Many in the anti-globalization movement, the World Social Forum, and various national social movements, such as the Zapatistas have subscribed to the slogan, "change the world without taking power."[28] To some extent this notion is understandable in a world in which the anti-capitalist socialist left (i.e., not the social-democratic left) has rarely managed to win democratic victories, especially in the industrialized North.

Venezuela, though, challenges the notion that the world cannot be changed by taking power. Of course, it still remains to be seen how successful the Bolivarian project will be in the long run or if it too will fail, either due to its internal problems or due to external assaults. The obstacles to creating long-lasting and transformative social change are truly formidable. It is thus unlikely that Venezuela will completely transcend capitalism or social democracy. But this is unnecessary for the historical significance of the project—the Bolivarian project is important also because it is currently practically the only project in the world that is in power and that challenges both the capitalist status quo and the state socialism of the past. That is, Venezuela is recuperating the utopian energies, which became exhausted with the failures of state socialism, of social democracy, and of neo-liberal capitalism, merely by trying a different and as yet relatively unexplored path.

If the Bolivarian project succeeds in the medium to long term and if it manages to overcome its internal obstacles, then it might very well forge a path towards a socialism of the twenty-first century, where economic and political democracy are participatory, mostly via cooperatives and self-management, and social justice and distribution are achieved via a participatory allocation process, instead of the market. The lack of a clear vision in Venezuela as to how the allocation problem is to be solved means, though, that in the medium-term market competition and private enterprise will still play an important role in Venezuela.

However, it is very possible that the Chávez government will not be able to implement its longer-term evolving vision. Chávez has repeatedly stated that it is his goal to eliminate poverty and to complete the Bolivarian revolution in Venezuela by the year 2021, exactly 20 years after the start of Chávez's first full term in office. This is a long time-span in which much can happen. As long as there is no concrete plan for how to overcome the obstacles mentioned in this chapter, it will be practically impossible for the project to succeed by 2021. That is, as long as there is no clear conception on how to overcome Venezuela's patronage culture, its weak rule of law, its over-dependency on oil revenues, its ossified public administration, and the attacks coming from an imperialist United States, the Bolivarian project is not going to achieve its goals. It is possible, though, that it can master the rough waters ahead, with the help of people around the world who are paying attention to what is happening in Venezuela, who make the Chávez government more aware of its shortcomings while also helping it ward off attacks from the outside.

Epilogue: 2007—Year of Transition to Twenty-first Century Socialism?

Following his re-election on December 3, 2006, with 62.9% of the vote, Chávez made a series of far-reaching policy announcements for his new term in office, which appeared to further radicalize his presidency. First, two weeks after his re-election, he announced the formation of a new socialist political party that would unite all the forces that support him.[1] Second, when he swore in his new cabinet in early January, he promised the nationalization of key sectors of the economy.[2] Third, he stated that the broadcast license of one of the country's main opposition-oriented television stations (RCTV) would not be renewed.[3] Fourth, he proposed the reform of the 1999 constitution to make it more socialist. And fifth, he asked the National Assembly for the power to pass laws by decree.[4] These were all dramatic new announcements that the Venezuelan opposition and foreign mainstream observers immediately characterized as changes that would definitively turn Venezuela into an "elected dictatorship."[5]

What, though, do these announcements really mean for Venezuela's future? Will they contribute towards the establishment of "twenty-first century socialism," will they turn Venezuela into the opposition's long-announced state socialist (or "Castro-communist") dictatorship, or will they lead Venezuela towards something completely different? To answer these questions, we need to briefly examine each of these announcements one-by-one and see how they fit or fail to fit with the ideals Chávez has set out for twenty-first century socialism.

A Unified Socialist Party of Venezuela

As has become normal for news coverage of Venezuela, Chávez's announcement that he wanted to create a "Unified Socialist Party of

Venezuela" (PSUV) was immediately misinterpreted in the most authoritarian terms possible, that he wanted to turn Venezuela into a one-party
state. Far from this, all he was calling for was for all parties that support
his presidency, which are his own MVR, the major coalition partners
PPT, Podemos, and PCV, plus the 20 or so tiny parties that support him,
to unify into one party.

Chávez explained his motivation for doing so as being based on the
need to both democratize the Bolivarian movement and to make its
decision-making processes more efficient and more transparent. Several
times in the past, Chávez had explained that he was "tired" of settling
disputes between factions that support him and of naming candidates for
mayor or other elected posts, based on a list that MVR and other party
leaders gave him. Instead, the new PSUV is supposed be "the most
democratic" party, in Latin America, in which all nominations and
policy goals are decided via internal party debate and elections.

Chávez placed tremendous pressure on all pro-government parties to
dissolve and to have their membership join the PSUV. However, the top
leadership of PPT, Podemos, and PCV, whose combined support was
around 15% in the December 2006 presidential elections, all said that
they would prefer to wait and see the new party's political program and
by-laws before taking the leap into the unknown. A less charitable
interpretation of their hesitation is that dissolving their parties would
potentially mean a tremendous loss of power for these party leaders.
They would not know if they would be elected to high office again and
would no longer be able to act as powerbrokers in the processes for
nominating ministers or candidates for elected office.[6] Supporting the
latter thesis is the fact that numerous prominent but out-of-power
members of these three parties publicly renounced their membership
of them and announced that they would join the newly forming PSUV.[7]
Meanwhile, Chávez has said those who did not join the PSUV are "free
to leave" the coalition[8] and are "cowards" and "counter-revolutionary."[9]
To organize the PSUV, Chávez outlined a nine-month process, from
March to December 2007.[10]

If the PSUV manages to take off as planned, as a grassroots democratic
party, where party bosses who manipulate nominations and elections
processes are a thing of the past, then the PSUV would indeed be the
"most democratic" party of Latin America. However, old habits die hard
and it is possible that the new PSUV will replicate patronage structures

within the party, despite Chávez's best intentions and despite carefully crafted by-laws. There is nothing—other than the party members themselves—that will prevent members from electing old-style party bosses, who then go on to trade influence for favors, making ill-conceived recommendations for candidates or policy platforms to Chávez and to voters in exchange for future support. In other words, only the degree of determination of Venezuelans to overcome patronage politics will determine the party's actual success in becoming truly democratic. While it has gotten off to a good start, with the naming of a non-party-bosses commission to start organizing the party, which way the party will eventually go is too early to tell at the time of writing.

Nationalizations

The second controversial announcement Chávez made upon his re-election was that "key sectors" of the Venezuelan economy would be nationalized. While Chávez has threatened to nationalize various sectors of the economy before, he did not announce any nationalizations prior to his re-election and so the announcement came as a bit of a surprise. The three sectors that would be nationalized immediately, said Chávez in January 2007, were telecommunications, energy, and oil production.

Once again, the private national and international media machines began speculating that Venezuela would now expropriate these sectors without compensation, thus furthering their argument that Chávez has now become the definitive "Castro-communist" dictator. However, two short months later, in March, the first outlines of the nationalization process were presented and in all cases, the owners of the affected companies would be compensated in accordance with a mutual agreement between the concerned parties.

The nationalization of the telecommunications sector actually only affected the former state-owned telephone company CANTV, whose main stock holder was the US-based company Verizon (28.5%), and not the two main competing cellphone networks. Verizon agreed to sell its CANTV stock to the government for $572 million.[11] The remaining shareholders were small investors, to whom a similar offer per share was made and who sold their shares to the government for just under $800 million.

The main rationale for the nationalization of CANTV was that in order to promote the development of the country, particularly of its interior, the government needed to ensure that land-based phone lines would be provided to less profitable areas. When CANTV was privatized in the 1990s it had committed itself to do this, but, government officials said, it had reneged on this commitment. Also, the government promised to lower phone rates, which had been climbing inexorably ever since the company was privatized. With CANTV back in state hands and an already existing state-owned fiber-optic network throughout the country, CANTV stands to become one of the more technologically advanced and powerful telecommunications companies in Latin America.

Next, the government proceeded to nationalize the regionalized electricity companies that are mainly responsible for the distribution of electricity, but not its generation, which is and always has been in state hands. The power companies quickly came to an agreement with the government and sold their stock at a mutually agreed price. Here too, the rationale for the nationalization was that the government wanted to ensure that electricity distribution would reach into the underserved interior of the country.

Symbolically, though, the most important nationalization was that of the remaining privately controlled oil fields, which were located in the extra heavy oil fields of the Orinoco Oil Belt. In the 1990s, during the so-called *apertura* or oil opening, the Venezuelan government had allowed foreign oil companies to invest heavily in the Orinoco Oil Belt, creating four joint ventures with six major transnational oil companies (Total, ChevronTexaco, ExxonMobil, British Petroleum, Veba Oel, Conoco-Phillips) and Venezuela's own PDVSA. In each of these joint ventures PDVSA had the minority participation of around 30%. As part of the objective of "renationalizing" Venezuela's oil production, Chávez said that PDVSA's minority participation would be turned into a minimum 60% participation, so that PDVSA would have a controlling share in each venture. On May 1 Chávez announced that all companies involved in these projects, except for ConocoPhillips, had agreed to the new arrangement.[12]

This nationalization process, while fairly moderate in its conception, in that it merely transformed minority state participation into majority participation, was enormous both in terms of its financial scope and its symbolic power. That is, financially it required PDVSA to spend billions of dollars and it is thus far more expensive to Venezuela than the other nationalizations.[13] And symbolically, the nationalization was significant because it represented the Venezuelan state's takeover of the last remaining foreign-controlled oil fields. This takeover was accomplished in three phases: first, with the defeat of the 2002/03 oil industry shutdown the Chávez government wrested control of the oil industry from the old neo-liberal oriented management. Second, it turned 32 "service agreements" for production in marginal oil fields into joint ventures with a majority PDVSA stake. Then, third, it turned the existing Orinoco Oil Belt joint ventures into PDVSA-controlled projects. Thus, as of May 1, Chávez was able to state, "Imperialism dominated our basic industry, our energy resources, and our natural resources for a long time. That is over today . . . Today is the end of that time when all our natural resources always ended up in the hands of anyone but the Venezuelan people."[14]

RCTV

Another announcement that proved to opponents of Chávez that he was leading the country towards dictatorship was the decision not to renew the broadcast license (or concession, as it is called in Venezuela) of the country's most popular television channel RCTV. To government critics this was the most definitive proof that freedom of expression was being limited in Venezuela. To the government and its supporters, though, the termination of RCTV's broadcast rights was long overdue because of the channel's participation in the coup attempt, in the oil industry shutdown, and because of its frequent violations of broadcast regulations.

International press freedom groups, such as the Inter-American Press Association (IAPA), Reporters without Borders (RSF), and the Committee to Protect Journalists (CPJ), among others, also condemned the government's decision. The IAPA said, "Venezuelan President Hugo Chávez's drive to suppress press freedom . . . is continuing with ever more serious and defiant threats and incidents. At this point, the president, who controls all branches of the government, moves directly to close media outlets, as in the case of Radio Caracas Televisión (RCTV), the most important channel in the country."[15]

The government's justification for not renewing RCTV's license is twofold. First, RCTV no longer deserves a broadcast license because of its participation in the coup and the oil industry shutdown and because of its many infractions of existing broadcast laws. Second, the measure itself is purely administrative—that is, no review process is legally required—because the decision to grant broadcast licenses is at the government's discretion. In other words, the opposition's argument that the Venezuelan government is violating norms of freedom of speech is based purely on ethical grounds, but not legal ones. One can see this even in RCTV's main defense argument, which does not challenge the government's discretion in renewing broadcast licenses, but which claims that its license does not expire until 2020.[16]

The "Organic Law on Telecommunications" states quite clearly that, "A concession for the use of the radioelectric spectrum will not be provided to those who, despite having been chosen in conformity with the modalities established in this law are, nonetheless, involved in the following situations: . . . . 5. When grave circumstances arise relating to the security of the state that, in the judgment of the President of the Republic, make the provision [of a concession] unsuitable."[17] Since no review process is indicated in the law, it would appear that the President's decision is somewhat discretional. RCTV is, of course, taking the matter to the Supreme Court, where it is also challenging the "non-renewal of its broadcast license." It is thus still theoretically possible that the Supreme Court will rule that the non-renewal is illegal.

With this argument the government could, in theory, refuse to renew the licenses of the remaining three coup-supporting TV stations: Venevisión, Globovisión, and Televen. Since the coup and especially since the 2004 presidential recall referendum, Venevisión and Televen, however, have significantly moderated their anti-government stance, thus making it difficult for the government to argue that these still represent a threat to the state. Globovisión, the 24-hour news channel, has continued on the same anti-government line as before and could thus face the possibility of losing its license. This is a long way off, though, because its license does not expire until 2014.[18]

Since the legal situation of this case is fairly clear (Chávez has the legal authority to not renew RCTV's license), the main question actually revolves around whether closing RCTV is good for freedom of speech in Venezuela. No doubt, denying RCTV its broadcast license will decrease the amount of dissent coming from the country's old elite.[19] But does this mean that freedom of speech is being restricted? Taking RCTV off the air does restrict freedom of speech if you believe that this is measured by the freedom of those who own the resources for using the airwaves. If, however, freedom of speech means that every view—regardless of its holder's personal wealth—has an equal opportunity to be broadcast, then the degree of freedom of speech in Venezuela actually depends on what RCTV will be replaced with.

This was once actually the philosophy with regard to the use of the airwaves in much of the world, especially in Western Europe prior to the 1980s. At that time, in Western Europe, private broadcast media were generally not even allowed and public radio and television dominated the airwaves. The complete prohibition of private broadcast media in many countries was never accompanied with the claim that these countries restricted freedom of speech. More than that, public media was believed to bring about more freedom of speech and more diversity than private media ever would. It was only in the 1980s, when neo-liberalism and privatization became ascendant, that restricting private broadcast media became synonymous with lack of freedom of speech.

In other words, if Venezuela were to replace RCTV with a truly public television channel, as opposed to a government TV channel (of which it now has several: VTV, Vive, ANTV, TeleSur, and Avila TV),[20] then freedom of speech would be enhanced in Venezuela, not lessened. This is exactly what the Chávez government has promised. Telecommunications Minister Jesse Chacón has explained on several occasions that the channel would be publicly controlled and not government controlled. By this he seems to imply that it would be more democratically controlled than either government TV or private TV are. Whether this will actually be the case is, as of this writing, too early to tell. It should be noted, though, just how strongly public opinion has been manipulated by the private media, both in Venezuela and around the world, so that replacing private TV with public TV could in any way be conceived of as a restriction of freedom of speech.[21] This judgment can only be made after the government presents the organization of the new channel, not before.

Aside from the free speech implications, RCTV's going off the air also has an unusual political ramification for Chávez. This is the first time in Chávez's presidency that he is pushing ahead with what seems to be a highly unpopular decision. According to a poll by the opposition-oriented polling company Datanalisis, about 70% of Venezuelans disapprove of RCTV's license not being renewed, even while Chávez himself continues to enjoy approval among 65% of the population.[22] The reason for this disparity is that RCTV is a channel that broadcasts some of the country's most popular television shows, such as the game show "Who Wants to be a Millionaire?" and numerous soap operas. That is, disapproval of the license non-renewal has nothing to do with the channel's politics, but with the potential loss of favorite programs. Taking RCTV off the air will thus probably mean a loss of popularity for Chávez. Early indications are, though, that the new channel, which is to be called "Venezuelan Social Television" (Tves), will attempt to replicate some of this popular programming.[23]

The Enabling law

As if party unification, nationalizations, and taking a private TV channel off the air weren't enough to push the buttons of the opposition and the world's mainstream media, Chávez also announced that he would ask the National Assembly for an "enabling law," which would allow him to "rule by decree" for a period of 18 months. Actually, "rule by decree" was a media misnomer that conjures images of dictators who are enabled to issue decrees on just about anything, without constitutional or political limits. In Venezuela, though, enabling laws, which have a long tradition,[24] are limited by the constitution, have a limited duration, and contain the possibility of revision or revocation by the National Assembly, the Supreme Court, or by popular referendum.

In this case, the enabling law that the National Assembly passed on January 31, 2007, allows Chávez to pass law decrees in eleven broadly defined areas for a period of 18 months. The areas cover practically everything, such as "transformation of the state," "popular participation" in social and economic policies, the fight against corruption, "economic and social policy," "finances and taxation," "citizen and judicial security," "science and technology," "territorial order," "security and defense," "infrastructure," and "energy policy."[25] Vice-president Jorge Rodriguez estimated that the final number of laws the president will pass will reach a similar amount as the last time Chávez had an enabling law, when he passed 49 laws. Chávez justified the law on the basis that the population had voted for twenty-first century socialism on December 3, 2006, and that this required too many changes in too little time for the slow-moving National Assembly to process.

As an example of the types of law decrees that needed to be introduced, Chávez mentioned Venezuela's Code of Commerce law, which is a "symbol of capitalism" and "was written over 100 years ago, in 1904 . . . . [the last modification] to the law was made in 1955, when Venezuela was governed by [dictator] General Marcos Perez Jimenez. What kind of socialism will we make with a Commerce Code of this type?"[26]

For the opposition and for outside observers, this enabling law was another affront to democracy because it circumvented the National Assembly. Considering that the National Assembly consists entirely of Chávez supporters because of the opposition's boycott of the December 2005 National Assembly elections, it is not too clear why having Chávez pass the laws instead of the assembly would make such a dramatic difference for democracy in Venezuela. Still, opposition leaders such as Teodoro Petkoff compared the enabling law to the enabling law that Adolf Hitler received from the German Bundestag when he became dictator.[27] There are many crucial differences, though, between that law and Chávez's law, which make them completely different types. First, and most importantly, Hitler's enabling law allowed him to pass laws that violated or even changed the constitution. Second, Hitler had already suspended civil liberties as a result of the Reichstags Fire Decree. Third, no revision or revocation of Hitler's decrees was possible. In all three cases, the opposite is the case with Chávez's enabling law. Petkoff's parallel between the two acts thus lacks any basis in reality.

The common opposition concern that Chávez might use the enabling law to pass repressive law decrees is perhaps more understandable, given that the Supreme Court and the National Assembly are controlled by Chávez supporters and thus appear unlikely to challenge Chávez's law decrees. However, there are at least two reasons to doubt this would happen. First, when Chávez had an enabling law in 2000/01, none of the forty-nine laws he passed then were repressive in any way. More than that, many of these laws ensured greater economic democracy in that they contributed to the redistribution of Venezuela's wealth, whether via the land reform law, the hydrocarbons law, or the fishing law, for example. Besides, with a very loyal National Assembly there is no reason to believe that if Chávez wanted to pass repressive laws, he would need an enabling law to do so.[28] Second, contrary to opposition analysts' thinking, there is a powerful force in Venezuelan politics that can rescind any law decree Chávez passes: the Venezuelan people. According to the 1999 constitution, any law may be put to a vote if 10% of registered voters petition for it. Law decrees have an even lower requirement, of only 5% of registered voters. If put to a vote, a simple majority can then decide to rescind the law decree.

There is, however, a more realistic concern about the enabling law, which has to do with its internal contradictions and the effect it has on Venezuelan politics. That is, first, one of the law's main purposes is to allow Chávez to pass laws that bring about twenty-first century socialism and participatory democracy more rapidly. However, there is an inverse relationship between the principles of participation and of efficiency and so the enabling law emphasizes efficiency at the expense of participation. It is thus justified to ask whether passing laws that are supposed to enhance participation and democracy via less deliberation and participation really makes sense and whether such a process will lead to good laws.

Second, by passing laws as decrees Chávez risks that these laws will have less legitimacy than they would otherwise have had, had they been passed via the normal legislative process. Even though the opposition is not represented in the National Assembly, the less national debate there is over any given issue, the more likely the opposition will attempt to challenge Chávez on that issue, just as they did with the forty-nine law decrees of 2001. Although the opposition, at the time of writing (May, 2007), appears to be too weak to mount an effective political challenge, it is precisely this weakness that could cause it to resort to extremist measures, such as violence. There are increasing indications that more radical sectors of the opposition might be seeking to assassinate Chávez or to initiate some sort of terrorist activity.[29] Such a development could eventually lead to the formation of a "contra" type of terrorist army, as existed in Nicaragua during the Sandinista government. In his effort to make more radical changes as quickly as possible, Chávez could very well end up with more problems than he bargained for.

Other Projects for 2007

The previously mentioned projects for 2007 were merely the most important ones that were part of a package of projects that Chávez announced at his inauguration in January 2007 and which he called the "five motors" for establishing twenty-first century socialism in Venezuela. The first motor is the previously mentioned enabling law, which included law decrees on nationalizing the remaining private oil projects, CANTV, and the electricity sector. The second motor is the reform of the 1999 constitution, the third is a public education campaign, the fourth is the reorganization of political jurisdictions within Venezuela, and the fifth is the "explosion of communal power."

Chávez immediately went about appointing presidential commissions to work on all five of these motors, but unfortunately did not provide specifics as to exactly what each one of them would do. The previously mentioned enabling law included law decrees on the nationalizations mentioned above, but beyond that he did not say exactly what the other laws would be. Similarly, Chávez provided only the most general outline for the constitutional reform, mainly mentioning the proposal to eliminate the limitation on allowing the president to be re-elected only once, for two consecutive six-year terms. Other issues Chávez suggested that would be in the constitutional reform were the introduction of a new form of collective property and a stronger prohibition on the nationalization of the country's oil industry. The proposed reform would be presented to the country sometime in mid-2007 and then voted upon, following a public debate, in early 2008.

The third "motor" of a socialist public education campaign (*jornada*), called "morals and enlightenment" (*moral y luces*) would send out "brigades" to teach the Venezuelan population about the thought of Simon Bolivar, of his teacher Simon Rodriguez, and Ezequiel Zamora. It would also teach about Latin American and socialist thought in general. According to Chávez, this project is an absolute necessity for creating twenty-first century socialism because, "There will be no revolution without revolutionary ideology, there will be no socialism without socialist, communitarian, and social consciousness that will allow us to heal the country."[30]

The education campaign will be organized via study circles of ten to thirty people who will discuss and study the seven strategic lines of the National Plan Simon Bolivar, 2007–2021: Socialist Ethics, Supreme Happiness, the Socialist Model of Production, Socialist Protagonist Democracy, New Internal Geopolitics, Energy Power, and Global Geopolitics.[31] The study groups are supposed to meet once a week for four hours. Also, thousands of promoters who are organized by the presidential commission "morals and enlightenment" have been assigned to fan out throughout the country to promote the organization of these study circles.

The fourth motor, "new geometry of power," Chávez described as the "socialist reordering of the nation's geo-politics." By this he meant the "politico-territorial division of the country,"[32] in terms of analyzing and possibly changing the boundaries of municipalities and potentially states. Venezuela's system of municipalities is very poorly organized in that some have over a million inhabitants and others have only a few thousand. The result is a very uneven distribution of state resources and public administration, since these are organized on the basis of municipalities. The idea would be to create a more even distribution of municipalities so that the political organization of the country is more even.

Finally, the fifth motor, "the explosion of communal power," Chávez said, is the most important motor because it represents popular (grassroots) power, which is, "the soul, nerve, bone, meat, and essence of Bolivarian democracy, of revolutionary democracy, of true democracy." As a step in the direction towards increasing the power of communities, Chávez proposed the creation of "federal cities," where the direct and participatory democracy of communal councils would replace the representative democracy of mayors and city councils. The idea would be to experiment with this type of governance and see if it could eventually be expanded to all of Venezuela. Parallel to this experiment, Chávez proposed the strengthening of the power of communal councils in the whole country, so that these go beyond the immediately local. Here the idea would be to create associations of communal councils on a state and national level.[33] Whether the communal councils on the state and national level would completely supplant the power of elected representatives or merely complement them is not clear yet. However, Chávez said that what needs to be done is to "head towards a social state and leave the old structures of the bourgeois capitalist state, which places brakes on revolutionary impulses."[34]

2007: Year of Transition to Twenty-first Century Socialism?

Few except for the most radical leftists would deny that Chávez's political program has radicalized significantly since he was re-elected in December 2006. He has moved forward with re-founding his political movement, launched new nationalizations, is promising a thorough reform of the constitution and the country's laws so as to further dismantle the country's old political and economic institutions, and continues to challenge the power of the country's old elite, by not renewing the license of RCTV. But does this apparent increased radicalism move the country closer towards something that could legitimately be called twenty-first century socialism?

Indeed, many of the measures only look radical given the conservative context of the early twenty-first century, in which privatization and political demobilization appear to be the norm in most countries around the world. If Chávez had not renewed RCTV's license to create a public TV channel and if he had nationalized key industries thirty years ago, hardly anyone would have considered the move radical or even dictatorial. It is thus fair to say that these two moves, by themselves, are hardly radical and not particularly deserving of the label twenty-first century socialism, because one of the things such a socialism was not supposed to involve was greater state control over civil society and the economy. However, one might consider these moves to be necessary pre-conditions for the establishment of twenty-first century socialism.[35]

Of course, without defining twenty-first century socialism it is impossible to say whether Venezuela is moving in this direction. Building on statements Chávez and many of the main intellectuals around him have made, though, it is possible to outline a few basic institutional elements that twenty-first century socialism ought to embody.[36] First, if twenty-first century socialism means the deepening of democracy, as Chávez says, it ought to enable every individual's ability to be self-managed, whether at work, as a consumer, or in the political sphere. Second, the previous point means that ownership and control of the means of production must be collective and democratic. Third—also deriving from the first point—is that the state must be organized so that it is truly independent of particular and powerful private interests and is only accountable to the people. Fourth, given the material inequality and thus private centers of power that markets produce, new mechanisms of distribution and allocation must be found that instead decrease inequality.

Using these four points as rough guidelines for the way towards twenty-first century socialism, one can say that self-management is certainly being strengthened in the political sphere, via the communal councils. However, so far, not much has happened recently to move the workplace in this direction. That is, even though CANTV, PDVSA, and the electric companies have been renationalized, little or nothing has happened in terms of internally democratizing these enterprises. While there has been a movement towards greater self-management in other areas, such as through the enormous growth of the cooperative movement and the worker takeover of several bankrupt factories, key sectors of Venezuela's economy are still managed in the typical capitalist top-down style. The same goes for the public administration in general.[37]

With regard to the democratization and self-management of the political sphere, the deepening of the communal councils in Venezuelan political life clearly continues to move forward in 2007, thereby potentially strengthening this aspect of twenty-first century socialism. The reason, though, this is still only a potential and not completely fulfilled is because one of the key issues about the communal councils has still not been resolved, which is the danger of patronage-clientelism. That is, as long as there is no impartial appeals process or other assurance that the councils' funding does not go only to pro-government councils, there is a very real and serious danger that old patronage-clientelist structures will be recreated, whereby government benefits are exchanged for political support.

However, on the positive side, the Venezuelan state is now more independent than ever of powerful private interests. There is no revolving door between private industry and the government as there used to be and big business, whether domestic or international, clearly has little power over the government, unlike during the pre-Chávez era. This greater independence creates space for greater citizen involvement and meaningful participation in self-governance. Also, whether the television channel that replaces RCTV will be truly plural and democratically controlled or merely another government channel will be a further indicator for how brave the government is in letting go of control and turning it over to the people.

Finally, regarding the fourth point, of developing non-market distribution and allocation mechanisms, the only one that has been strengthened in 2007 is the role of the state, through its redistribution of wealth via nationalization, taxes, social programs, and land reform. Non-state-based and non-market-based forms of allocation (such as presented in the appendix, in the form of participatory economics) are still nearly entirely outside the scope of discussion, let alone implementation.

Aside from the question about the extent to which the new policies move towards twenty-first century socialism, one should also examine whether these policies help overcome the obstacles to twenty-first century socialism that were described in Chapter 6 of this book. In particular, do these recent moves help overcome the three key internal obstacles of personalism, patronage, and top-down management?

The most important recent development in this regard is the creation of the United Socialist Party of Venezuela (PSUV), which has the potential to overcome personalism and top-down management, if the party is organized in a truly grassroots democratic fashion. That is, if party leaders and the party program are directly accountable to the party's membership, then this would go a long way towards diminishing the Bolivarian movement's dependence on Chávez and thus counteract his top-down leadership style. Party leaders would rise more on the basis of their personal abilities and in consonance with the members that elect them than on the basis of their uncritical support of Chávez. Also, the Socialist Bolivarian movement would have an organizational and ideological coherence that no longer depends on Chávez's leadership for its unity.

Unfortunately, while the creation of the PSUV helps move the Bolivarian movement beyond its dependence on Chávez, this same movement is also proposing an amendment to Venezuela's constitution, so that the president may be re-elected more than once. Allowing for an indefinite number of re-elections would postpone the movement's need to overcome its dependence on Chávez and would potentially reinforce the negative consequences this dependence brings with it.

With regard to overcoming Venezuela's political culture of patronage, it is quite possible that even a highly democratically organized PSUV could evolve into a patronage vehicle, as long as the state is not reformed. Patronage culture is deeply embedded in Venezuela and in Latin America in general and Venezuela has had a long history in which patronage did not depend so much on support for the president, but on membership of one of the two dominant parties, AD and Copei. If the PSUV becomes the dominant political force in Venezuela, it will be very tempting for managers in the public administration to ensure loyalty by hiring only party members (currently, membership in any of the governing parties does not play this role). More than that, it could even become a means for deciding who receives state services.

Whether Venezuela and the Bolivarian Socialist movement overcome this temptation will depend on a reform of the state, such that public servants implement government policies regardless of their own personal political affiliations and so that those hiring public servants also do so regardless of political affiliation.[38] This means that the reform of the state will depend more on the training of new public servants than on actual structural changes (although these are needed too). One of the areas of the 2007 enabling law precisely covers reform of the public administration. However, since the law decrees covering this area have not yet been presented, it is not possible to know whether they will address the problems mentioned here.

The source of many of the above mentioned problems is directly related to the Bolivarian movement's success until now: President Hugo Chávez. While some analysts would say that his success comes from his populism,[39] it seems more useful to see it as being rooted in his charisma. Certainly, these two concepts are closely related, in that charisma is generally seen as an essential component of populism, but by emphasizing the role of charisma, we can more clearly see how it creates problems of personalism, patronage, and *caudillismo*, while at the same time it also makes possible a radical transformation of the society.[40]

It is Chávez's charisma that managed to unify an otherwise extremely internally divided left in Venezuela and which to a large extent has contributed to his winning one election after another (the other key factor being his government's actual policies that promoted the social and political inclusion of the country's poor majority). At the same time, it is this charisma that creates an overdependence of the movement on Chávez, for giving it unity, and it thus creates a very personalistic politics, where faithfulness to the Bolivarian project, loyalty to Chávez, and uncritical acceptance of all of Chávez's policies are seen to be one and the same thing. This personalism, together with the subversive efforts by opposition sectors to overthrow Chávez, produces a need to protect the government from subversion and combines with the pre-existing patronage culture to reproduce patronage structures within the new society that Chávez and his supporters want to create.

In other words, the Bolivarian project faces a contradictory situation in which, on the one hand, it would never be where it is without Chávez, his charisma, and his strategic vision, and on the other hand, the movement's dependence on Chávez and his charisma reproduces some of the worst aspects of the previous regime that the movement set out to overcome. Still, despite this contradictory situation, Venezuela's Bolivarian and—as of recently—Bolivarian Socialist project, remains one of the best beacons of hope for a newly reinvigorated left in Latin America. As the Chávez government moves forward and experiments and sometimes stumbles with new forms of politico-economic organization, it leads by example and provides inspiration that a better world is indeed possible.

Appendix:
What is Twenty-first Century Socialism?

A veces pienso que todo el pueblo
es un muchacho que va corriendo
tras la esperanza que se le va
la sangre joven y el sueño viejo
pero dejando de ser pendejo
esa esperanza será verdad [1]

—Alí Primera,
Canción Mansa para un Pueblo Bravo

Within Venezuela, there is no real answer to or consensus about what twenty-first century socialism is. Rather, there are some indicators as to what President Chávez and his supporters might mean by the term. As we will see shortly, though, Chávez's rather vague definition, which he says is deliberate, provides us only with a set of ideals or goals that do not give us enough material to evaluate whether Venezuela is actually heading towards something that merits the designation of twenty-first century socialism.

Thus, so as to provide a stronger basis for comparing government policies with a desired outcome, this appendix will provide a proposal of what kinds of institutions a society might need to fulfill the ideals Chávez mentions. Before we speculate about a possible outline for the institutions of twenty-first century socialism, though, it makes sense to first take a closer look at what kinds of ideals Chávez talks about that society's institutions ought to fulfill. Next, so as to have a clearer understanding of why the institutions of capitalism do not fulfill these ideals, we need to take a brief look at the core institutions of capitalism and how and why these fail to fulfill our conception of an ideal society. There are at least four principal conceptions of socialism, though, that claim or once claimed to fulfill the ideals of socialism. To the extent that these have been tried out in various countries, regions, or periods of history, it makes sense to examine their limitations, to see how these experiments can help in the formulation of twenty-first century socialism.

Having laid the groundwork, via an examination of the ideals we might want, what institutions we don't want, and of the socialist alternatives that have been tried or at least conceived, we can then proceed to a rough outline of twenty-first century socialist institutions that might actually fulfill the ideals of socialism. This is not meant to provide a blueprint, but is merely an attempt to provide a proposal that could be used for debating the contours of twenty-first century socialism. After all, if one of socialism's main hallmarks is supposed to be the democratic participation of the people in the polity and in the economy, then one cannot claim to have a blueprint for the ideal society. Presumably everyone, though, including this author, would be invited to make proposals for what such a socialism ought to look like.

Chávez's Ideals for Twenty-first Century Socialism

On January 30, 2005, in a speech to the fifth World Social Forum, President Hugo Chávez announced that he supported the creation of socialism of the twenty-first century in Venezuela. According to Chávez, this socialism would be different from the socialism of the twentieth century. Chávez said twenty-first century socialism would not be a state socialism as was practiced in the Soviet Union and Eastern Europe or as is practiced in Cuba today. Rather, it would be a socialism that would be more pluralistic and less state-centered. "There is no solution within capitalism, one must transcend capitalism. Nor is it about statism or state capitalism, which would be the same perversion of the Soviet Union, which was the cause of its fall. We must reclaim socialism as a thesis, as a project and a path, but a new socialism. Humanism, putting humans and not the machine ahead of everything, the human and not the state," said Chávez.[2]

On another occasion, in May 2006, Chávez specified the ideals of such a new socialism: "We have assumed the commitment to direct the Bolivarian revolution towards socialism and to contribute to the socialist path, with a new socialism, a socialism of the twenty-first century, which is based in solidarity, in fraternity, in love, in justice, in liberty, and in equality."[3]

Also, on various occasions Chávez mentioned that this socialism is not just economic, but also political, saying, "Socialism of the political: this has a combination of elements, but one is central: participatory and protagonist democracy. This is the central axis of socialism in the political [realm], democracy from below, from inside, full democracy . . ."[4]

Chávez often mentions that one of his most important ideological influences, Simon Bolivar's teacher Simon Rodriguez, was an early socialist, a utopian socialist in the tradition of Robert Owen and Charles Fourier. "If Simon Bolivar had lived like Simon Rodriguez, for thirty years more . . . [he] would have been one of the precursors of utopian socialism, here in the lands of the Americas . . ."[5]

When specifying what he means by twenty-first century socialism, Chávez goes on to mention that it means, "transformation of the economic model, increasing cooperativism, collective property, the submission of private property to the social interest and to the general interest . . ."[6] Further, such a socialism is community-based, the center-piece of the project, the new "communal system of production and consumption" must be created "from the popular bases, with the participation of the communities, through the community organizations, the cooperatives, self-management, and different ways to create this system."[7]

Also, this socialism is not pre-defined. Rather, says Chávez, we must, "transform the mode of capital and move towards socialism, towards a new socialism that must be constructed every day."[8] Repeatedly Chávez emphasizes that this socialism has to be home-grown and must be developed gradually.

At other times Chávez makes a strong connection between the values of Christianity and socialism, saying that Christ was the world's first socialist: "The symbol of capitalism is Judas and of socialism it is Christ."[9]

Finally, another aspect that Chávez mentions this type of socialism should have is that it enables "human and social development."[10] In this aspect Chávez reiterates aspects of Venezuela's 1999 constitution, which states, for example, "everyone has the right to the free development of his or her own personality," (Art. 20) and that Venezuela's education system should be devoted to "developing the creative potential of every human being and the full exercise of his or her personality in a democratic society" (Art. 102).

In other words, according to Chávez, twenty-first century socialism would, in essence, value the traditional values of the French Revolution, of liberty, equality, and fraternity. Also, he emphasizes its compatibility with Christian values of love and solidarity and its relationship to the constitutional values of human and social development.

The problem with such a definition of socialism that is based almost entirely on values, ideals, and goals, is that it makes it indistinguishable from a wide variety of other economic and political projects. First off, one could argue that twentieth-century socialism wanted to achieve these ideals too. Not only that, but many who support capitalism and liberal democracy believe in these ideals too. Thus, what is needed is an institutional definition or at least set of defining features of socialism in order to know what socialism really means. This has, however, been hard to come by in Venezuela (and elsewhere).

The problem is that on the Venezuelan left, just as on the left around the world, there is no real consensus about what constitutes socialism, in terms of its institutions. In Venezuela this problem has its roots, at least partly, first, in the rather late debate about socialism because prior to 2005 socialism was not seriously on the national agenda. Second, there is no real structured debate on the concept in Venezuela because so far there has been no national organization or other structure that would channel such a debate. Chávez's MVR party, which is now the largest party in Venezuela, is not suited to the task because it is primarily an electoral vehicle for Chávez. Finally, Chávez's strong leadership of his movement and of the country tends to stifle debate because his proposals are all too often adopted as the last word on any topic.

Despite this lack of clarity about the institutions of twenty-first century socialism, can we nonetheless develop some ideas, in the abstract, about what such institutions might look like? One place to start would be by looking at what institutions clearly do not fulfill the ideals of socialism. Once we are clear about that, we can begin outlining what alternative institutions that do fulfill the ideals might look like.

What is Capitalism?

While there is uncertainty as to what kinds of institutions Chávez and his supporters envision for twenty-first century socialism, the type of institutions they are opposed to is very clear: they are opposed to the institutions and values of capitalism. But what are these?

Key Institutions of Capitalism

The definition of capitalism varies by almost as much as there are theorists of capitalism, with many even arguing that there is no such thing as capitalism or that the concept of capitalism is useless because most definitions cover such a wide variety of human practices that the idea has no analytic value. Despite this, there are two key institutions of capitalism that most definitions seem to refer to.[11] First, in capitalism production is organized through private ownership (and thus control) of the means of production, that is, of land, factories, and other forms of capital that allows the production of sellable goods and services.

Second, products and labor are exchanged and distribution is regulated in a competitive market. Competitive markets are an essential and integral aspect of capitalism, which help regulate not only distribution, but also prices and thereby guide what things are or are not produced. As long as owners are interested in making sure that they do not lose their investment to competitors who try to outsell them and who reinvest their profit in their business, so as to improve it, all owners must aim to maximize and reinvest profits (unless they have ways to distort the market situation). That is, private ownership of production combined with competitive markets also necessarily implies the pursuit of profit maximization.

The third institutional element to capitalism, which is often forgotten, is that capitalism needs a state that helps adjudicate contract disputes, that guarantees property rights, and that corrects capitalism's frequent dysfunctions and erratic behavior. Capitalism needs a state to act as a mediator in social conflicts, usually between owners and non-owners, who enter into frequent conflicts over issues relating to material inequality. While social movements have historically managed to demand that capitalist states respond better to their needs, mostly by democratizing the state, the state in most capitalist countries is to a very large extent influenced and shaped by the owners of capital because they can lobby, finance political campaigns and mass media, and generally wield much more power in capitalist democracies than ordinary citizens do.

On a non-institutional level, that is, on the level of the individual, capitalism consists of individuals who seek to rationally maximize their material gains, within the institutional framework described earlier. That is, capitalism fosters and depends on individualism. More pro-capitalist interpretations would argue capitalism is based on individual liberty. Chávez, many government officials in Venezuela, and socialists in general, thus also argue that another important defining feature of socialism, in contrast to capitalism, is that it places greater emphasis on the collective good instead of individual selfishness.

Key Negative Consequences of Capitalism

For critics of capitalism, the main reasons to move away from capitalism have to do with the negative consequences of the above-named institutions and social practices. There are at least five main negative consequences that are generally listed in this connection.[12] One of the most common consequences, according to most critical analysts of capitalism, is that capitalism inherently produces social inequality. Those who already have much are in a position to gain more in capitalism because they can invest more and are in a better position to beat their competition. Those who have little usually end up with less because limited resources go to the winners in market competition.[13]

Not only does wealth give an unfair advantage in capitalism, but it also makes the exploitation of those who work for a wage or salary easy. Those who work for a living are in competition with one another for jobs and, due to the existence of unemployment, are usually pushed into a position where their labor sells for far less than what it produces for the employer. According to most critics of capitalism, the fruit of one's labor ought to belong entirely to the employee or the worker, but it is kept by the employer and is thus exploitation. This then further contributes to inequality.

A second important negative consequence of capitalism is that, in Karl Marx's terminology, it creates alienation. Those who do not own productive capital or who do not manage it and have to work for a wage or salary are in control of neither the production process (because they have to obey a manager/boss) nor of the products they produce (because they don't own the production process). In other words, capitalism is a basic source of lack of freedom in society and an essentially undemocratic process, where the owners and managers have far more control and freedom over the production process and its products than those who work for owners and managers.

The third negative consequence of capitalism is that it is inherently unstable. As Marx explained in great detail, capitalism is an inherently unstable and self-contradictory economic system, with constant boom and bust business cycles, growing conflict between workers and capital owners, and increasing tensions between the development of new technology and the organization of the production process, among other problems. Marx probably underestimated, however, just how malleable and flexible capitalism is, so that it has so far, contrary to his expectations, not collapsed. On the other hand, these contradictions lead to constant suffering, mostly for workers, via their dislocation and unemployment or via defeats in labor struggles and the subsequent lowering of their standard of living.

A fourth negative consequence of capitalism, which is one that eco-socialists have pointed out, is the ecological destruction that capitalism provokes.[14] This destruction takes place, first, because capitalism needs constant economic growth in order to survive and increasing growth generally means the increasing use of non-renewable resources and increasing pollution. Second, the pricing and cost allocation mechanisms of the free market allow businesses to "externalize" costs, such as environmental pollution and other forms of destructive behavior. That is, the costs that environmental destruction causes to society and to nature are generally not included in production costs and this thus encourages polluters to continue their environmentally destructive activity. The most glaring and dangerous example of this practice is the emission of carbon dioxide into the atmosphere, which is rarely included in production costs, but which is now causing global warming and which is on its way to leading to a global ecological catastrophe.

Finally, a fifth negative consequence of capitalism is that it encourages racism, sexism, and other forms of discrimination and marginalization. That is, businesses often find that it is to their advantage to encourage divisions among workers, so that these do not unite and organize against their employer. One of the best ways for employers to encourage divisions among workers is to subtly promote racism, sexism, and other discriminatory "isms" at the workplace. Similarly, discrimination in employment practices divides not just the workplace, but the entire working class, making class unity more difficult and thus further enabling the continued exploitation of all workers. This does not mean that capitalism is the cause of racism and sexism and other "isms" in society in general, but that it thrives on and promotes all forms of discrimination and marginalization. [15]

Ideals of Twenty-first Century Socialism

As stated earlier, the ideals of twenty-first century socialism, as described by Chávez, are basically the same ideals as those that most of humanity has sought to fulfill at least ever since the French Revolution: liberty, equality, and social justice/solidarity. However, since most twentieth-century socialists, capitalists, conservatives, anarchists, etc., would probably agree with these ideals, these ideals, by themselves, do not distinguish twenty-first century socialism from anything else. Rather, it is the analysis of contemporary society and the recommended path and solutions for achieving these ideals that distinguishes different ideologies from each other. Certainly, the exact meaning of each of these three concepts also varies from one ideology to another. It thus makes sense to briefly clarify what is meant here by each of them.

Liberty in this context refers to a combination of what has been called negative liberty and positive liberty. That is, both the individual's freedom "from" outside constraints (negative liberty), such as from repression or hardship, and the individual's freedom "to" engage in political activity, such as organizing, running for office, or having an influence on matters that concern him or her. Of course, liberty is always constrained by the rights of others. That is, individuals should not be free to prevent the exercise of other people's liberty.

Second, equality refers to formal equality in this discussion; that everyone enjoys equal rights and duties, that no-one has a privileged status with regard to the law. This concept is different from, but closely related to, substantive equality (or equality of conditions or material equality). It is one matter for a political or economic system to treat everyone equally (formal equality) and a completely different matter to live in a condition of substantive or material equality with everyone else, in terms of one's material wealth. People who use the slogan of equality often do not differentiate the two forms of equality, which leads to much confusion. For this reason this analysis will reserve the term equality for formal equality and the term social justice for substantive equality.

The third ideal of the French Revolution, *fraternité*, brotherhood, has a wide range of possible meanings, but in this context it makes sense to equate it with the demand for social justice and for solidarity. In other words, it reflects the general human desire that no-one should be much worse or much better off than anyone else—that all have more or less equal conditions for life and that inequality of conditions should be the result of an individual's personal effort and decisions and not the result of good or bad fortune. Solidarity and social justice, while distinct, are closely related because it is the sense of solidarity with others that produces the demand for social justice for others.

Finally, many political philosophers have recognized that these three classical demands of the French Revolution are not enough for today's world because we are threatened by the possibility of extinction, due to humanity's own actions in destroying the planet's ecological balance. A fourth ideal thus becomes necessary, which could be called sustainability. Under the heading of sustainability we can also include the ideals of efficiency (no waste), diversity (which greatly aids sustainability), and the ideal of promoting the greatest development for the greatest number of beings (extending solidarity beyond the realm of humans).[16]

Varieties of Socialism

Since the Chávez government says it is working towards a new socialism, it makes sense to briefly also look at what socialism meant in the 20th century. Just as now, socialism was meant to address all five of capitalism's negative consequences and thereby create a society in which the ideals of the French Revolution, of liberty, equality, and of social justice (fraternity/solidarity) and the ideal of sustainability would be fulfilled. However, socialists disagreed vehemently as to what kinds of non-capitalist institutions would be necessary to fulfill these ideals. At least four different varieties of socialism emerged in the 20th century, each with very different proposals. The four main types of socialism were social democracy, state socialism, market socialism, and libertarian socialism. Of these, only two—social democracy and state socialism—were practiced in countries over extended periods of time, allowing us to analyze whether these were actually able to achieve their ideals. Market socialism was practiced to some extent in Yugoslavia, Hungary, and in a small region of Spain. The problems with these forms of socialism can help us identify what might be wrong with other proposed forms of socialism, insofar as their solutions may replicate problems of the tested forms of socialism.

Social Democracy

Keeping the institutions of capitalism in mind, one can identify the types of socialism in relation to the extent to which they accept or reject each of capitalism's key institutions, of the private ownership of means of production, of the market, and of the capitalist state. Applying this relationship to the varieties of socialism, one can see that social democracy is the variant of socialism that accepts the largest number of capitalist institutions. Social democracy accepts the existence of the private ownership of the means of production and of the market. In contrast to capitalism's advocates, though, social democracy also accepts Marx's and other socialists' basic thesis of a fundamental clash of interests between capital and labor. Thus, according to social democrats, the state, instead of functioning in the interests of private capital, should function in the interests of labor and the people in general. As a result, social democracy advocates that the state should intervene in markets and regulate privately owned and controlled production. This can be done via regulations (for workplace safety or the environment), redistributing wealth (via progressive taxation and social programs), and state support for national economic development (via subsidies, trade protection, etc.).

During the twentieth-century social democracy was no doubt the most successful variant of socialism, although many would question whether it deserves the label of socialism because it accepts so many of capitalism's key institutions. Still, between the 1950s and 1970s social democracy was extremely successful at creating greater income equality while also contributing to economic growth.[17] However, with the collapse of the Bretton Woods system of fixed exchange rates in 1973, international capital flows and globalization intensified, making it increasingly difficult for countries to protect themselves from capital flight and to maintain social democratic welfare states. The ideological onslaught of neo-liberalism, combined with First and Third World debt crises, the collapse of the state socialist economies, and the structural adjustment programs of the International Monetary Fund, pushed social democracy aside in the 1980s and 1990s.[18]

Part of the problem was that social democracy left the market and the capitalist class structure in place, which made it possible for capital to eventually break the global system that had been functioning until 1973 and that had largely made social democracy feasible. In addition to this, social democracy did not solve many of the other negative consequences of capitalism, such as alienation and ecological destruction.

State Socialism

Meanwhile, in the Soviet Union, Eastern Europe, China, and several other places, a much more radical approach to socialism—state-social-ism, sometimes also known as communism—attempted to achieve socialism's ideals by instituting a complete break with capitalism. The means of production were turned over to the state or to "collectives," markets were replaced with central planning, and the state was under the total control of the communist party, supposedly in the name of the country's workers. In the end, the only socialist ideal that state socialism achieved was to create a larger degree of social justice than exists in capitalism, but it did not fulfill the ideal of political liberty and did not do well with the ideal of formal equality, since communist party members generally received preferential treatment. Ecological sustainability was never on state socialism's agenda.[19] In the end, it too collapsed nearly everywhere, partly because of the pressures of globalization, of an inability to compete militarily, unpopularity, and due to internal economic problems.

The reasons state socialism failed to fulfill the ideals of socialism were varied, but to a large extent had to do with its prioritizing of social justice and social rights over liberty and individual rights. As a result, the lack of true democracy made the system unresponsive to people's needs. Also, perhaps more importantly, the state-socialist analysis, mostly because of its reliance on Marx, failed to recognize that classes are not just a function of ownership of the means of production, but also of control. That is, even though ownership was supposedly collective, it was still being controlled by an unelected elite. Finally, a third crucial reason for state socialism's collapse was that central planning was not able to compete with capitalist societies on a global scale, thus causing it to bankrupt itself in the arms race and to fall behind in its appeal for consumers.

Market Socialism

Market socialism was developed as a much more democratic socialist solution to capitalism that does not have the problem of central planning. The main institutional difference from capitalism is that the workplace is run in the form of democratic worker cooperatives. In other words, the means of production are in the hands of the workers directly and not in the hands of capital owners, as in capitalism, or of the state's coordinators, as in state socialism. Also, ideally (even if not always in practice), the state would be a representative democracy or some other form of democracy. The main experiments with this type of system existed in Yugoslavia and Hungary and still exist in the Mondragon region of Spain.

While this type of socialism has been tried only on a limited basis, it is recently acquiring more adherents, in light of the blatant failures of social democracy and of state socialism.[20] However, critics of market social-ism[21] argue that by keeping the market in place, the main problems of the market, which are its inducement to cut-throat competition, its mechanism for pricing products and services in ways that ignore costs external to the transaction, and the injustice of remunerating people based on market value remain in place. As a result, market socialism tends to continue to contribute towards a class division between coordinators, who have more market power, and workers, who have less market power. Market socialism only gets rid of owners of productive capital, but does not get rid of all of the polarizing tendencies of markets because these naturally tend to provide greater benefits to those who have more and less benefits to those who have less. Employers, even if they are cooperatives, have strong incentives to give highly valued employees far higher wages than less valued employees. The better valued will end up coordinating and, in the end, coordinators dominate, just as they did in state socialism. Also, since markets foster competition, they end up fostering individualism and break down cooperation and solidarity.[22]

Certainly, a redistributive state that is combined with a market socialist economy could counter-act polarizing tendencies, such as via progressive taxation. As such, market socialism in a democratic context would almost certainly be better than pure capitalism or social democracy. However, its insufficient ability to fulfill the ideals of social justice and solidarity should be cause for people to seek a better solution to solving the allocation problem than socialist markets.

Libertarian Socialism

The fourth type of socialism, libertarian socialism, has rarely been tried, largely because it is the least theorized school of socialism and because those who have advocated it were either in a minority relative to other strands of socialism or, when they were not a tiny minority, they were brutally squashed, as was the case in revolutionary Russia in the 1920s or in revolutionary Spain in the 1930s. However, it is precisely this relative lack of success and a practical experience base that provides the opportunity to define its concrete institutional model. Also, libertarian socialism is one of the most interesting branches of socialism because it attempts to address all of the problems of capitalism as well as the problems of the other three socialist traditions.

Libertarian socialism includes a wide diversity of sub-groups, such as anarcho-syndicalism, mutualism, social ecology, council communism, and others. As such, it is rather difficult to clearly identify a single institutional model that its proponents advocate. However, unlike social democracy, state socialism, and market socialism, one can say that its main aim is to get rid of all three of the key institutions of capitalism: private ownership or control over the means of production, markets, and a state that is in the hands of powerful private interests. In lieu of private productive property libertarian socialists propose the establishing of cooperatives and in lieu of the liberal democratic state, they propose more direct forms of participatory democracy. However, with regard to the allocation mechanism, the solution is not that clear. Some have proposed participatory planning, others propose a gift economy, and yet other libertarian socialists advocate the limited use of markets. An important element in all of their proposals, though, is the avoidance of the development of a managerial or coordinator class that would introduce social injustice.

In effect, the success or failure of libertarian socialism will largely depend on whether it manages to find a solution to the non-market based allocation problem. If it can, then it could very well be the only form of socialism that is capable of fulfilling the ideals of socialism.

A Proposal for Institutions that Fulfill Socialism's Ideals

Rather than examine Venezuela's policies on the basis of whether they fulfill or fail to fulfill the ideals of twenty-first century socialism, this discussion proposes to examine whether they help create institutions that are capable of fulfilling the ideals of twenty-first century socialism. But what, exactly, are the institutions that could fulfill these ideals? Proposed here is a model that is inspired by libertarian socialism in its general contours, by participatory economics[23] (Parecon, for short) in its details, that also includes some considerations about a better political sphere, and five guiding principles for developing an institutional model.

Five Guiding Principles for Institution Building

Given the all too often tragic history of socialism in the 20th century, it is important that we learn some of its lessons if we hope to avoid repeating its mistakes. The following five guiding principles for institution-building could serve as five of the main lessons to be learnt from that history.

First, and perhaps most importantly, we cannot build institutions where we say that the ends justify the means. If there is any lesson to be learned from the horrors of the 20th century, where noble ideals were sacrificed in the present for a better tomorrow, it is this. Rather, new institutions should embody and pre-figure our values and ideals. If they do not, we risk creating institutions that might appear to be necessary for a better future, but that in the long run undermine our efforts to reach our goals. In other words, institutions that are supposed to work towards a better future, such as social movement organizations, should embody our ideals of liberty, equality, social justice, and sustainability to the greatest extent possible. This is not always possible, due to circumstances beyond our control, but to the extent that we can control them, this is what we ought to strive for if we are to have any hope of actually creating this better society. This means that this principle precludes the establishment of discriminatory or authoritarian structures, such as democratic centralism, and of exploitation within our own institutions today, just as much as it precludes them from institutions of the future.

Second, ideas for developing institutions for a better future cannot be dogmatic. That is, they cannot treat texts, ideas, or leaders' statements about anything as unquestionable dogma. Another way of putting this is to say that the model and its analysis and justifications must be based on an open mind and must be open to revision and modification in light of new ideas and new evidence. Too many movements for a better society have deteriorated because they took the ideas of a certain individual or text as the last word on all matters. Also, dogma leads to authoritarianism and thus violates the ideals sought.

Third, we should try to avoid privileging one ideal over the other. If we agree that we all want liberty, equality, social justice, and sustainability, we should not say that one of these is much more important than the other and that we thus ought to be satisfied if we achieve one or two of these ideals at the expense of the others. Rather, we need to recognize that these ideals are all fundamentally inter-linked and that the denial of any one of them implies the lessening of all of them. It is the privileging of liberty over social justice that allows capitalism to provide neither for the poor and it was the privileging of social justice over liberty that allowed state-socialism's oppression of nearly everyone. Also, if we say today, in light of the ecological crisis, that we must privilege sustainability over the other ideals, we might survive the ecological crisis in the short term, but at the cost of living in an eco-fascist society, which is not sustainable in the long run.

Fourth, closely related to the previous point, we should avoid privileging either the individual or the collective because privileging one leads to the neglect of the other. Rather, we need to recognize that one cannot thrive without the other, which means that both must be fostered simultaneously. For too long have political ideologies favored either the collective or the individual, when, in actuality, we need to live up to Marx's dictum where, "the free development of each is the condition for the free development of all." Anarchism, libertarianism, and capitalism, for example, have generally favored the the individual, while socialism and Christian conservatism have traditionally favored the needs of the collective. Another way of putting this distinction is to contrast individual freedom with social order. Again, both are needed for a functioning society.

Fifth, as we build institutions, we should pay attention to their place in the existing network of relationships and of meaning. In other words, institutions, just as individuals, do not exist in a vacuum, but are embedded in webs of relationships and of meaning. What happens in one institution has effects on others. In practice, this means, for example, that if we create economic institutions, such as cooperatives, which contribute to the fulfillment of our ideals, we also ought to be simultaneously building political institutions that complement and support the economic institutions we create. Similarly, we cannot create new institutions without paying attention to the meaning-making, the values, culture, and world-views of the people who will be working inside of these. If the participants in the new institutions have values and world views that are at odds with the goals of the new institution, then these will fail in the long run. This means that we need to pay an equal amount of attention to how institutions are organized as we do to their organizational culture.

This last point also implies that the institutions we build cannot be utopian. Instead, they should recognize the historical, social, psychological, cultural, and physical realities of today's society. This point is rather similar to Friedrich Engels' critique of utopian socialism, which he contrasted to scientific socialism, saying that we need a careful analysis of what is possible in a given moment in history, not just fantasies of what we would like.[24] Certainly, institutions can change the way we think about things, but this causal relationship where institutions create new forms of consciousness has its limits. Institutions can push people towards new forms of consciousness, but not if too many of those in those new institutions have values that are diametrically at odds with the ideals embedded in the new institutions.

Armed with the ideals for a better society, these five guidelines for institution-building, and the history of past and present efforts to create a better society, it is now possible to venture some ideas about what the institutions for a better society ought to look like. The proposal can then serve as a means for evaluating the probabilities of success or failure for the Chávez government in moving towards a society with liberty, equality, social justice, and sustainability for all its citizens.

New Economic Institutions[25]

I. SELF-MANAGEMENT
Based on the fact that privatized means of production will almost always mean greater inequality, due to the owners' unearned income, and

greater unfreedom, due to the owners' (or managers') ability to control all aspects of the workplace, it makes sense to call for the socialization of the means of production. In practice, this means, first and foremost, self-managed cooperatives, where all workers have an equal voice in the management of their enterprise and an equal share in the revenues it generates. Cooperatives have over and over again proven to be every bit as—or more—efficient and productive as traditional capitalist enterprises, so there is no reason to be concerned that cooperatives would lead to economic stagnation and decline, as is sometimes argued.

2. BALANCED JOB COMPLEXES
However, as many observers of the cooperative movement around the world have noticed, cooperatives easily fall into typical corporate divisions of labor, whereby managers end up controlling or manipulating with far more power than is accorded to them by the one person, one vote principle of cooperatives. The reason for this dynamic is simple: managers tend to centralize information and gradually acquire essential skills that make them indispensable for the running of the cooperative, so that, even though they are elected, they wield far more power than they should. The solution to this problem is to rotate or balance tasks within the cooperative, so that everyone has an equal opportunity to do the work that is empowering and the work that is less empowering. In other words, all cooperative members would engage in so-called "balanced job complexes."

The creation of such job complexes is often one of the most controversial aspects of the participatory economics proposal, perhaps because it is extremely difficult for people who are involved in high-skilled and high-responsibility tasks to imagine balancing their work with that of the janitor or the secretary. In other words, much of the criticism probably comes from resistance to the idea that they too should be involved in such menial work. However, if one is serious about creating a society with social justice, where everyone enjoys similar degrees of freedom and power, then there is no way around balancing work between empowering and non-empowering tasks.

3. REMUNERATION FOR EFFORT AND SACRIFICE
Another source of inequality in society is income differential. The simple solution to this problem is to make sure everyone enjoys the same

income. Here, though, critics rightly point out that if that happens, then there could be insufficient incentives to ensure that people do not simply "free-ride" and not do their work. The alternative, of letting the labor market determine incomes, tends to lead to enormous income differentials, which are mostly based on luck of birth, such as talent or having a family that could afford to provide for an expensive education. Such family or genetic luck should surely not be a justifiable basis for income differentials. Instead, most progressives would probably agree that the only justifiable basis for income differentials is effort and sacrifice. That is, if you work more or in jobs that are riskier or that require other kinds of sacrifice (such as not being with your family for months at a time because you are at sea), then you deserve to earn more than someone who does less work or does work that requires less sacrifice. A key principle of participatory economics is thus income based on effort and sacrifice, not on talent, skill, or family luck.[26]

4. PARTICIPATORY PLANNING (COOPERATIVE ALLOCATION)

The fourth institutional proposal is perhaps the most controversial and complicated of Parecon, which is to replace markets with participatory planning. If we agree that markets exacerbate inequality, reduce solidarity, and increase ecological destruction, especially with the severe degree of global inequality we have today and the risks we face of ecological catastrophe, then we must seriously re-think markets. One reason this is rarely done, though, is because it is generally assumed that markets are "natural" and that there is no alternative to markets, other than central planning, which, as is generally assumed, failed miserably. However, what if there is an alternative to market allocation?

The main known remedy for the problems of the market has already been in effect for almost as long as market economies have been in existence: state regulation. Progressive taxation can, in theory, correct for inequality and regulations and taxes on the externalization of costs can correct for ecological damage. The problem with these solutions, while better than "pure" markets, is that they do not eliminate the root of the problem, which is the market itself. As long as the problem's root remains, there is an opening for the more market-powerful to expand their power and to gradually eliminate the regulations and taxes, as indeed happened from the 1970s to the 1990s. Furthermore, markets fundamentally undermine the principle of rewarding according to effort and sacrifice, which no amount of government regulation can correct. Also, taxing externalities is extremely difficult to do on a broad scale because businesses have an almost infinite variety of cost externalization mechanisms, which cannot be dealt with by an infinite variety of taxes. Finally, no amount of taxation or regulation is going to correct for markets' undermining of solidarity. As long as everyone is pitted against everyone else in a market situation, the incentives to act only in one's self-interest will be stronger than the interest in helping others.

What is the solution then, if "pure" markets (there is no such thing), regulated markets, and central planning cannot fulfill our ideals? Participatory economics proposes participatory planning, where workers and consumers jointly and in a decentralized process develop a production plan. Allocation, in other words, would be based on cooperation instead of competition. That is, rather than having consumers compete against each other for products and having producers compete against each other for consumers, the operating principle for allocation and production would be cooperation. In participatory planning workers and consumers deliberate within their respective consumer or producer councils to determine consumption and production targets. These targets are then matched, via gradual revisions and corresponding price adjustments.

Social costs are taken into account, in that the production and consumption process is collective, involving all those affected by these processes and not just the individual consumer and producer, as is the case in a market system. That is, if a particular consumer council feels that some of the consumption requests of its members have too high a social cost, they can collectively decide to change the consumption plan.

The producer councils would be based on workplaces, with smaller ones for work teams and larger ones for industries. Consumer councils would go from the individual, to family, to neighborhood, to city, etc. Each side (consumers and producers) draws up their proposals for what they would like to consume/produce and these are then passed on up to the appropriate level and then matched to the appropriate counterpart, which, in turn, modifies its proposed plan until the plans of the two sides match.

The process might sound complicated, but does not have to be, if one uses computer technology, to indicate what one wants to consume or produce. The resulting balancing of supply and demand might not be perfect, but neither is it in a competitive market economy. More importantly, with participatory planning, self-management, cooperation, solidarity, equity, and sustainability are all assured because everyone has a collective say in how much can and should be produced/consumed at what price.[27]

Since this process is somewhat unfamiliar to most people, here is another explanation, provided by Albert and Hahnel, the theorists of participatory planning:

> The participants in the planning procedure are the workers' councils and federations, the consumers' councils and federations, and an Iteration Facilitation Board (IFB). Conceptually, the planning procedure is quite simple. The IFB announces what we call "indicative prices" for all goods, resources, categories of labor, and capital stocks. Consumer councils and federations respond with consumption proposals taking the indicative prices of final goods and services as estimates of the social cost of providing them. Workers' councils and federations respond with production proposals listing the outputs they would make available and the inputs they would need to make them, again, taking the indicative prices as estimates of the social benefits of outputs and true opportunity costs of inputs. The IFB then calculates the excess demand or supply for each good and adjusts the indicative price for the good up, or down, in light of the excess demand or supply. Using the new indicative prices consumer and worker councils and federations revise and resubmit their proposals.
>
> Essentially the procedure "whittles" overly optimistic, infeasible proposals down to a feasible plan in two different ways: Consumers requesting more than their effort ratings[28] warrant are forced to reduce their requests, or shift their requests to less socially costly items, to achieve the approval of other consumer councils who regard their requests as greedy. Workers' councils whose proposals have lower than average social benefit to social cost ratios are forced to increase either their efforts or efficiency to win the approval of other workers. As iterations proceed, proposals move closer to mutual feasibility and indicative prices more closely approximate true social opportunity costs. Since no participant in the planning procedure enjoys advantage over others, the procedure generates equity and efficiency simultaneously.[29]

5. FREE KNOWLEDGE

Now we turn to an economic institution that is not part of Parecon, but that has in recent years acquired an increasing number of adherents and which promises to greatly contribute to self-management, equality, and social justice. The Free Software Movement proposes that software knowledge should be "free" to be used, reproduced, modified, and distributed as users of the software see fit. Under normal copyright and patent provisions, this not possible, which can make the developers of important and widely used software unusually rich, while those who wish to remain competitive in the free market are often forced to adopt that software at high personal cost. The result of the existing system for distributing useful knowledge thus strongly contributes to social inequity. Also, having limitations placed on the use of proprietary software/ knowledge reduces one's options for self-management, and gives the owner more rights than the mere user, thus distorting formal equality.

The concept of free software, however, does not have to be limited to software. Already creative artists have initiated an "Open Content" (similar to "free content") movement, which allows people to freely use, reproduce, modify, and distribute artistic content, such as music, articles, pictures, and videos. The concept can be taken even further, to processes, which are currently governed by patent law. For example, medications are often released of their patent restrictions, so that generic medications can be made at a much cheaper price than those of the original developer. It makes sense then, to extend the concept of "free" or "open" to all forms of knowledge. The Open Knowledge Foundation thus provides the following definition "A work is *open* if it is accessible, reproducible and re-usable without legal, social or technological restriction."[30]

Since knowledge is an essential aspect of contemporary society, how this knowledge is used and distributed has a significant impact on social life. In a participatory society, where people would be rewarded according to effort and sacrifice, it would not make any sense to impose copyright or patent restrictions, since their main purpose is to provide an incentive and income to those involved in creative work. However, on our way to such a society, it makes sense to support and expand institutions such as the open/free knowledge movement, so as to help create the better society today.

New Political Institutions

It would not be of much use if we managed to establish the above-named new economic institutions, but political institutions that reward power with more power, that undermine solidarity, and that institutionalize social injustice remained in place. The new economic institutions would probably never get off the ground and, even if they did, they would probably be reversed in short order. It is thus absolutely necessary to think about whether our existing political institutions contribute towards the ideals of liberty, equality, social justice, and sustainability and, if they do not, how we could create institutions that do contribute towards these ideals.

I. FROM REPRESENTATIVE DEMOCRACY TO PARTICIPATORY DEMOCRACY

The problems with representative democracy—the most prevalent form of democracy in the world today—are becoming increasingly obvious. As economic power grows and the means for manipulating the electorate become increasingly more sophisticated, representative democracy is ever more held hostage to powerful economic interests. Powerful lobbies and economic interest groups exist in most representative democracies that manage to sway elected representatives on crucial pieces of legislation, who end up listening to these lobbies more than to their constituents because they have to depend on these only once every election cycle. Second, elected representatives do not even need to truly listen to constituents because the electoral process has become very removed from debating actual issues of import, relying instead on images and "character." This usually happens via the private mass media, which exert a powerful sway over public opinion.

Third, and perhaps most importantly, the decisions of elected representatives do not necessarily reflect what citizens themselves would choose, if given a chance to debate the issues. Democracy, in its original intention of "rule by the people" meant that political decisions reflect the desires of the people, but if representatives make the decisions, this is not guaranteed. Already Max Weber pointed out that elected leaders, due to the need to maintain party discipline, do not really deliberate in parliament anymore. Rather, decisions are generally made behind closed doors by party leaders. The result is what Weber called an "elected dictatorship." For this reason, a number of political theorists have recently been suggesting that a more democratic form of governance, short of unmanageable direct democracy, would be deliberative democracy.[31] In a deliberative democracy emphasis is placed on citizens' discussion and deliberation of issues, with decisions emanating from these deliberations either directly or indirectly. Exactly how deliberation is institutionalized and how decisions are made varies from one theorist to the other.

The concept of participatory democracy builds on the idea of deliberative democracy and argues that citizens should be active participants in politics for real democracy to be possible. However, for this participation to be real and effective, they need to engage on a relatively small scale. One concrete institutionalization of this idea is Steven Shalom's proposal[32] that people be organized in nested councils of twenty-five to fifty people, depending on the total size of the society, with up to five levels. Councils of fifty with five nested levels could thus encompass a society of over 300 million people. Issues could be discussed on a relatively small scale at each level, with representatives being sent on a short-term basis from one level to the other. An important aspect of this idea is that the representatives maintain close connections to their lowest level council and that they do not serve for extended periods of time, so that they do not become removed from the general population, as is usually the case in representative democracy. Also, whenever a decision is close (e.g. does not have a two thirds majority) or when lower councils feel that that they might object to a decision, the decision of a higher council can be brought back to the next lower one. That is, contrary to representative democracy, the lower councils' decisions have more weight than a higher council's decision.

The main principle of this type of participatory democracy is the continuous participation and deliberation of citizens in the political will formation process. This is quite different from contemporary democracy, where voters vote once every four years or so and that is the extent of participation for the vast majority of citizens. The constant participation and deliberation of all citizens as equals would provide a better basis for ensuring self-determination. Also, social justice would be better served because powerful economic interests (insofar as they would still exist, if at all) would have a much harder time swaying councils and influencing their deliberations than they do now, when they have to influence voters only occasionally and a handful of powerful politicians continuously.

2. FROM FORMAL EQUALITY TO JUSTICE

The second key political institution is the legal system. In most western societies it is based on the principle of equal rights, or formal equality. All citizens enjoy the same rights and duties in a state that is governed by the rule of law, regardless of class, gender, race, ethnicity, or other characteristics. However, as feminists and other critics of the principle of equal rights point out, formal equality results in greater material or substantive inequality when those who are being treated equally are materially unequal.[33] The classical example of this is that if a poor person and a rich person commit the same crime and both have exactly the same rights in court, chances are that the rich person will receive a better verdict than the poor person because the rich person has more resources to defend themselves with. This is why social justice is often seen as an absolutely necessary additional ideal for meaningful formal equality.

One important way for the legal system to provide for social justice in addition to formal equality, is to make sure that social justice is a part of the legal system's operating principles. For example, Venezuela's 1999 constitution states, in its second article, that Venezuela is governed by the rule of Law *and Justice*. The implication is that the legal system seeks not only to apply the law equally, but that it also seeks substantive social justice. Affirmative action programs are the best example of this type of justice. In this way the legal system becomes committed not only to the ideal of equality and formal justice, but also to social justice.

However, so that the legal system is also committed to the ideal of sustainability or of ensuring the greatest development for the greatest number of beings, further modifications to the legal principles of a country might be necessary. As we will see, here too, Venezuela's new 1999 constitution provides an example of how such an ideal might be incorporated into the legal system. That is, various articles of Venezuela's constitution (articles 20, 62, and 299) affirm that the full development of all Venezuelans is a goal of the country's legal and political system.[34] Exactly what development might mean here will be explored at the end of this appendix.

3. FROM IDENTITY POLITICS TO UNIVERSAL SOLIDARITY

Civil society, defined as the free association of citizens outside of formal government or economic institutions, has in recent years been increasingly recognized by political theorists as being a crucial element of a functioning polity.[35] Normally, civil society organizations and movements have, in the western world at least, been organized around what has sometimes been called "identity politics" lines. That is, people organize on the basis of identification with one's ethnic group, gender group, or class group (although, the latter is generally not included), such as women's rights groups, groups representing ethnic or racial minorities, groups representing a particular sexual orientation, or similar types of groups. While this type of civil society organization was necessary to call into question the false universalism of civil society groups that made universalistic claims, such as that of leftist political parties or socialist movements, and of the supposedly universalistic principles of the political system in general, the time has come to transcend identity politics in many countries. Identity politics tends to be based on and to foster a type of solidarity that is limited to one's own identity group and thus severely limits the potential power of mass movements based on solving problems of social injustice in general.

Instead, in order to create broad-based and powerful movements, it is necessary to incorporate the concerns articulated by identity politics in a generalized movement for social justice. This also means that the sense of solidarity that a movement feels must transcend all boundaries and encompass all who are the victims of injustice, wherever they are in the world, and not just those of one's own ethnic, gender, or class group. This might seem obvious to most people, but despite this it rarely has the practical consequences it should. Applied to the foregoing institutional model for a better society, this implies, among other things, the advocacy for remuneration based on effort and sacrifice, and not based on market value, in-born talent, or skill that comes from having the luck of coming from an advantaged family.

Also, a truly universal solidarity means letting go of the notion that some are destined to perform menial and unempowering labor and others are destined to perform intellectually rewarding labor (or that society is better off if this is the case). Instead, universal solidarity would require us to give everyone the opportunity to perform intellectually rewarding and empowering labor. In other words, universal solidarity means making sure that we are involved in job complexes that are balanced in terms of the degree of empowerment they provide.

Next, the ideal of social justice can only become a reality if we indeed feel a universal solidarity with all and are thus able to support the principle of making sure that universal formal equality is complemented with universal social justice, as it is in affirmative action programs.

Finally, a truly universal solidarity would require us to feel for other non-human beings on the planet and for the eco-sphere in general, which is continuously being destroyed. Our self-interest in survival could be sufficient to make us reverse course, as we acquire more information about how we are participating in the eco-sphere's destruction and our own extermination. However, we do not always have the necessary scientific knowledge for saving ourselves. Besides, it would be more morally mature if we were interested in preserving nature for its own sake.

A New Form of Communication—Peer-to-Peer

The German social philosopher Jürgen Habermas points out that our society and all of its institutions are based on and held together via communication. The implication of this is that if the mode of communication of a society changes, then this will have a profound effect on how society's institutions function. That is, just as Marx argued that every society has a mode of production, which consists of the technology for production and the social relations in which production occurs, so one could say that every society has a particular mode of communication. This mode of communication also consists of the technology that enables communication (such as telephones, Internet, TV, printing press, etc.) and the relations of communication (hierarchical or participatory, for example).

More and more social theorists are observing that contemporary societies are changing their mode of communication,[36] which some are describing as a transition from communication based on center to periphery messages, to one that is based on peer-to-peer messages, which is having a profound impact on consciousness and on social institutions. This is not to say that we are entering into a glorious brave new world because of technology. Rather, the new form of communication is creating an amazing enabling potential for transforming economic and political institutions in the direction mentioned in the earlier sections of this chapter.

For most of the twentieth century mass communication was largely based on the technologies of television, radio, and the printing press.

This technological platform combined very well with hierarchical forms of organization because they encouraged communication from a knowing and powerful center to an ignorant and powerless periphery. Recipients of TV, radio, and printing press messages had relatively little control over what was being broadcast. They could choose to remain ignorant and thus relatively unaffected by this centralized form of communication, but in a technologically advanced society ignorance is an even worse option than receiving centralized forms of communication. However, with the proliferating use of the internet in the last decade of the twentieth century, a fundamentally new mode of communication was being developed, which has the *potential* to help generate and support the participatory kinds of transformations we have been discussing about earlier in this chapter. What, though, exactly is peer-to-peer?

According to one definition, "It is a specific form of relational dynamic, is based on the assumed equipotency of its participants, organized through the free cooperation of equals in view of the performance of a common task, for the creation of a common good, with forms of decision-making and autonomy that are widely distributed throughout the network."[37] The internet itself is the best example of peer-to-peer communication. Via email, chatrooms, websites, and file sharing internet users communicate directly with one another, largely past centers of power or hubs (or straight through them, with minimal interference).

This is not to say that peer-to-peer is purely a result of a new technology. Rather, it is the confluence of a new technology with a more participatory-minded consciousness. It is perfectly possible to use the internet in the old hierarchical, center-to-periphery forms. As a matter of fact, many large corporations try to deploy the internet in this way. However, the more participatory consciousness that peer-to-peer (P2P) technology enables reinforces both the technology and the consciousness. The following conceptualization of P2P is not, for example, purely technology-driven:

> [P2P] does not deny "authority", but only fixed forced hierarchy, and therefore accepts authority based on expertise, initiation of the project, etc . . . P2P may be the first true meritocracy. The threshold for participation is kept as low as possible. Equipotency means that there is no prior formal filtering for participation, but

rather that it is the immediate practice of cooperation which determines the expertise and level of participation. Communication is not top-down and based on strictly defined reporting rules, but feedback is systemic, integrated in the protocol of the cooperative system. Techniques of 'participation capture' and other social accounting make automatic cooperation the default scheme of the project. Personal identity becomes partly generated by the contribution to the common project.[38]

As such, the principles embodied in P2P are also an integral part of the previously discussed free culture, free knowledge, and free software movements. More than that, P2P systems are ideally suited for the development of participatory economics and of participatory politics. Just as in P2P, participatory economics and participatory politics involve everyone's equal opportunity to participate, automatic feedback systems, and decision-making that is widely distributed instead of top-down.

The perhaps most significant aspect for the feasibility of P2P communication and a participatory society in general is that these are not incompatible with contemporary capitalism. That is, many alternatives to capitalism are often completely antithetical to capitalism, such as state socialism, which then leads to a fundamental conflict between the interests of capital and the interests of those promoting state socialism. P2P, however, as has already been proven in the realm of the free software movement, is in many ways quite compatible with capitalism and even thrives in it. For example, major corporations, such as IBM, have incorporated and promoted many products coming out of the free and open source software movements, such as the Linux operating system. While this might seem to open the system to cooptation, this is not necessarily the case because P2P production is quite capable of producing products more efficiently than is possible with the normal capitalist production process.

Some might conclude that P2P thus is merely a new phase within capitalism. Such a claim misses, though, that P2P production transcends capitalism's core institutions of private ownership, the market, and capitalist governance. The means of production, which currently, in the P2P realm, involves the internet's infrastructure and the software developed under P2P principles, is not privately owned/controlled. Also, given the unrestrained access, reproduction, and modifiability of P2P products, one cannot say that it is distributed via market mechanisms. Finally, the governance principles of P2P (such as the free software license) emerged cooperatively, outside of the realm of capitalist governance principles (there is no free software law). Certainly, government is still needed to help enforce the license, but when it does so, it is forced to operate outside of capital's normal interests.

Given P2P's simultaneous compatibility with and undermining of capitalism, the expansion of this type of production could create a situation similar to the one Marx described as having caused the downfall of feudalism and that would cause the fall of capitalism. That is, new forces of production (the internet) are gradually creating new relations of production (P2P) that clash with the old capitalist forces and relations of production (mass production industry and private property/market). However, capitalist production is eager to make use of this new form of production, until, perhaps, it is eventually completely displaced. This is not to say that there are or will be no conflict between the two systems, but there is a good possibility that capitalism's resistance to change will be significantly weaker because of the initial compatibility of P2P with capitalism.

A fuller analysis of the relationship between P2P, participatory economics, and capitalism is still needed for a fuller understanding of how these dynamics are playing and will play out. The outline here is merely meant to be suggestive of what might be possible and how this potentiality is and could be applied to Venezuela's transformation.

Utopianism and Human Development

Given how far most societies are from the institutional model for a participatory society that is described here, it would not be surprising if readers believed that this proposal violates the fifth guideline for institution building that I described earlier, that the proposed institutions should not be utopian. In other words, are the institutions proposed here too far removed from contemporary society to ever have a realistic chance of being implemented? Hopefully the last point about the increasing use of peer-to-peer communication and the analysis of the Venezuelan experience will show that these institutions for a participatory society are much more feasible and realistic than at first seems.

However, when building new institutions for a participatory society we should keep in mind that the proposal, by itself, is insufficient. What is also needed is a critical mass of people who share the values and interpretations underlying these institutions so that the people who populate the institutions end up strengthening them instead of undermining them. What kind of consciousness, though, is necessary for or compatible with the institutions for a participatory society?

One way to describe this consciousness is to contrast it with the type of consciousness that prevails in capitalism. Capitalism, as mentioned earlier, promotes and requires an individualistic consciousness, which sees the world in an atomistic and reductionist manner. In contrast, the participatory institutions described here promote and require a consciousness that is inclusive, capable of including others' perspectives. This also means that this consciousness needs to be capable of systems thinking instead of atomism and of integrating perspectives instead of using reductionism to make sense of the world.[39]

If we look at society historically, we can see that each major epoch in human history corresponded to a particular form of consciousness. In simplified form, one can say that feudalism corresponded to a conformist and dogmatic religious consciousness, while capitalism corresponds to individualist and strategic-rational consciousness. The challenge for social change movements is to promote the type of integrative consciousness necessary for a participatory society. As suggested earlier, a participatory society promotes integrative consciousness, but it will not come into being without a critical mass of individuals who already operate from this type of consciousness. Also, the persistence of dogmatic pre-capitalist and of individualist capitalist forms of consciousness constantly threaten to derail and undo projects for a participatory society. As we saw in this book, this is one of the main challenges that the Bolivarian project for twenty-first century socialism faces in Venezuela.

Notes

Introduction

1 The truth of Venezuela/one does not see in the Country Club/the truth one can see in the hills/with the people and their unrest [Note: The poor majority of Caracas lives in the "hills," while many of the city's rich live in a part of the city known as the "Country Club"].
2 Weisbrot and Rosnick (2003).
3 A more detailed overview and analysis of this history is available at www. venezuelanalysis.com.

Chapter 1

1 Those who have read my account of the history of the Chávez presidency (Wilpert 2007) should feel free to skip this chapter, as it merely summarizes what is contained in that book.
2 Those who die for life/cannot be called dead/and from this moment on/it is forbidden to cry for them [Inscription on the Puente Llaguno Bridge memorial to those who died April 11, 2002].
3 Tugwell (1975), p. 182.
4 Karl (1997).
5 Hellinger (2000) takes issue with the argument that the Dutch Disease is a serious issue for Venezuela, dismissing it as a neo-liberal analysis and adding that if it does apply then it would have to be applicable to all Third World societies, since they all have imbalances in their economic activity. While it might very well be true that many Third World societies suffer from this problem, countries suffer far more from it the more one sector predominates. Since Venezuela is exceptionally dependent on oil, it is particularly applicable to Venezuela. Karl's (1997) comparative analysis of oil-producing countries and of other countries in which oil is dominant shows very well how the Dutch Disease affects all of these countries.

6 World Bank (2000). Uruguay is the most urbanized, with most of its population in Montevideo.

7 Terry Lynn Karl (1997), p. 234: "In the twenty years between 1960 and 1980, which included two booms, Venezuelans enjoyed almost double the resources for investment, a significantly faster growth in salaries, a longer life expectancy, lower infant mortality, and more education than their Latin American neighbors—and they did so without paying close to comparable taxes (Baptista 1984, p. 26, Table 3). These economic outcomes underwrote political stability."

8 The pact was named after the house in which it was signed, the Quinta Punto Fijo, in Caracas.

9 "The key players of 1958 became a frozen status quo. The institutional arrangements they set in place allowed them to control policy making, exclude new groups from participating, and kept new issues off the agenda" (Crisp 2000, p. 173).

10 Real per capita income (Real GDP Chain per equivalent adult, in 2000 constant dollars) declined from $11,869 in 1979 to $8,675 in 1999 (Penn World Table Version 6.1, Center for International Comparisons at the University of Pennsylvania (CICUP), accessed September 2006). Only Peru suffered a decline, of 17%, while Argentina, Bolivia, Brazil, Colombia, and Ecuador increased their per capita GDP in that time period. Venezuela's real GDP per worker declined far more dramatically, by 36% (compared to 27% for Peru), indicating that inequality also increased during this time period.

11 Universidad Católica Andrés Bello, "Proyecto Pobreza", http://www. ucab.edu.ve/investigacion/iies/pobreza.htm.

12 Buxton (2001) and Crisp (2000) both make this argument.

13 For a fuller description of Chávez's life story, see: Muñoz (1998), Harnecker (2002), Gott (2000), Chávez and Guevara (2005), and Elizalde and Baez (2004).

14 Blanco Muñoz (1998), pp. 56–7.

15 This summary is provided by Samuel Moncada (2003).

16 Lopez-Maya (1999) says that the most credible figure, provided by the human rights group COFAVIC, stands at 396 deaths.

17 See Gott (2005) for a brief overview of Miquilena and others around Chávez at the time.

18 Marta Harnecker first coined this term with regard to events in Venezuela in her book-length interview with Chávez (Harnecker, 2003).

19 In some of Venezuela's poorer states establishment candidate Henrique Salas Römer beat Chávez, such as in Delta Amacuro by 52–46, in Amazonas he beat Chávez 54–44, and in Apure 60–39. Chávez, though, beat Salas Römer in wealthier states, such as Carabobo (Salas's home state), by 53–44, in Miranda 51–43, and in Zulia 55–41.

20 For example, in the poor states that Salas Römer won in 1998, Chávez got overwhelming majorities in the recall referendum. In Apure he was confirmed with 68% of the vote (compared to 39% in 1998), in Amazonas with 70%, and in Delta Amacuro 70%. In the wealthier states that Chávez won in

1998, he got smaller percentages, such as in Carabobo (57%), Miranda (51%), and in Zulia (53%). This hypothesis that Chávez was elected by the middle class in 1998 and confirmed by the poor in 2004 still needs more research, but a preliminary investigation of the electoral data suggests that there is good reason to believe it is true.

21 For a more detailed rebuttal of the fabricated reasons for opposing Chávez, see: *Extra!*, special issue on Venezuela, November/December 2006.

22 The most notable exceptions are the studies by Duno (2004) and Herrera Salas (2004), which clearly demonstrate the racism and classism against Chávez.

23 Venezuela's new 1999 constitution provided for five branches of government instead of the usual three, adding an independent electoral branch and an independent prosecutorial branch (the "moral power").

24 The pro-Chávez slate said that the AD-dominated slate had committed fraud and Chávez subsequently refused to recognize the election. The issue was never truly resolved.

25 For a full account of the 2002 coup attempt, see Wilpert 2007.

26 The president may only be recalled once half of his term has expired. The Supreme Court thus ruled that recall referendum petition signatures that are collected before the halfway point, such as the ones collected on February 2, 2003, were invalid.

27 The final official result would increase the margin of Chávez's victory slightly, with 59% for "no" and 41% for "yes"—many of the additional no votes came from the countryside, where the vote had to be counted manually and which went 70–30 in favor of Chávez.

28 See, for example: "Poll: Chávez Enjoys 71.8% Approval Rating in Venezuela," Venezuelanalysis.com, July 27, 2005 (http://www.venezuelanalysis.com/news.php?newsno=1702).

29 Hugo Chávez, "Palabras desde el Balcon del Pueblo," August 16, 2004 (http://www.gobiernoenlinea.ve/misc-view/sharedfiles/Palabras_Balcon_del_Pueblo_16ago2004.pdf).

30 The reason for the shift within the opposition has to do with more moderate factions gaining an upper hand, which is directly related to the discrediting of the more radical factions in the opposition, due to their long string of failures in the previous eight years.

Chapter 2

1 The other countries that Simon Bolivar liberated are Colombia, Ecuador, Peru, and Bolivia. In theory, however, any country that subscribes to the principles or goals of Simon Bolivar, which included the unification of all of Latin America, could consider itself a "Bolivarian Republic."

2 See, Carol Delgado, *Response Magazine*, June, 2003, "The Non-Androcentric Constitution of Bolivarian Republic of Venezuela."

3 For example, the German constitution refers to the German state as a "*Rechtsstaat*," a "state of law," implying that the rule of law is supreme.

4 Constitución de la República Bolivariana de Venezuela, Exposición de Motivos, Titulo 1, Principios Fundamentales.

5 Practically no-one in Venezuela argues that there is censorship. Rather, they argue that the government has "intimidated" the private mass media by threatening to withhold government advertising or fining or closing broadcasters for violating the law on social responsibility in the media.

6 Article 91.

7 Article 118.

8 Article 274.

9 This means that the terms for Attorney General Isaias Rodriguez, Human Rights Defender German Mundarain, and Comptroller General Closbaldo Russián are up in 2007.

10 Rafael Caldera was president during 1969–1974 and 1994–1999; Carlos Andres Perez during 1974–1979 and 1989–1993.

11 Blanco (2002), *Revolución y Desilusión*, 2002, Libros de Catarata, p. 245.

12 In addition to Blanco (2002), see Harald Trinkunas, a Latin America military expert of the US navy, author of "Civil—Military Relations in Venezuela after April 11": *http://www.ccc.nps.navy.mil/rsepResources/si/may02/latinAmerica.asp*. Other English-language sources on Venezuela's civil—military relations include: Daniel Levine and Brian Crisp, "Legitimacy, Governability and Reform in Venezuela," in Goodman et al., *Lessons of the Venezuelan Experience*; Moisés Naím, "The Real Story Behind Venezuela's Woes," *Journal of Democracy* 12 (April 2001): 17–31; Winfield Burggraaff and Richard Millett, "The Crisis in Venezuelan Civil—Military Relations" in Goodman et al.; Felipe Agüero, "Debilitating Democracy: Political Elites and Military Rebels," in Goodman et al.; Deborah Norden, "Democracy and Military Control in Venezuela," *Latin American Research Review* 33 (2): 143–165, 1998; Harold Trinkunas, "The Crisis in Venezuelan Civil—Military Relations: From Punto Fijo to the Fifth Republic," *Latin American Research Review* 37 (2002): 41–76.

13 More on the military in the government comes below, in this chapter.

14 The previous constitution required the legislature to approve of ministerial appointments.

15 Previously presidents could only be re-elected after being out of office for ten years.

16 See: www.transparency.org.

17 Survey can be found at: www.latinobarometro.org.

18 Roland Denis in an interview with Raul Zelik, originally published in German in: *Subtropen*. Reprinted also at: *http://www.venezuelanalysis.com/articles.php?artno=1006*, September 3, 2003.

19 "Halfway to Reform: The World Bank and the Venezuelan Justice System", August 1996, at: *www.lchr.org/pubs/descriptions/halfway.htm*.

20 Source: Evaluación 2000 de la Comisión Coordinadora de Evaluación y Concursos para el Ingreso y Permanencia en el Poder Judicial (also: *www.cajpe.org.pe*).

21 Taken from the 2002 report: www.cajpe.org.pe/rij/bases/reforma/ven6.htm.

22 Full text, *Ley Orgánica del Tribunal Supremo de Justicia:* http://www.asam-bleanacional.gov.ve/ns2/leyes.asp?id=531.

23 Human Rights Watch's 2005 country report on Venezuela (http://hrw.org/english/docs/2006/01/18/venezu12258.htm) mentions the judiciary as a human rights problem area, claiming that 80% of judges are temporary. This is a claim that Judge Mora categorically rejected, saying that it proved HRW's opposition bias with regard to Venezuela.

24 Venezuela's Supreme Court is divided into six "chambers," each of which deals with different types of legal issues: constitutional, electoral, social, administrative, civil, and penal. Also, there is the plenary of the court, which attends to impeachments and disputes between the chambers. Each chamber consists of five judges, except the constitutional, which has seven.

25 Article 23, section 4 of the *Ley Organica del Tribunal Supremo de Justicia.*

26 Human Rights Watch, unfortunately, does not take such arguments into consideration in their reports on Venezuela.

27 *El Universal,* August 26, 2004, "Ministros a granel."

28 For example, a speech given on April 26, 1999 at a forum on "Civilian—Military Unity and National Development," reprinted in: Hugo Chávez (2003), *Discursos Fundamentales: Ideología y acción política.* Caracas: Foro Bolivariano de Nuestra América, p. 124.

29 Ibid., p. 122.

30 Ibid., p. 127.

31 Prior to the creation of Misión Miranda there were only 5,000 reservists in total (http://www.misionvenezuela.gov.ve/12Miranda/12Ejercitodepueblo.htm).

32 See Chapter 11 for details on the new strategic plan.

33 *El Universal,* March 13, 2005, "Defensa Endogena."

34 *Ley Orgánica de la Fuerza Armada Nacional.*

35 In speeches, Chávez makes frequent reference to himself as being a "soldier" and as someone whose life experience was shaped by the military.

36 Chapter 4, section 1 ("on political rights"), paragraphs 3 and 4, of the Exposition of Motives of the Constitution of the Bolivarian Republic of Venezuela (CBRV).

37 Terms used in chapter 4, section 1, paragraph 11 of the CBRV.

38 Increasingly, though, in the US, Venezuela, and throughout the world, there is an emerging "healthy communities movement" that is pushing for communities to solve their own problems, largely based on self-reliance rather than on help from national governments. See, International Healthy Cities Foundation (www.healthycities.org), for example.

39 The full list of functions in the CLPP law includes 22 functions altogether.

40 See: Wagner, Sarah, "Problems and Opportunities for Citizen Power in Venezuela," Venezuelanalysis.com (http://www.venezuelanalysis.com/articles.php?artno=1331).

41 Ibid.

42 Taken by Roland Denis and the *Movimiento 13 de Abril.*

272 NOTES

43 Taken, for example, by former Planning and Development Minister Felipe Perez and the group *ConexiónSocial.*
44 *Ministerio de Participación Popular y Desarrollo Social* (Minpades).
45 "Venezuelan Government Announces $5 Billion for Communal Councils in 2007," Venezuelanalysis.com, January 10, 2007 (http://www.venezuelanalysis.com/news.php?newsno=2188).
46 "Más fondos para consejos comunales," *El Universal,* January 12, 2007 (http://buscador.eluniversal.com/2007/01/12/eco_art_138895.shtml).
47 Jesús Rojas, of the Ministry of Popular Participation and Social Development, in a personal interview.
48 See "Chávez Announces Nationalizations, Constitutional Reform for Socialism in Venezuela," Venezuelanalysis.com, January 8, 2007 (http://www.venezuelanalysis.com/news.php?newsno=2187).
49 Ley Organica de la Administración Pública, Article 138.
50 Constitución de la República Bolivariana de Venezuela, articles: 51, 62, 178, 184; Ley Orgánica de la Administración Pública, articles: 1, 135, 138; Ley Orgánica de Planificación Pública, articles: 14, 58, 59; Ley Orgánica de la Contraloría General de la República y del Sistema Nacional de Control Fiscal, articles: 1, 6, 14 sec. 9, 24 sec. 4, 25 sec. 7, 75, 76; Ley De Los Consejos Locales De Planificación Pública, articles: 5 sec. 21, 8, 24.
51 Article 98 of the *Ley de Participación Ciudadana,* introduced to the Nacional Assembly November 29, 2001.
52 For more information on the land committees, see Chapter 4.
53 Kuiper, Jeroen and Gregory Wilpert (2005), "Interview with Jacqueline Faria, Minister for the Environment: The Many Tasks of Environmental Protection in Venezuela," Venezuelanalysis.com (http://www.venezuelanalysis.com/articles.php?artno=1508).
54 Piñero Harnecker, Camila (2005), "The New Cooperative Movement in Venezuela's Bolivarian Process," Venezuelanalysis.com (http://www.venezuelanalysis.com/articles.php?artno=1631).
55 "Proyecto de ley establece "control obrero" en empresas," *El Universal,* January 13, 2007 (http://buscador.eluniversal.com/2007/01/13/pol_art_140072.shtml).
56 The *Ley Orgánica de Participación Ciudadana* (Constitutional Law for Citizen Participation) is scheduled to be passed sometime in 2005.
57 "Deepening the Bolivarian revolution: Program 2007–2013," unpublished first draft manuscript.

Chapter 3

1 "Líneas Generales del Plan de Desarrollo Económico y Social de la Nación 2001–2007," Ministry for Planning and Development—www.mpd.gov.ve.
2 Ibid., p. 56.
3 "Venezuela Creates New State-Owned Petrochemical Company," Venezue-

lanalysis.com, June 27, 2005 (http://www.venezuelanalysis.com/news.-php?newsno=1674).

4 This figure is according to an interview with Chávez's brother, Adán Chávez, who was the president of the National Land Institute in 2002.

5 Banco Central de Venezuela (www.bcv.org.ve/c2/indicadores.asp).

6 Ibid.

7 For example, the explanation for the motives for changing the FEM in 2001 stated it was to, "liberate the national oil company from the obligation to save, in order to dispose and take advantage of a more efficient use of its resources." Exposición de Motivos del Proyecto de Reforma del Decreto con Rango y Fuerza de Ley del Fondo de Inversión para la Estabilización Macroeconómica.

8 "Condicionan aportes al FEM," *El Universal,* February 9, 2005.

9 The reason bank reserves have already been spent is that when a country earns foreign currency, via international trade, such as from oil, the dollars are first exchanged by the Central Bank into Bolivars and the Central Bank keeps the dollars, to be used when other banks or the government need to purchase dollars. If the executive takes a portion of the hard currency reserves and exchanges them into Bolivars, it is actually printing more national currency, since the hard currency would merely end up in the Central Bank reserves again.

10 The revised Central Bank Law now states: "The resources transferred to the fund . . . only may be used by it, in foreign currency, for the financing of investment projects in the real economy, and in education and in health; for the improvement of the profile and balance of the external public debt; as well as for attending to special and strategic situations." Source: "Venezuela's Central Bank Law Reform Allows Limited Government Use of Reserves," Venezuelanalysis.com, July 22, 2005 (http://www.venezuelanalysis.com/news.php?newsno=1698).

11 Actually, most of Venezuela's foreign reserves are now held in euros because, in mid-2005, over the course of several months, the Central Bank, at the urging of Chávez, exchanged $20 billion of its $30 billion in reserves into Euros. See: "Venezuela's Central Bank Confirms It Deposited $20 Billion in Swiss Bank," Venezuelanalysis.com, October 5, 2005 (http://www.venezuelanalysis.com/news.php?newsno=1777).

12 On various occasions Chávez cited from Sunkel's work and even invited Sunkel onto his weekly television program *Aló Presidente.*

13 Sunkel, quoted in Lebowitz (2006). Lebowitz points out very well how limited this strategy was.

14 A sixth, the creation of SARAOs (*Sistema de Asociaciones Rurales Auto-Organizados*—System of Self-Organized Rural Associations), was originally part of the social economy concept. A handful of these projects were organized in Zulia, Táchira, Miranda, Apure, and Lara states. These are essentially agricultural communities of 650 to 1,900 individuals that are supposed to be ecologically sustainable and egalitarian, in some ways similar

to Israeli kibbutzim. In a speech Chávez gave in July 2003, he pointed out that until that point 40,700 families had benefited from the SARAOs throughout the country. Given that the average Venezuelan family has about five members, this means that approximately 200,000 individuals are living in SARAOs now. Unfortunately, no serious evaluation of the SARAOs has been made so far, so it is not possible to say how viable these communities are as a serious project for expanding the social economy in Venezuela. It seems, though, given how little attention the government has placed on the SARAOs since 2003 that this program has fallen by the wayside, in favor of the NUDEs and the social production enterprises, largely because these were central government planned communities, whose organizing principle contradicts the more participatory approach the government has advocated for community development.

15 Banks also have to maintain at least 16% of their credit portfolio for agricultural loans, 10% for home loans, and 2.5% for tourism.

16 According to the magazine *America Economia*, Sept. 23, 2005.

17 Sunacoop data (http://www.sunacoop.gov.ve/estadisticas/cuadro1.htm).

18 Numerous articles analyzing Venezuela's promotion of cooperatives can be found in the economy section of Venezuelanalysis.com.

19 For a review of these efforts, see Jonah Gindin (2005), "Made in Venezuela: The Struggle to Reinvent Venezuelan Labor," in *Monthly Review*, Vol. 57, No. 2.

20 For a discussion of the problems with co-management, see "Constructing Co-Management in Venezuela: Contradictions along the Path," by Michael Lebowitz, Venezuelanalysis.com, Oct. 27, 2005 (http://www.venezuelanalysis.com/articles.php?artno=1587). See also "Invepal: desorden administrativo o algo más," by Luisana Ramirez, Aporrea.org, Aug. 8, 2006 (http://www.aporrea.org/endogeno/a24269.html).

21 Based on a presentation given by the Ministry for the Popular Economy at the Regional Andean Conference on Employment in Lima, Peru, November 22 and 23, 2004.

22 According to an interview with Popular Economy Minister Elias Jaua, www.revoltaire.net, "El pueblo es el principal actor del camino hacia el progreso," March 11, 2005.

23 Ministry of the Popular Economy, Misión Vuelvan Caras (http://www.minep.gov.ve/).

24 Jaua interview, www.revoltaire.net.

25 Lebowitz (2006) quotes Chávez's June 2005 speech in Paraguay, where Chávez said, "Workers often demand a fair salary and other benefits, and they have the right to demand this. But the working class is obliged not just to demand its rights, but to constitute itself into a factor for the transformation of society." Chávez went on to add the analogy, "If you are traveling with your three children and your wife in your air conditioned car and pass by an eight-year-old child, that is on the street, at midnight, isn't this a problem of yours too?"

26 Mészáros (1995), p. 758, also cited in Lebowitz (2006). Chávez referred to Mészáros in his Alo Presidente program of July 17, 2005.

27 Article 3 of Decree No. 3,895, of September 13, 2005, published in Gaceta Oficial No. 38,271.

28 "Empresas de Producción Social," article in PDVSA's corporate magazine, *Siembra Petrolera*, issue No. 1, Jan.–Mar. 2006, p. 55.

29 Source: personal communication with PDVSA's public affairs department.

30 For a recent study of Mondragon see: Cheney (1999).

31 While many different models of local currency or LETS systems exist, where some work better than others, in the best case they indeed promote solidarity and cooperation and move exchange away from competition, which is one of the main factors that undermines cooperative culture and functioning. See www.lets-linkup.com for a directory of LETS systems.

32 See the appendix or Albert (2003) and Hahnel (2005) for an explanation of what a participatory economy could look like.

33 Data based on Finance Ministry and *El Universal*, March 27, 2005, "Gobierno que se niega a ahorrar" and Ministry of Finance data (www.mf.gov.ve).

34 Venezuela's total public debt (foreign and domestic) of 32% compares favorably to that of Colombia (44.2%), Brazil (50.2%), US (64.7%), Germany (68.1%), and Argentina (69.7%). Only Guatemala (26.9%), Mexico (21.2%), and Chile (8.1%) have lower rates of public indebtedness in Latin America (Source: CIA World Fact Book).

35 In 1998 foreign debt was 25.2% of GDP and domestic was 4.4%. By 2004 foreign was at 25.1% and domestic debt at 13.9% of GDP (source: Finance Ministry).

36 In 1983 Venezuela's debt to GDP ratio was 22%, according to Karl (1997), p. 268.

37 Draft of the 2007–2013 Government Program.

38 Tugwell, Franklin (1975), *The Politics of Oil in Venezuela*, Stanford University Press, p. 182.

39 For example, while Venezuelan individual income taxes during the '70s made up only 4.1% of total tax income and corporate taxes made up 70.3%, in neighboring Colombia, the tax burden is distributed much more evenly among different sources, so that individual income tax makes up 11% and corporate tax 12.8% of total tax income. (Source: Terry Lynn Karl, 1997, *The Paradox of Plenty: Oil Booms and Petro States*, University of California Press, p. 89.)

40 Mommer (2003) says, "Nationalization changed the ownership of the oil industry but not, for the most part, management" (p. 132). Bernard Mommer is now vice-minister for hydro-carbons in the Chávez government. Carlos Mendoza Potellá, a long-time analyst of Venezuela's oil industry, and others who write for the website www.soberania.org also make this argument.

41 Ibid., p. 135.

42 See "Cuentas Crudas, Precios Refinados," *El Nacional*, November 17, 1998.

43 For 2001 outsourced oil fields have a cost of $10.94 per barrel of oil equivalent produced, while non-outsourced oil fields have a cost of only $2.03 per barrel of oil equivalent (in 1997 dollars). Source: Weisbrot and Baribeau (2003). Another drawback of these agreements is that any change in legislation that are "detrimental" to the partners would mean that Venezuela would have to pay an indemnity. Also, for the first time in Venezuela's history, PDVSA accepted outside arbitration in the case of any contract disputes.

44 Ramirez, Rafael (2005), "A National, Popular, and Revolutionary Oil Policy for Venezuela," posted on Venezuelanalysis.com (http://www.venezuelanalysis.com/articles.php?artno=1474).

45 Ibid., p. 137.

46 www.americaeconomia.com.

47 PDVSA ranks #24 in terms of return on assets, #49 in terms of return on sales, and #50 in terms of return on fixed assets (*patrimonio*).

48 Source: Weisbrot and Baribeau (2003) (their figures are based on SEC filings).

49 Carlos Rossi, "PDVSA's Labor Problems," *The Daily Journal*, April 18, 2002.

50 Chávez's visits to Saddam Hussein and Muammar Qaddafi would come to haunt him over and over again, as his opponents would cite these visits as reasons for their dislike of Chávez.

51 Alí Rodríguez, the former president of OPEC and current president of PDVSA provides a good summary of the policy in: "La Reforma Petrolera Venezolana de 2001" in *Revista Venezolana de Economía y Ciencias Sociales*, No. 2/2002, May/August 2002.

52 Constitution of the Bolivarian Republic of Venezuela, Article 303. However, successful PDVSA influence in the constitutional assembly left open a back door to privatization because the constitution also says that the state shall own all shares of PDVSA, "except those of subsidiaries, strategic associations, businesses, and whatever other that has constituted or constitutes PDVSA as a result of the development of its business." Since PDVSA itself does not produce any oil—only its affiliates do—PDVSA could, in theory, sell off its subsidiaries one by one. PDVSA is mostly a holding company and so not much of it would be left should a government decide to pursue this route.

53 Article 5 of the "Ley Organica de Hidrocarburos."

54 Alí Rodríguez (2002, p. 204).

55 Chávez's visits to Iraq—the first of any head of state since the Gulf War—and to Libya, both members of OPEC, would later be used repeatedly by his opponents at home and in the US as proof of his unreliability and dangerous tendencies.

56 Ultimately, the renaissance of OPEC could be a large part of what motivated the US to attack Iraq. That is, if OPEC had remained as defunct as it was when Chávez came to power, it is quite possible that the Bush administration would never have considered controlling Iraq's oil reserves to be much of an

issue. But with the return of OPEC, the consequent rise in oil prices, and the general lack of control the US government felt in the face of an energy crisis and the attack on the World Trade Center, "breaking OPEC's back" became a top priority.

57 See www.soberania.org/tercerizacion_portada.htm. The excess costs averaged about $90 million per year for 1998 to 2000.

58 See Alexander Foster and Tulio Monsalve, "Quien Maneja las Computadoras de PDVSA?", *Venezuela Analitica*, December 17, 2002, www.analitica.com/bitbiblioteca/tulio_monsalve/computadoras_pdvsa.asp.

59 According to the PDVSA website (www.pdvsa.com).

60 In 2000 Chávez had renewed the San José pact with the Caracas accords, which included more countries, including Cuba, which eventually led to the exchange of Venezuelan oil for Cuban doctors.

61 President Hugo Chávez, November 6, 2004, during the press conference following the signing of the energy agreement with the Dominican Republic, quoted in www.pdvsa.com.

62 "Chávez Announces that Venezuelan State Will Switch to 'Free Software'," Venezuelanalysis.com, September 29, 2004 (http://www.venezuelanalysis.com/news.php?newsno=1373).

63 Another related area where the government has also made moves towards transforming the use of knowledge and technology is with regard to medical patents, where it is pushing for international norms that would place the right to certain life-saving or essential medicines above the right to profiting from intellectual property.

64 According to PDVSA, revenues were $30 billion higher than they would have been without the changes from 2004 to 2006. PDVSA (2007) *Siembra Petrolera*, No. 3, Caracas: PDVSA.

Chapter 4

1 The Gini Index goes from 0, meaning complete equality (all incomes the same), to 1, meaning complete inequality (all income held by one individual). Source: Francisco Rodriguez (2000).

2 Ibid., p. 5.

3 Rodriguez: "If our calculations are correct, Venezuela today is one of the most unequal countries in the world, with its 1997 Gini [of 62.6] surpassing that of South Africa (62.3) and Brazil (61.8)." Ibid., p. 6.

4 OPEC Statistical Bulletin, 2001.

5 In 1985 dollars. Own calculations, based on value of oil exports (IMF, *International Financial Statistics Yearbook 1993*), population (Instituto Nacional de Estadistica, Venezuela: www.ine.gov.ve), and 1985 exchange rate (Banco Central de Venezuela: www.bcv.org.ve).

6 According to the income-based poverty line used by the Poverty Project of the Catholic University Andres Bello (Matias Riutort, "El Costo de Eradicar la Pobreza" in *Un Mal Posible de Superar*, Vol. 1, UCAB, 1999).

7 The official poverty statistic of Venezuela's Institute of National Statistics (INE) states that the poverty level in 2003 was 54%. *Reporte Social, 2004*, www.ine.gov.ve.

8 Kenneth Roberts, "Social Polarization and the Populist Resurgence in Venezuela," p. 59, in *Venezuelan Politics in the Chávez Era*, edited by Steve Ellner and Daniel Hellinger (2002), Lynne Rienner Publishers.

9 Portions of this section were previously published in Wilpert (2003) and in Wilpert (2005b).

10 Articles 305 and 306 of the Constitution of the Bolivarian Republic of Venezuela. According to Adán Chávez, the brother of President Hugo Chávez and former president of the National Land Institute, the institution in charge of redistributing land, the government has set the goal of increasing agriculture's share of GDP by one percent in 2002 and to double it to 12% by the end of Chávez's first term in office, by 2007.

11 Censo Agricola 1998.

12 P. 2 of the exposition of motives for the Land Law. This motive is also based in article 307 of the constitution, which says:
> The predominance of large land estates (*latifundios*) is contrary to the interests of society. Appropriate tax law provisions shall be enacted to tax fallow lands and establish the necessary measures to transform them into productive economic units, likewise recovering arable land. Farmers and other agricultural producers are entitled to own land, in the cases and forms specified under the pertinent law. The State shall protect and promote associative and private forms of property in such manner as to guarantee agricultural production. The State shall see to the sustainable ordering of arable land to guarantee its food-producing potential.

13 "The data indicate clearly that all other things being equal, the family farm is still the most efficient and sustainable. This does not emerge through romantic wishful thinking but rather through the fact that, on average, a family farm achieves a much higher density of management than do any other types of farm enterprise arrangement. This greater density of management exists because there is motivated family labor available on a continuous basis." FAO Paper, "Contemporary Thinking on Land Reform," March 2000, by J. Riddell and the staff of the Land Tenure Service in the Rural Development Division www.fao.org/sd/ltdirect/ltan0037.htm.

14 Personal interview with author in October, 2003.

15 Olivier Delahaye, "La discusión sobre la ley de tierras: Espejismos y realidades" in *Revista SIC*, August 2002, No. 647, pp. 351–354. Caracas: Centro Gumilla (web: http://www.gumilla.org.ve/SIC/SIC2002/SIC647/SIC647_Delahaye.htm).

16 Parts of this section were reprinted without the author's authorization or attribution in Michael McCoughan's book, *The Battle of Venezuela*, Latin America Bureau, 2004. The Seven Stories Press edition of the same book does not have the unauthorized sections.

17 Hernando de Soto (2000), *The Mystery of Capital*.

18 Source: World Development Report 2000/20001. For all of Latin America, the percentage of urban population is 75% and for the whole world it is 46% (for 1999, World Development Report 2000/2001, World Bank).

19 In December 1999 a constant torrential rain that lasted about a week, caused massive mudslides, which led to the deaths of over 10,000 people and made over 150,000 people homeless. This was one of the worst natural disasters in the history of Latin America.

20 Currently land invasions are mostly tolerated and on those occasions when they are not tolerated, the squatters are simply evicted from the land.

21 Source: "Venezuela's Quiet Housing Revolution: Urban Land Reform," Venezuelanalysis.com, Sept. 12, 2005 (http://www.venezuelanalysis.com/articles.php?artno=1551).

22 Source: Ministry for Planning and Development, Sistema Integrado de Indicadores Sociales para Venezuela (sisov.mpd.gov.ve).

23 A slightly larger number attended private schools in this time-period, going from 1.2 million in 1992 to 1.5 million in 1998. Figures taken from: Provea Informe Anual 2003–2004, p. 162 (available at: www.derechos.org.ve).

24 Public spending on education continued to grow, even during the crisis years of 2002 and 2003, so that by 2005 it reached $273 per capita, or 4.9% of GDP, which was 44.5% higher than in 1990.

25 In an interview with the author, March 2005, posted on www.venezuelanalysis.com ("Now We Must Consolidate This Bolivarian Educational System," April 12, 2005).

26 Ibid.

27 *2004: Año de logros bolivarianos*, p. 118.

28 *Provea Informe Anual, 2003–2004*, p. 168.

29 Based on a primary school population of 4.085 million (grades 1–6), according to statistics of the Ministry of Education.

30 Taken from an Education Ministry brochure on Bolivarian schools.

31 Source: Ministry of Planning and Development, www.sisov.mpd.gov.ve.

32 *Provea Informe Anual, 2003–2004*, p. 171. Unfortunately, data reaching further back is not available.

33 These missions are: Robinson I II (adult elementary education), Ribas (adult high school education), Sucre (university education), Barrio Adentro I, II, III (comprehensive health care), Mercal (subsidized food stores), Vuelvan Caras (employment), Habitat (housing), Guaicaipuro (indigenous rights), Zamora (land reform), Piar (small mining), Identidad (identity papers), and Miranda (military reserves).

34 Figures taken from the government's website on the missions: www.misionvenezuela.gov.ve.

35 The opposition and a study conducted by Ortega, Rodriguez, and Miguel (2006), economists sympathetic to the opposition, contradict this claim, saying that the literacy program had practically no effect on reducing illiteracy.

36 Ibid., p. 197.

37 Ministry of Education brochure, *Liceo Bolivariano*, pp. 28–29.

38 Ibid, p. 51.

39 Ibid., p. 52.

40 One of these few translations is available through UNESCO: *Seven Complex Lessons in Education for the Future* (http://unesdoc.unesco.org/images/0011/001177/117740eo.pdf).

41 See: 3 Años de la Quinta Republica (http://www.mpd.gov.ve/3%20A%D1OS/3AnosdelaVRepublica.pdf).

42 According to Aló Presidente, #168, of October 19, 2003.

43 In 2005 the Bolivarian University system underwent a significant change, with a new director and an intense internal power struggle over the educational philosophy behind the university. Some observers said that the aim was to make the university less "post-modern" in Edgar Morin's sense and more traditional than it had initially been.

44 *Documento Rector: Universidad Bolivariana de Venezuela*, p. 16.

45 *Provea: Informe Annual 2003–2004*, p. 187.

46 In per capita terms, real public expenditures on health also declined by over 50%, from $91 per capita in 1990 to $43 per capita. Source: Sistema Integrado de Indicadores Sociales para Venezuela (SISOV), www.sisov.mpd.gov.ve.

47 Similarly, in 1995 real per capita expenditures dropped to 55% of the level they were in 1990, recovering slightly in 1998, to 66.8% of the level of 1990 (ibid.).

48 The four national systems are: Ministerio de Salud y Desarrollo Social (MSDS), Instituto Venezolano de los Seguros Sociales (IVSS), Instituto de Previsión de Asistencia Social del Ministerio de Educación (IPASME), and Instituto de Previsión Social de la Fuerza Armada Nacional (IPSFA).

49 Source: author's calculations, based on data provided by SISOV (www.sisov.mpd.gov.ve).

50 *Instituto Venezolano de Seguridad Social*—Venezuelan Institute for Social Security.

51 Provea, Informe Annual 2003–2004, p. 136.

52 Ibid., p. 139.

53 World Health Organization immunization statistics (www.who.int).

54 All statistics from Provea and www.misionvenezuela.gov.ve.

55 Fonden is the Fondo para el Desarrollo Nacional (Fund for National Development), which was created from "excess" foreign currency reserves. $6 billion were allocated to Fonden in 2005.

56 Ministry of Planning and Development: www.sisov.mpd.gov.ve.

57 Based on figures from CONAVI (*Consejo Nacional de la Vivienda*), cited in Provea, Informe Anual, 2003–2004, p. 203.

58 Ibid., p. 207.

59 Ibid., p. 205.

60 *Aló Presidente*, February 27, 2005.

61 *Agencia Bolivariana de Noticias*, March 20, 2005.

62 Source: "Persiste escasez de insumos para construir," *El Universal*, August 23, 2006 and "215,000 viviendas ejecutadas en 8 años," *El Universal*, January 15, 2007.

63 The term "popular" is generally used to refer to the barrios or the poor. Quoted in Provea: http://www.derechos.org.ve/actualidad/coyuntura/2005/coyuntura_152.htm#13.

64 *Provea Informe Annual, 2003–2004*, p. 213.

65 "Organic" means that the law is directly mandated by and derived from the constitution.

66 The six laws that needed to be passed for the social security system to take effect were: Ley del Régimen Prestacional de Empleo; Ley del Régimen Prestacional de los Servicios Sociales al Adulto Mayor; Ley de Salud y Sistema Público Nacional de Salud; Ley de Reforma de la Ley Orgánica de Prevención, Condiciones de Medio Ambiente y Trabajo; Ley del Régimen Prestacional de Vivienda y Hábitat; Ley del Régimen Prestacional de Pensiones. Of these, only the ones involving health care and retirement had not yet been passed by late 2006.

67 Stating that Venezuelans' human rights were being violated, the human rights group Provea filed a motion with the Supreme Court in 2003 to compel the legislature to pass the laws. It was twenty-three months after introducing the motion that the Supreme Court finally responded and required the National Assembly to pass the necessary laws, which it then did.

68 Source: www.sisov.mpd.gov.ve. Per inhabitant, this represents an increase, in real terms, of over 400%, relative to 1990.

69 Ibid.

70 Source: www.sisov.mpd.gov.ve. More recent data for the period of economic recovery was not available.

71 Ibid.

72 All figures taken from: www.misionvenezuela.gov.ve.

73 *Provea, Informe Annual 2003–2004*, p. 61.

74 "Venezuela Launches Primary Health Program for Extreme Poor," Vene-zuelanalysis.com, April 22, 2006 (http://www.venezuelanalysis.com/articles.php?artno=1712).

75 For a detailed examination of how this myth evolved and continued to be propagated by the international media, see: "Poverty Rates in Venezuela: Getting The Numbers Right," CEPR Research Paper, by Weisbrot et al. (2006).

76 Source: National Institute of Statistics, www.ine.gov.ve.

77 1997–2004 data is from the National Institute for Statistics (www.ine.gov.ve); 1970–1995 data from the UNDP (www.undp.org).

78 Instituto Nacional de Estadisticas (INE): www.ine.gov.ve.

79 Weisbrot *et al.* (2006). This figure is the middle estimate of how much the health care program benefits the poor.

80 16% is the total percentage decline in GDP between 2001 and 2003. By 2005 GDP had recovered so that it was 8.4% higher than in 2001 and 28.8% higher than in 2003. Source: Banco Central de Venezuela (www.bcv.org.ve).

81 It should be noted that just because someone signed the petition, it does not automatically mean that they are opposed to the government. It is entirely conceivable that some Chávez supporters wanted a recall referendum not to get rid of Chávez, but to confirm his continuation in office and to defeat the opposition in a democratic contest (instead of via a coup or a general strike).

Chapter 5

1 *Líneas Generales del Plan Nacional de Desarrollo Económico y Social de la Nación 2001–2007*, posted at: www.mpd.gov.ve (Ministry of Planning and Development).
2 Ibid., p. 156.
3 Article 153 of the Constitution of the Bolivarian Republic of Venezuela. Article 73, though, specifies that such treaties must be approved by the general population in an "approbatory" referendum.
4 *Últimas Noticias*, December 18, 2003.
5 The following discussion of ALBA is largely based on a description provided by Venezuela's Import—Export bank (Bancocx), which can be found at: http://www.venezuelanalysis.com/articles.php?artno=1100.
6 Though, during the last round of WTO negotiations in Cancún, Mexico, in September 2003, the Minister of Production and Commerce almost signed an agreement that would have ratified the WTO rules on intellectual property rights, against the stated policy of the Chávez government. For this reason, shortly after his return from Mexico Minister Ramón Rosales was dismissed from his post.
7 "What is the Bolivarian Alternative for Latin America and the Caribbean?" by Bancoex, posted February 5, 200 http://www.venezuelanalysis.com/articles.php?artno=1100.
8 This failure led Bolivar to famously state, "I have ploughed the sea."
9 Instituto Nacional de Estadisticas, www.ine.gov.ve.
10 Also, in an effort to further strengthen cross-border collaboration in late 2004 PDVSA opened two gas stations in Argentina, where it established its first foothold in directly selling gasoline to consumers of another Latin American country.
11 A more detailed description of this project was provided in Chapter 11.
12 The 2005 State Department report on terrorism (caracas.usembassy.gov/wwwh2642.html) repeats the charge: "Venezuela continued in 2004 to be unwilling or unable to assert control over its 1,400-mile border with Colombia. Consequently, Colombia's three US-designated Foreign Terrorist Organizations (FTOs)—the Revolutionary Armed Forces of Colombia (FARC), the National Liberation Army (ELN), and the United Self-Defense Forces of Colombia (AUC)—continued to regard Venezuelan territory near the border as a safe area to conduct crossborder incursions, transship arms and drugs, rest, and secure logistical supplies, as well as to commit kidnappings and extortion for profit. Weapons and ammunition—

some from official Venezuelan stocks and facilities—continued flowing from Venezuelan suppliers and intermediaries into the hands of Colombia's FTOs."

13 Source: CIA World Factbook (http://www.cia.gov/cia/publications/factbook/index.html).

14 According to the probably biased estimates of the US Defense Department, Venezuela spent $4.3 billion on arms in 2005 and 2006. (Source: "Venezuela's Arms Purchases Since 2005 Top China, Iran, Pakistan," Bloomberg, January 22, 2007.)

15 During a speech held in Havana, April 29, 2005.

16 The *Acuerdo Energetico de Caracas* is an accord Venezuela signed on October 19, 2000, with ten Caribbean and Central American countries (Belize, Costa Rica, El Salvador, Guatemala, Haiti, Honduras, Jamaica, Nicaragua, Panama, Dominican Republic) for Venezuela to provide below-market priced oil to these countries, with 15-year financing at a 2% annual interest rate. The total volume of oil supplied to these countries is 80,000 barrels per day. The Caracas Accords are in addition to the Accords of San José that Venezuela and Mexico signed with various Caribbean countries in 1980. Mexico is not a signer of the Caracas Accords because it refused to expand on its 1980 commitment.

17 See: "Felix's Miracle and the Convenio Cuba—Venezuela," Venezuelanalysis.com, Aug. 24, 2006 (http://www.venezuelanalysis.com/articles.php?artno=1804).

18 The treaty's text can be found at: http://www.venezuelanalysis.com/articles.php?artno=1789.

19 Personal interview in March 2002 with a delegation of inhabitants of the Sierra de Perija region, who came to Caracas to inform the national government of developments in their area.

20 Chávez has on several occasions, though, urged the FBL to demobilize and to turn in their weapons, saying that his government does not need their help.

21 "Weapons and ammunition—some from official Venezuelan stocks and facilities—continued flowing from Venezuelan suppliers and intermediaries into the hands of Colombia's FTOs [Foreign Terrorist Organizations]. It is unclear to what extent and at what level the Venezuelan Government approves of or condones material support to Colombian terrorists. President Chávez's close ties to Cuba, a US-designated state sponsor of terrorism, continue to concern the US Government." Country Reports on Terrorism, 2004, US State Department, p. 87 (http://www.state.gov/documents/organization/45322.pdf).

22 In April 2005 Venezuelan security forces arrested five Colombian soldiers who had crossed the Venezuelan border without proper authorization. They were returned to Colombia a few days later.

23 Colombia is Venezuela's second largest trade partner after the US

24 Recounted in: Golinger (2005), *The Chávez Code*, pp. 52–53, Havana: Editorial José Martí.

25 Eva Golinger cites a June 2000 cable sent by the military section of the US embassy in Venezuela that instructed: "Expand United States government

access and influence at all levels of the Venezuelan Armed Forces . . . Increase the number of Venezuelan Armed Forces Officers at all levels receiving instruction in US military schools . . ." (Ibid., p. 58).

26 It is thanks to the efforts of Jeremy Bigwood and Eva Golinger in requesting and publicizing countless documents in countless US government agencies that at least some of the scope of US operations in Venezuela has come to be known. The documents were obtained through numerous Freedom of Information Act requests (FOIA) and the investigation of these documents is still in progress. One result of the investigation has been to impact US–Venezuela relations. Most of these documents are posted on the website www.venezuelafoia.info.

27 These figures are combined funds provided by the National Endowment for Democracy and USAID. Ibid., p. 83.

28 "US Aid Stirs Venezuela's Suspicion," Associated Press, August 27, 2006.

29 Personal communication with Eva Golinger, who has been researching the most recent appropriations for Venezuela.

30 Robinson, (1992).

31 Agee, Philip (1975), *Inside the Company: CIA Diary*.

32 *www.dai.com* (exact reference: http://www.dai.com/work/project_detail.php?pid=53).

33 *www.usaid.gov.*

34 Golinger (2005), p. 245 According to the OTI website, its Venezuela program has so far spent $6 million on OTI projects. According to Golinger, OTI was to spend $7 million on projects, which probably means that $1 million has not yet been distributed and $3 million is to be used by OTI and DAI directly as operating costs and not for projects.

35 www.venezuelafoia.info/usaid.html.

36 That same month, a failed kidnapping attempt was made against Ortega Diaz. In February 2006, before the trial had concluded, a judge declared it be a mistrial because the presiding judge had not allowed a jury trial to take place for the four Sumate leaders. Attorney General Rodriguez said that he would re-launch the trial. In mid–2006 Venezuela's National Assembly launched its own investigation of Súmate's funding and said that it had bank records that confirmed that Súmate received $300,000 from the US Department of Health and Human Services. Bush administration officials denied the claim.

37 Golinger (2005), p. 163.

38 Ibid., p. 193.

39 Posted at: *http://www.venezuelafoia.info/usaid.html* under project : G–3822–101–043. The name of the organization that benefited from the project was blacked out.

40 This group was often mis-named and mis-construed as a Group of Friends of Venezuela.

41 Quoted in Golinger (2005), p. 139.

42 Palast, Greg (2004), *The Best Democracy Money Can Buy* (Rev. Ed.), Plume Books.

43 "Chávez reta a Bush," *El Universal,* February 29, 2004.

44 The fact that the US military has been conducting war exercises off the coast of the Caribbean island of Curaçao in early 2006 further inflames suspicions that the US is preparing for an invasion.

45 Chávez, though, often criticizes social justice issues within the US. Venezuela's heating oil program also shows practical solidarity with the poor in the US.

46 A simple comparison of Amnesty International's Report 2006, on the human rights record in Belorussia, Iran, Syria, China, Zimbabwe, and Russia, for example, with that of Venezuela ought to dispel any notion that Venezuela's human rights record is in any way comparable to that of the above mentioned countries.

Chapter 6

1 Let us make history/and others write it/in a better world/Find, find the struggle within/for transforming the world/means love.

2 See: www.latinobarometro.org, 2006 report and "Poll: Venezuelans Have Highest Regard for Their Democracy," Venezuelanalysis.com, December 20, 2006 (http://www.venezuelanalysis.com/news.php?newsno=2179).

3 See "The Real Fracture in Venezuela's Labor Movement is Ideological," by Steven Mather, Venezuelanalysis.com, July 10, 2006 (http://www.venezue-lanalysis.com/articles.php?artno=1775), and Ellner (2003c).

4 The appendix presents a more detailed proposal for what the institutions of twenty-first century socialism might look like. In short, in the appendix, I propose that to replace capitalist economic institutions we need institutions that support self-management, balanced job complexes, remuneration based on effort and sacrifice, participatory planning, and free knowledge. In the polity, we would need participatory democracy, a legal system that prioritizes both formal equality and justice, supports human development, and solidarity that is truly universal.

5 Source: www.sisov.mpd.gov.ve.

6 In visits to China, Chávez regularly invokes Mao, apparently believing that the Chinese leadership is still interested in pursuing Mao's social vision. With regard to the leaders of Belarus, Zimbabwe, and Iran, Chávez has praised these as progressive and revolutionary leaders.

7 Or Iteration Federation Board (IFB), as it is known in the Parecon literature (Albert, 2003; Hahnel, 2005).

8 The analysis of this type of problem was continued in the middle third of the twentieth century and beyond by Friedrich von Hayek, Talcott Parsons, Niklas Luhmann, and Samuel P. Huntington, among others, for the conservatives and for the left by the so-called Frankfurt School, such as Theodor Adorno, Walter Benjamin, Max Horkheimer, Herbert Marcuse, Erich Fromm, and Jürgen Habermas, among others.

9 Both quotes from "Taller de Alto Nivel," November 12–13, 2004, p. 17, Ministerio de Comunicación e Información.

10 Venezuela scores 2.3, on a scale of 1 to 10, one of the lowest scores, placing Venezuela at rank 114 out of 146 surveyed countries. See: Transparency International, Corruption Perceptions Index 2004 (http://www.transparency.org).

11 Romero (1997), pp. 20–21.

12 Source: www.latinobarometro.org, 2005 report.

13 "Taller de Alto Nivel," p. 12, November 12–13, 2004, Ministerio de Comunicación e Información.

14 "Con Chávez gobernamos todos," seen on the bottom of countless government posters and newspaper advertisements.

15 Partial reform of the penal code, in effect since April 13, 2005 (Gaceta # 5,768).

16 This is based on experiences recounted to the author by several people who have been close to the president and who wish to remain anonymous.

17 With regard to taxation, the Venezuelan state is now enforcing tax laws more strictly than ever. In June 2005, for example, Venezuela's tax authority, Seniat, closed several international automakers for a few days because they owed back taxes. Similarly, Seniat also closed Coca-Cola for two days for not paying their full tax bill ("Venezuela's Tax Agency Shuts Down Coca Cola for 48 Hours," Venezuelanalysis.com, February 16, 2005, www.venezuelanalysis.com/news.php?newsno=1509).

18 In the case of Venezuela, Foreign Direct Investment (FDI) reached $4.9 billion in 1998 and held more or less steady until 2002, when it dropped dramatically to $782 million, but then recovered again, reaching $2.6 billion for 2003, $1.5 billion for 2004, and $2.9 billion for 2005. (Source: Banco Central de Venezuela.)

19 See Harvey, David (2004), *The New Imperialism*, for a good dissection of how Clinton, as a neo-liberal, represented the logic of capital while Bush, as a neo-conservative, represents the logic of territory or empire.

20 William Robinson (1996).

21 Prominent works in this area include: Jean Cohen and Andrew Arato (1992), *Civil Society and Political Theory*, Cambridge, MA: MIT Press; Jürgen Habermas (1998), *Between Facts and Norms*, Cambridge, MA: MIT Press; John Keane (2003), *Global Civil Society?*, Cambridge: Cambridge University Press; Antonio Negri and Michael Hardt (2004), *Multitude*, New York: Penguin Press.

22 This debate began in Venezuela in 2006, with the National Assembly's discussion of a new law to regulate international funding of Venezuelan NGOs. See: "Heritage Foundation and Venezuela's International Cooperation Law," Venezuelanalysis.com, August 1, 2006. (http://www.venezuelanalysis.com/articles.php?artno=1785).

23 While the institution of "social comptrol" had improved such accounting in Venezuela, there still is tremendous room for improvement.

24 Buxton (2001) and Karl (1997) provide good overviews of these earlier reform efforts.

25 Shortly before completing this manuscript, I received an unofficial draft of Chávez's 2007–2013 program, which places a strong emphasis on the need to "transform the state apparatus," which aims to make the state more efficient and less corrupt. The specific strategies outlined in the plan are too vague, though, to allow an evaluation as to how, exactly, Chávez proposes to do this, other than to place stronger emphasis on the creation of a "Bolivarian ethic" and to increase transparency.

26 See: "Chávez Scolds Own Party as Internal Squabble Continues," Venezuelanalysis.com, April 26, 2005 (http://www.venezuelanalysis.com/news.-php?newsno=1601).

27 Tariq Ali has, in particular, pointed out the importance of this aspect of what is happening in Venezuela. See: "Venezuela: Changing the World by Taking Power," interview with Tariq Ali by Jonah Gindin and Claudia Jardim, July 22, 2004 (http://www.venezuelanalysis.com/articles.php?art-no=1223).

28 A slogan encapsulated in the book by John Halloway (2002), *Change the World Without Taking Power: The Meaning of Revolution Today*, London: Pluto Press.

Epilogue

1 "Chávez Calls for United Socialist Party of Venezuela," Venezuelanalysis.com, December 18, 2006 (http://www.venezuelanalysis.com/news.-php?newsno=2177).

2 "Chávez Announces Nationalizations, Constitutional Reform for Socialism in Venezuela," Venezuelanalysis.com, January 8, 2007 (http://www.vene-zuelanalysis.com/news.php?newsno=2187).

3 "Venezuelan Government Will Not Renew 'Coup-Plotting' TV Station's License," Venezuelanalysis.com, January 3, 2007 (http://www.venezuelana-lysis.com/news.php?newsno=2182).

4 "Chávez Announces Nationalizations, Constitutional Reform for Socialism in Venezuela," Venezuelanalysis.com, January 8, 2007 (http://www.vene-zuelanalysis.com/news.php?newsno=2187).

5 One of the first to make use of this term was conservative *Miami Herald* columnist Andrés Oppenheimer: "Hugo Chávez moves ahead with elected dictatorship," by Andrés Oppenheimer, *Miami Herald*, September 19, 2004, p. 16A.

6 See: "Venezuela's PSUV and Socialism from Below," by George Ciccariello-Maher, in *MR Zine*, March 28, 2007 (http://mrzine.monthlyreview.org/cm280307.html); and "Political Parties and Social Change in Venezuela," by Sujatha Fernandes, in *ZNet*, March 19, 2007, (http://www.zmag.org/con-tent/showarticle.cfm?SectionID=45ItemID=12379).

7 The prominent party members tended to be ones who did not enjoy significant office any longer in their respective parties, such as former education minister Aristobulo Isturiz and former PDVSA president Ali

Rodriguez, both of the PPT, or former National Assembly vice-president Ricardo Gutierrez of Podemos.

8 "Chávez: Parties That Don't Join Unified Socialist Party of Venezuela are Free to Leave," Venezuelanalysis.com, March 19, 2007 (http://www.venezuelanalysis.com/news.php?newsno=2244).

9 "Formation of the United Socialist Party of Venezuela Moves Forward," Venezuelanalysis.com, April 21, 2007 (http://www.venezuelanalysis.com/news.php?newsno=2276).

10 "Hugo Chávez: En nueve meses será gestado el PSUV," Radio Nacional de Venezuela, March 5, 2007 (http://www.rnv.gov.ve/noticias/index.php?act=STf=2t=44529).

11 "Venezuelan Government and Verizon Agree to Telecom Nationalization," Venezuelanalysis.com, February 13, 2007 (http://www.venezuelanalysis.com/news.php?newsno=2218).

12 "Venezuela Takes Control of the Orinoco Oil Reserves," Venezuelanalysis.com, May 2, 2007 (http://www.venezuelanalysis.com/news.php?newsno=2288).

13 However, given that the oil policy changes Chávez has promoted so far have brought in more than $23 billion between 2002 and 2006 that would otherwise have remained in the hands of transnational oil companies, the government's "re-nationalization" strategy has more than paid off. (Source: PDVSA.)

14 Ibid.

15 IAPA Mid-year meeting report on Venezuela, March 16–19, 2007, (http://www.sipiapa.com/pulications/informe_venezuela2007ca.cfm).

16 The exact reasoning for this is based on the fact that in 2000 a new telecommunications law was passed and that, according to RCTV, this means that its license was automatically renewed for another 20 years with the passage of the law. The government, though, says that this argument has no basis in the 2000 law, which merely states that existing licenses will be brought into conformity with the 2000 law, not that they are automatically renewed.

17 Ley Organica de Telecomunicaciones, March 28, 2000, Article 108.

18 This is based on the fact that it was first granted a 20-year license in 1994.

19 RCTV will not go off the air completely, though, because it will almost certainly continue its programming via satellite and cable. Also, a large part of its revenues come from selling soap operas to the rest of Latin America, so it won't even have to scale back its operations all that much.

20 It should be noted that despite this recent increase in state TV channels, and RCTV's going off the air, private TV stations still dominate Venezuela's airwaves, both in terms of the numbers of broadcast licenses and in terms of audience share.

21 This manipulation appears to be even more surprising with regard to press freedom groups, such as IAPA, RSF, and CPJ. However, it should not be all that surprising in the former two (IAPA and RSF) because these are actually associations of self-interested private broadcasters and not groups that disinterestedly protect the principle of freedom of speech for everyone.

22 "Poll: Chávez Approval 65%, Despite 70% Rejection of TV Channel's Non-Renewal," Venezuelanalysis.com, April 26, 2007 (http://www.venezuelanalysis.com/news.php?newsno=2281). That the opposition is not taking advantage of this disapproval is remarkable. In theory, the opposition could easily have organized a consultative referendum (with support from 10% of registered voters) against the license non-renewal and embarrassed Chávez with the vote. The reason the opposition did not do this can probably be traced to its general unwillingness to do anything that strengthens the impression that Venezuela is a democratic country.

23 "El nuevo canal 2 comenzará con una película: Bolívar eterno," Panorama, May 12, 2007, reprinted in Aporrea.org (http://www.aporrea.org/medios/n94778.html).

24 This was the third time that Chávez was granted an enabling law and he was the fifth president in Venezuela's democratic history to have one. The first enabling law in Chávez's presidency was in 1999, under the 1961 constitution, to pass a law on taxation. The second was in 2000, under the new constitution, which permitted Chávez to pass 49 laws on a wide variety of issues, to bring Venezuela's legal framework up to date with the 1999 constitution.

25 "Venezuelan Legislature Allows President to Pass Laws by Decree for 18 Months," Venezuelanalysis.com, January 31, 2007 (http://www.venezuelanalysis.com/news.php?newsno=2207).

26 Quoted in a brochure produced by the Ministry of Communication and Information, "Primer motor: ley habilitante."

27 Teodoro Petkoff, "Heil Hugo!" *Tal Cual*, February 2, 2007.

28 One could say that the pro-Chávez National Assembly is less sensitive to the charge of authoritarianism than Chávez because it has passed or considered repressive laws in the past, such as the penal code reform or the law on social responsibility in radio and television, which were both passed in 2004 or the anti-terrorism law, which was considered by the National Assembly for a long time, but was never passed. In the case of the penal code reform, which indeed stiffened penalties for insulting high government officials, Chávez and the Attorney General have challenged the law for its draconian aspects and as of this writing it is being reviewed by the Supreme Court. See: "Venezuela's Attorney General Mounts Legal Challenge to Controversial Penal Code," Venezuelanalysis.com, November 23, 2005, (http://www.venezuelanalysis.com/news.php?newsno=1824).

29 On May 5, 2007 Chávez said state security forces had arrested someone, who supposedly works with the opposition, with five rifles with telescopic lenses. (Source: "Chávez anuncia incautación armas vinculadas a complot en su contra," Milenio.com, May 6th, 2007, http://www.milenio.com/index.php/2007/05/05/65937/.)

30 Juramentación del Consejo Presidencial Moral y Luces, January 25, 2007, www.alopresidente.gob.ve. Workshops on these issues will take place in communities, workplaces, schools, universities, and state broadcast media.

Chávez's brother, Adán Chávez, who was named Minister of Education earlier in the year, will head up the program. According to Adán Chávez, the objective is to "turn every corner of the country into a school . . . to achieve a level of consciousness, of capability that the people need to form a new homeland, the socialist homeland." Source: " 'Toda la Patria una Escuela, la autentica educación popular,' "Radio Nacional de Venezuela, May 3, 2007 (www.rnv.gov.ve).

31 This plan has, as of this writing, not yet been officially released.

32 Quoted in the Ministry of Communication and Information brochure, "Cuarto Motor: La nueva geometria del poder" (www.minci.gov.ve).

33 This proposal had actually already been developed in the new "Organic Law on Citizen Participation," which, at the time of writing, the National Assembly has not yet passed, but which is scheduled to pass in the course of 2007. For a detailed analysis of this law, see Gregory Wilpert (2008) "Venezuela's Experiment in Participatory Democracy," forthcoming in an as yet untitled book edited by Jonathan Eastwood and Thomas Ponniah.

34 Quoted in Ministry of Communication and Information brochure, "Quinto Motor: Explosión del poder comunal" (www.minci.gov.ve).

35 Chávez says as much when he says that the fifth motor of Bolivarian Socialism is the most important, but that it depends for its success on the previous four.

36 See the appendix of this book for a much fuller explanation of what twenty-first century socialism could mean.

37 The Communist Party of Venezuela (PCV) recently proposed the creation of socialist worker's councils, though, which would have an important co-management role in all private and public institutions. The opposition and many unions have criticized this proposal as merely being a way to undermine the role of unions in the workplace, something the PCV of course denies. "Proyecto De Ley—Ley Especial De Los Consejos Socialistas De Trabajadores Y Trabajadoras," presented to the National Assembly in April 2007. Chávez seems to support the proposal and there is a good chance that it will pass sometime in 2007.

38 One of the things that Chávez critics regularly omit when they correctly criticize the government for political hiring is that too many public servants are guilty of sabotaging the public administration because they do not want to carry out the government's policies. Such sabotage, of course, forces managers to hire along political criteria. In other words, both sides are complicit in the politicization of the public administration.

39 Analysts who have made this argument include, Raby (2006), Ellner (2001, 2005), Hawkins (2003), and Parker (2001). A general analysis of populism in Latin America that tries to explain its ability to mobilize large segments of the population is that provided by Laclau (2005).

40 Max Weber (1947) was the first to see this dual potential of charisma.

Appendix

1 Sometimes I think all the people/is a boy that runs/after hope that goes/ young blood and old dream/but leaving behind foolishness/this hope will come true.

2 Press conference, Porto Alegre, Brazil, January 30, 2005 (transcript: www.go-biernoenlinea.gob.ve).

3 Linking Alternatives II Conference, Vienna, May 13, 2006 (transcript: www.gobicrnoenlinea.gob.ve).

4 Swearing in ceremony of pro-Chávez candidates for the National Assembly, Sept. 13, 2005.

5 Ibid.

6 Ibid.

7 Aló Presidente, No. 229, July 17, 2005.

8 Op. cit., swearing-in ceremony of candidates.

9 Groundbreaking ceremony for the Refinery of Pernambuco, in Brazil, December 16, 2005.

10 Op. cit., swearing in ceremony of candidates.

11 For a collection of common dictionary definitions, see "Definitions of Capitalism" in Wikiquote (en.wikiquote.org/wiki/definitions_of_capital-ism).

12 Capitalism also has positive consequences, which critics such as Marx recognized (especially in the *Communist Manifesto*) and which the cheerlea-ders of capitalism (such as Friedrich von Hayek, Ayn Rand, and Milton Friedman) celebrate. These positive consequences include its dynamism in the face of changing circumstances and the steady stream of innovation that it enables. Other claimed positive consequences, such as greater individual liberty and rising standards of living, are more questionable because critics argue that this is usually only possible in some countries because others are being exploited elsewhere in the world.

13 Many supporters of capitalism counter this argument by pointing out that in the most capitalist countries in the world, such as in the US, living standards for the vast majority have dramatically increased in the past two centuries. While this might be true, if one looks at capitalism as a global system of economic organization, inequality has increased dramatically throughout the world in the 20th century and the poor have become more numerous and poorer.

14 Some of the more important eco-socialists include Joel Kovel (2002), James O'Connor (1998), and Rudolf Bahro (1984).

15 For a perspective that combines anti-racism and anti-capitalism, see Cornel West (1988).

16 This last ideal, of promoting the greatest development for the greatest number of beings, actually ends up encompassing all the other ideals, insofar that liberty, equality, social justice, efficiency, and diversity are needed for this ideal to be possible. It is, in a sense, a mega-ideal. Ken Wilber (2000) has

expounded the basis for this type of universal ethics in great detail. Also, Marx echoed this ideal when he said that communism sought to create a society in which "the free development of each is a condition for the free development of all." Marx (1998), p. 62.

17 Weisbrot and Rosnick (2003) show that this was especially true for Latin America in this time period.

18 See Harvey (2005) and Amin (1997) for two excellent accounts of how this happened.

19 This changed to some extent in Cuba in the 1990s, when it was forced to develop more ecological awareness, due to the economic problems it was having.

20 Three of the more prominent proponents in the English-speaking world are David Schweickart (2002), John Roemer (1994), and Alec Nove (1991).

21 See, for example: Ollman (1998), Robin Hahnel (2005), pp. 170–181, and Albert (2003), pp. 79–80.

22 For a recent analysis of the problems in one of the main experiments in market socialism, see Cheney (1999) on Mondragon. Similarly, Lebowitz (2006) argues that Yugoslav market socialism fostered individualism and not solidarity between cooperatives, and it fostered class distinctions between managers and workers.

23 Participatory economics was developed by Michael Albert and Robin Hahnel over the course of numerous books. The most recent are: Albert (2003, 2006) and Hahnel (2005).

24 Friedrich Engels, "Socialism: Utopian and Scientific."

25 The following outline of new economic institutions is based on Albert and Hahnel's conception of Participatory Economics. For a full discussion of Parecon and criticisms and responses, see: www.parecon.org. The presentation of Parecon here is meant to be suggestive, not a blueprint.

26 This principle assumes that people are also paid to learn, so that they don't need to justify higher incomes for higher skill levels, based on earlier unremunerated sacrifices.

27 There are other, less participatory and more hierarchical, models for democratic planning, such as the one developed by Cockshott and Cottrell (1993), but which does not deal much with issues of workplace hierarchy, remuneration, or self-management. It might be conceivable, if a society wanted to, to combine elements from different economic democracy models.

28 Every workplace and every industry assigns "effort ratings" to workers and to cooperatives, which reflect the amount of effort these generally expend in their work, in terms of hours worked and the degree of sacrifice or burdensomeness of the work.

29 Albert and Hahnel, "Socialism As It Was Always Meant to Be" at www.parecon.org.

30 www.okfn.org. The terms "open" and "free" are used more or less interchangeably.

31 This concept has been promoted particularly by Jon Elster, Jürgen Habermas, Joshua Cohen, and Amy Gutman, among others. See: Bohman (1997).
32 A full summary of his conception is available at: www.zmag.org. "A Political System for a Good Society," Stephen Shalom, 2006.
33 See, for example, Weisberg (1993).
34 Lebowitz (2006) highlights the importance human development has for a conception of twenty-first century socialism.
35 See, especially: Habermas (1996) and Arato and Cohen (1992).
36 See, for example, Poster (1990), Turkle (1995), and Castells (2000).
37 Definition provided in the P2P Foundation Wiki (http://www.p2pfoundation.net/index.php/Peer_to_Peer), by Michel Bauwens.
38 Ibid.
39 Theorists who describe this type of consciousness very well are Wilber (2000), Gebser (1984), Kegan (1994), and Torbert (2004). They each use different terms for this type of consciousness, but essentially point to the same type.

References

Agee, Philip (1976) *Inside the Company: CIA Diary*, New York, NY: Bantam Books

Albert, Michael (2003) *Parecon: Life After Capitalism*, London: Verso Books

Albert, Michael (2006) *Realizing Hope*, London: Zed Books

Amin, Samir (1997) *Capitalism in the Age of Globalization*, London: Zed Books

Anderson, Jon Lee (2001) "The Revolutionary" in: *The New Yorker*, 10–9–2001

Anderson, Perry (1988) *Democracia y Dictadura en America Latina*, Cuadernos de Sociología No. 2: Universidad de Buenos Aires

Bahro, Rudolf (1984) *From Red to Green*, London: Verso Books

Blanco Muñoz, Augustin (1998) *Habla el comandante*, Caracas: Fundación Catedra Pio Tamayo

Blanco, Carlos (2002) *Revolución y Desilusión*, Caracas: Libros de Catarata

Bohman, James (ed.) (1997) *Deliberative Democracy*, Cambridge, MA: MIT Press

Boudin, Chesa, Gabriel Gonzalez, and Wilmer Rumbos (2006) *The Venezuelan Revolution: 100 Questions—100 Answers*, New York: Thunder's Mouth Press

Bourdieu, Pierre (1984) *Distinction: A Social Critique of the Judgement of Taste*, Cambridge, MA: Harvard University Press

Buxton, Julia (2001) *The Failure of Political Reform in Venezuela*, Aldershot, England: Ashgate

Buxton, Julia (2003), "Economic Policy and the Rise of Hugo Chávez," in: *Venezuelan Politics in the Chávez Era*, edited by Steve Ellner and Daniel Hellinger, p. 114

Carmona Ulloa, Ernesto (2004) *Los Dueños de Venezuela*, Caracas: Editorial Question

Cartay Ramirez, Gehard (2000) *Política y Partidos Modernos en Venezuela*, Caracas: Fondo Editorial Nacional

Carter Center (2004) *Observing the Venezuela Presidential Recall Referendum—Comprehensive Report*, Carter Center (www.cartercenter.org)

Castells, Manuel (2000) *The Rise of the Network Society*, London: Blackwell Books

Catala, José Augustin and Eleazar Díaz Rangel (2003) *De Pérez Jiménez a Hugo Chávez: Censura y Autocensura*, Caracas: El Centauro

Ceresole, Norberto (1999) "Caudillo, ejército, pueblo" Venezuela Analítica (www.venezuelanalitica.com)

Chávez, Hugo (1996) *Agenda Alternativa Bolivariana*, Caracas, pamphlet

Chávez, Hugo (2003) *Discursos Fundamentales: Ideología y acción política*, Caracas: Foro Bolivariano de Nuestra América

Cheney, George (1999) *Values at Work: Employee Participation Meets Market Pressure at Mondragon*, Ithaca: Cornell University Press

Cockshott, Paul and Allin Cottrell (1993) *Towards A New Socialism*, Nottingham: Spokesman Books

Cohen, Jean and Andrew Arato (1992) *Civil Society and Political Theory*, Cambridge, MA: MIT Press

Coppedge, Michael (1994) *Strong Parties and Lame Ducks: Presidential Partyarchy and Factionalism in Venezuela*, Stanford: Stanford University Press

Coronil, Fernando (1997) *The Magical State*, Chicago: University of Chicago Press

Crisp, Brian (2000) *Democratic Institutional Design: The Powers and Incentives of Venezuelan Politicians and Interest Groups*, Stanford: Stanford University Press

de Soto, Hernando (2000) *The Mystery of Capital*, New York: Basic Books

Delahaye, Olivier (2002) "La discusión sobre la ley de tierras: Espejismos y realidades," *Revista SIC*, Caracas: Centro Gumilla

Delgado, Carol (2003) "The Non-Androcentric Constitution of Bolivarian Republic of Venezuela," *Response Magazine*

Derham, Michael (2002a) "Contemporary Politics in Venezuela: Introduction" in: *Bulletin of Latin American Research*, Vol. 21, No. 2, pp. 191–198, Blackwell Publishers

Derham, Michael (2002b) "Undemocratic Democracy: Venezuela and the Distorting of History," *Bulletin of Latin American Research* Vol. 21, No. 2, pp. 270–289, Blackwell Publishers

Duno, Luis (2004) "Mob Outrages: Reflections on the Media Construction of the Masses in Venezuela" (April 2000–January 20003) *Journal of Latin American Cultural Studies* Vol. 13, No. 1, pp. 115–135, Carfax Publishing

Elizalde, Rosa and Luis Baez (2004) *Chávez Nuestro*, Havana: Casa Editorial Abril

Ellner, Steve (2001) "Hugo Chávez: Radical Populist or Neopopulist?", paper presented at the 2001 meeting of the Latin American Studies Association (http://136.142.158.105/Lasa2001/EllnerSteve.pdf)

Ellner, Steve (2003b) "Organized Labor and the Challenge of Chavismo," in: *Venezuelan Politics in the Chávez Era*, London: Lynne Rienner Publishers

Ellner, Steve (2003c) "Tendencias recientes en el movimiento laboral Venezolano: Autonomia vs. control político," *Revista Venezolana de Economia y Ciencias Sociales*, 3/2003, Caracas: Universidad Central de Venezuela

Ellner, Steve (2005) "Revolutionary and Non-Revolutionary Paths of Radical Populism: Directions of the Chavista Movement in Venezuela," in: *Science and Society*, Vol. 69, No. 2, April 2005, pp. 160–190.

Ellner, Steve and Daniel Hellinger (eds.) (2003) *Venezuelan Politics in the Chávez Era: Class, Polarization, and Conflict*, London: Lynne Rienner Publishers

Ellner, Steve and Miguel Tinker Salas (2005) "The Venezuelan Exceptionalism Thesis: Separating Myth from Reality," *Latin American Perspectives*, Vol. 32, No. 2, London: Sage

Francia, Nestor (2003) *Que Piensa Chávez*, Caracas: Ediciones del Autor

Garcia Ponce, Guillermo (2004) *El Golpe de Estado del 11 de Abril*, Caracas: Comando Político de la Revolución

Garrido, Alberto (2002) *Testimonios de la Revolución Bolivarinana*, Caracas: Editiones del Autor

Gebser, Jean (1984) *The Ever-Present Origin*, Athens, OH: Ohio University Press

Giddens, Anthony (1984) *The Constitution of Society*, Berkeley: University of California Press

Golinger, Eva (2005) *The Chávez Code: Cracking US Intervention in Venezuela*, Havana: Editorial José Martí

Gott, Richard (2000) *In the Shadow of the Liberator*, London: Verso Books

Guevara, Aleida (2005) *Chávez, Venezuela and the New Latin America*, New York: Ocean Books

Habermas, Jürgen (1985) *Theory of Communicative Action*, Boston: Beacon Press

Habermas, Jürgen (1989) "The Crisis of the Welfare State and the Exhaustion of Utopian Energies," in: *Jürgen Habermas on Society and Politics*, Boston: Beacon Press

Habermas, Jürgen (1990) *Die Nachholende Revolution*, Frankfurt/Main: Suhrkamp Verlag

Habermas, Jürgen (1998) *Between Facts and Norms*, Cambridge, MA: MIT Press

Hahnel, Robin (2005) *Economic Justice and Democracy*, London: Routledge

Handelman, Howard and Mark Tessler (eds.) (1999) *Democracy and its Limits: Lessons from Asia, Latin America, and the Middle East*, Notre Dame: University of Notre Dame Press

Harnecker, Marta (2002) *Hugo Chávez Frías: Un hombre, un pueblo*, Caracas: Associacion Civil Universitarios por la Verdad, translated as: *Understanding the Venezuelan Revolution: Hugo Chávez talks to Marta Harnecker*, New York: Monthly Review Press

Harnecker, Marta (2003) *Militares junto al pueblo*, Caracas: Vadell hnos.

Harrison, Lawrence E. and Samuel P. Huntingon (2000) *Culture Matters: How Values Shape Human Progress*, New York: Basic Books

Harvey, David (2004) *The New Imperialism*, Oxford: Oxford University Press

Hawkins, Kirk (2003) "Populism in Venezuela: the Rise of Chavismo" in: *Third World Quarterly*, Vol. 24, No. 6, pp. 1137–1160.

Hellinger, Daniel (2000) "Understanding Venezuela's Crisis," in: *Latin American Perspectives* Vol. 27, No. 1, pp. 105–119, London: Sage

Herrera Salas, Jesus Maria (2004) "Racismo y discurso político en Venezuela," in: *Revista Venezolana de Economia y Ciencias Sociales*, No. 2, Vol. 10, Caracas: Universidad Central de Venezuela

Heydra, Pastor (2003) *Las Promesas de Hugo Chávez*, Caracas: Los Libros de *El Nacional*

Hillman, Richard (1994) *Democracy for the Privileged: Crisis and Transition in Venezuela*, Boulder: Lynne Rienner

Holloway, John (2002) *Change the World Without Taking Power: The Meaning of Revolution Today*, London: Pluto Press

Huber, Evelyne, Dietrich Rueschemeyer, and John D. Stephens (1999) *The Paradoxes of Contemporary Democracy: Formal, Participatory, and Social Dimensions*, New York: Columbia University Press

Human Rights Watch (2004) "Chávez Allies Pack Supreme Court," on: www.hrw.org

Ingelhart, Ronald (2000) "Culture and Democracy," in: *Culture Matters: How Values Shape Human Progress*, pp. 80–97, New York: Basic Books

Instituto Nacional de Estadisticas (2004) *Reporte Social*, www.ine.gov.ve

Ishibashi, Jun (2003) "Hacia una apertura del debate sobre el racismo en Venezuela," in: *Politicas de indentidades y diferencias sociales en tiempos de globalización*, Caracas: Universidad Central de Venezuela

Kaiser, Patricia (2003) "Estrategias discursivas antichavistas de los medios de comunicación," in: *Revista Venezolana de Economia y Ciencias Sociales*, No. 3, Caracas: Facultad de Ciencias Económicas y Sociales, UCV

Karl, Terry Lynn (1997) *The Paradox of Plenty*, Berkeley: University of California Press

Keane, John (2003) *Global Civil Society?*, Cambridge: Cambridge University Press

Kegan, Robert (1994) *In Over Our Heads*, Cambridge, MA: Harvard University Press

Knight, Alan (2001) "Democratic and Revolutionary Traditions in Latin America," *Society for Latin American Studies*, Vol. 20, No. 2, New York: Blackwell Publishers

Kovel, Joel (2002) *The Enemy of Nature: The End of Capitalism or the End of the World?*, London: Zed Books

Kozloff, Nikolas (2006) *Hugo Chávez: Oil, Politics, and the Challenge to the US*, New York: Palgrave Macmillan

Laclau, Ernesto (2005) *On Populist Reason*, London: Verso Books

La Fuente, Sandra and Alfredo Mesa (2004) *El acertijo de abril: Relato periodistico de la breve caida de Hugo Chávez*, Caracas: Editorial Debate

Lebowitz, Michael (2006) *Build it Now: Socialism for the Twenty-first century*, New York: Monthly Review Press

Leighley, Jan E., and Jonathan Nagler (1992) "Socioeconomic class bias in turnout, 1964–1988: The voters remain the same," *American Political Science Review* 86(3), 725–736

Levine, Daniel H. (1977) *Venezuelan Politics: Past and Future Contemporary Venezuela and its Role in International Affairs*, New York University Press

Lopez Sanz, R. (1993) *Parentesco, etnia, y clase social un la sociedad venezolana*, Caracas: Universidad Central de Venezuela

Lopez-Maya, Margarita (1999) *La protesta popular en Venezuela entre 1989 y 1993 Lucha popular, democracia, neo-liberalismo*, Caracas: Nueva Sociedad

Mainwaring, Scott (1999) "Democratic Survivability in Latin America," in: *Democracy and its Limits: Lessons from Asia, Latin America, and the Middle East*, Notre Dame: Notre Dame University Press

Martz, John D. (1984) *Venezuela, Colombia, and Ecuador Latin America: Its Problems and Its Promises*, Boulder: Westview Press

Marx, Karl (1998 [1848]) *The Communist Manifesto*, London: Verso Books

McCoy, Jennifer (2004) "From Representative to Participatory Democracy? Regime Transformation in Venezuela," in: *The Unraveling of Representative Democracy in Veneuzela*, Baltimore: Johns Hopkins University Press

McCoy, Jennifer and David Myers (eds.) (2004) *The Unraveling of Representative Democracy in Venezuela*, Baltimore: Johns Hopkins University Press

Medina, Medófilo (2001) *El elegido Presidente Chávez: Un nuevo sistema político*, Bogota: Ediciones Aurora

Medina, Medófilo and Margarita Lopez-Maya (2003) *Venezuela: confrontación social y polarización*, Bogota: Ediciones Aurora

Mészáros, István (1995) *Beyond Capital*, London: Merlin Press

Ministerio de Comunicación e Información (2004) *Taller de alto nivel: "El nuevo mapa estragégico,"* Caracas: Ministerio de Comunicación e Información

Ministerio de Comunicación e Información (2005) *2004: Año de logros bolivarianos*, Caracas: Ministerio de Comunicación e Información

Ministerio de Planificación y Desarrollo (2001) *Líneas Generales del Plan de Desarrollo Económico y Social de la Nación 2001–2007* (www.mpd.gov.ve)

Mommer, Bernard (2003) "Subversive Oil," in: *Venezuelan Politics in the Chávez Era*, edited by Ellner, Steve and Daniel Hellinger, London: Lynne Rienner

Moncada, Samuel (2003) "Ponencia en el Encuentro Mundial de Solidaridad con la Revolución Bolivarian" (http://www.analitica.com/bitblioteca/samuel_moncada/bolivarianismo.asp)

Montañez, Ligia (1993) *El racismo oculto en una sociedad no racista*, Caracas: Fondo Editorial Tropykos

Naím, Moisés (2001) "The Real Story Behind Venezuela's Woes," *Journal of Democracy*, Vol. 12, No. 2, pp. 17–31, Washington: Johns Hopkins University Press

Naím, Moisés and Ramón Piñango (1989) "El caso Venezuela: una illusión de armonía," in: *El caso Venezuela: una ilusión de armonía*, pp. 539–579, Caracas: Ediciones IESA

Negri, Antonio and Michael Hardt (2004) *Multitude*, New York, NY: Penguin Press

Norden, Deborah (2003) "Democracy in Uniform: Chávez and the Venezuelan Armed Forces," in: *Venezuelan Politics in the Chávez Era*, edited by Ellner, Steven and daniel Hellinger, pp. 93–112

Nove, Alec (1991) *The Economics of Feasible Socialism Revisited*, New York: Unwin Hyman

O'Connor, James (1998) *Natural Causes: Essays in Ecological Marxism*, New York: Guilford Press

Ollman, Bertell (1998) *Market Socialism: The Debate Among Socialists*, London: Routledge

OPEC (2003) *OPEC Statistical Bulletin*, Vienna: OPEC

Ortega, Daniel, Francisco Rodriguez, and Edward Miguel (2006), "A Closer Look at Venezuela's Robinson Literacy Campaign," http://frrodriguez.web.wesleyan.edu/docs/working_papers/Freed_from_Illiteracy.pdf

Palast, Greg (2004) *The Best Democracy Money Can Buy*, New York: Plume Books

Parker, Dick (2001) "El Chavismo: Populismo Radical y Potencial Revolucionario" in: *Revista de Economia y Ciencias Sociales*, vol. 7, No. 1 (Enero—Abril), pp. 13–44

Piven, Francis Fox and Richard Cloward (1988) *Why Americans Don't Vote*, New York: Pantheon Books

Poster, Mark (1990) *The Mode of Information*, Chicago: University of Chicago Press

Provea (2005) *Informe Anual, 2003–2004*, Caracas: Provea

Raby, D. L. (2006) *Democracy and Revolution: Latin America and Socialism Today*, London: Pluto Press

Riddell, J. (2000) "Contemporary Thinking on Land Reform," Food and Agriculture Organization (www.fao.org/sd/ltdirect/ltan0037.htm)

Riutort, Matias (1999) *El costo de eradicar la pobreza un mal posible de superar, Vol. 1*, Caracas: Universidad Católica Andrés Bello

Roberts, Kenneth (2001) "La descomposición del sistema político venezolano visto desde un análisis comparativo," in: *Revista Venezolana de Economía y Ciencias Sociales*, pp. 183–200, Caracas: Universidad Central de Venezuela

Roberts, Kenneth (2003) "Social Polarization and the Populist Resurgence in Venezuela," in: *Venezuelan Politics in the Chávez Era*, edited by Ellner, Steven and Daniel Hellinger

Robinson, William I. (1992) *A Faustian Bargain*, Boulder, CO: Westview Press

Rodriguez, Francisco (2000) "Factor Shares and Resource Booms: Accounting for the Evolution of Venezuelan Inequality," World Institute for Development Economics (http://www.wider.unu.edu/publications/wp205.pdf)

Roemer, John E. (1994) *A Future for Socialism*, Cambridge: Harvard University Press.

Romero, Anibal (1997) "Rearranging the Deck Chairs on the Titanic: The Agony of Democracy in Venezuela," *Latin American Research Review*, Vol. 32, No. 1, pp. 7–36, Austin: University of Texas Press

Romero, Carlos (2004) "The United States and Venezuela," in: *The Unraveling of Representative Democracy in Venezuela*, Baltimore: Johns Hopkins University Press

Rueschemeyer, Dietrich, Evelyne Huber Stephens, and John Stephens (1992) *Capitalist Development and Democracy*, Chicago: University of Chicago Press

Sanz, Rodolfo (2003) *Dialéctica de Una Victoria*, Caracas: self-published

Scheer, André (2004) *Kampf um Venezuela*, Essen: Neue Impulse Verlag

Schweickart, David (2002) *After Capitalism*, Lanham, Md.: Rowman and Littlefield

Sen, Amartya (1999) *Development as Freedom*, London: Anchor Books

Skocpol, Theda (1979) *States and Social Revolutions: A Comparative Analysis of France, Russia, and China*, Cambridge: Cambridge University Press

Teixeira, Ruy A. (1987) *Why Americans Don't Vote: Turnout Decline in the United States 1960–1984* (New York: Greenwood Press)

Therborn, Göran (1979) "The Travail of Latin American Democracy," in: *New Left Review*, pp. 113–114, Oxford: Alden Press

Torbert, Bill et al. (2004) *Action Enquiry: The Secret of Timely and Transforming Leadership*, San Francisco: Berrett-Kohler Publishers

Trinkunas, Harold A. (2004) "The Military: From Marginalization to Center Stage," in: *The Unraveling of Representative Democracy in Venezuela*, pp. 50–70, edited by Jennifer McCoy and David Myers, Baltimore: Johns Hopkins University Press

Turkle, Sherry (1995) *Life on the Screen*, New York: Simon and Schuster

Universidad Bolivariana (2004) *Documento Rector: Universidad Bolivariana de Venezuela*, Caracas: Universidad Bolivariana de Venezuela

Vallenilla Lanz, Laureano (1991[1919]) *Ceasarismo democratico y otros textos*, Caracas: Biblioteca Fundayacucho

Vilas, Carlos M. (2001) "La sociología política latinoamericana y el 'caso' Chávez," *Revista Venezolana de Economía y Ciencias Sociales*, 2001/2, pp. 129–145, Caracas: Universidad Central de Venezuela

Weber, Max (1947), *The Theory of Economic and Social Organization*, New York: Free Press

Weisberg, D. Kelly (1993) *Feminist Legal Theory: Foundations*, Philadelphia: Temple University Press

Weisbrot, Mark and David Rosnick (2003) "Another Lost Decade? Latin America's Growth Failure Continues into the Twenty-first century," research paper (www.cepr.net), Washington, DC: Center for Economic and Policy Research

Weisbrot, Mark and Simone Baribeau (2003) "What Happened to Profits?: The Record of Venezuela's Oil Industry" (www.cepr.net), Washington, DC: Center for Economic and Policy Research

West, Cornel (1988) "Towards a Socialist Theory of Racism" accessed at: http://race.eserver.org/toward-a-theory-of-racism.html

Weyland, Kurt (2003) "Economic Voting Reconsidered: Crisis and Charisma in the Election of Hugo Chávez," in: *Comparative Political Studies*, Vol. 36, No. 7, pp. 822–848, London: Sage Publications

Wilber, Ken (2000) *Sex, Ecology, Spirituality*, Boston: Shambhala Books

Wilpert, Gregory (2003) "Collision in Venezuela," in: New Left Review, No. 21 (May/June 2003), Oxford: Alden Press

Wilpert, Gregory (2005a) "Venezuela's 'Other Path' " in: *Dissent*, Spring 2005

Wilpert, Gregory (2005b) "Venezuela: Participatory Democracy or Government as Usual?" in: *Socialism and Democracy*, Vol. 19, No. 1, March 2005, pp. 7–32, Abingdon: Taylor and Francis Group

Wilpert, Gregory (2007) *Venezuela During the Chàvez Presidency: A History*, forthcoming, self-published, available at: www.venezuelanalysis.com

World Bank (2002) *World Development Report 2000/2001*, Washington, DC: World Bank

Wright, Winthrop (1990) *Café con Leche: Race, Class, and National Image in Venezuela*, Austin, TX: University of Texas

Zelik, Raul, Sabine Bitter, and Helmut Weber (2003) *Made in Venezuela: Notizen zur "Bolivarischen Revolution"*, Berlin: Assoziation A

Index